IMAGINING NEW NORMALS

A NARRATIVE FRAMEWORK FOR HEALTH COMMUNICATION

Lynn M. Harter, Ph.D., and Associates

Kendall Hunt
publishing company

Forewords by
Pete Anderson, M.D., Ph.D.
Professor, University of Texas
and Laura L. Ellingson, Ph.D.
Professor, Santa Clara University

Book Team

Chairman and Chief Executive Officer	Mark C. Falb
President and Chief Operating Officer	Chad M. Chandlee
Vice President, Higher Education	David L. Tart
Director of Publishing Partnerships	Paul B. Carty
Senior Editor	Angela Willenbring
Vice President, Operations	Timothy J. Beitzel
Assistant Vice President, Production Services	Christine E. O'Brien
Senior Production Editor	Mary Melloy
Permissions Editor	Patricia Schissel

Cover designed by Lisa Villamil and Larry Hamel-Lambert

Kendall Hunt
publishing company

www.kendallhunt.com
Send all inquiries to:
4050 Westmark Drive
Dubuque, IA 52004-1840

Printed in the United States of America
10 9 8 7 6 5 4 3 2 1

DEDICATION

In memory of my father
Richard W. Harter

...because the detour became more meaningful than the planned route...

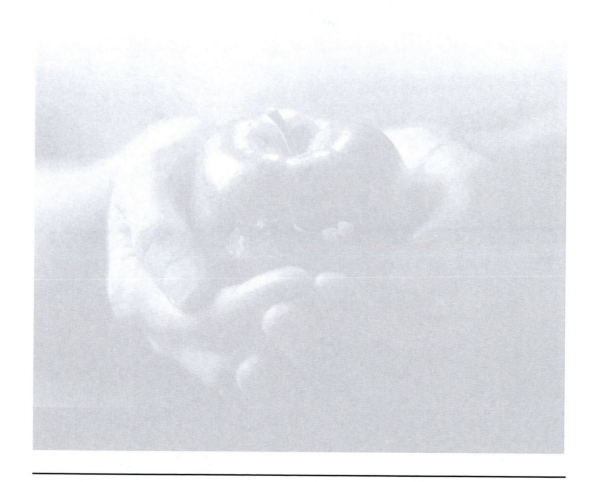

CONTENTS

ACKNOWLEDGMENTS

Countless individuals have informed and supported the development of this book. I first acknowledge the extraordinary generosity of families and care providers who invited me into their lives and showed me what it means to live well in the midst of illness. Your stories are far richer than my writing can convey. I hope the book stands as a testament to your courage and compassion. To Diane Moore and Rhonda and Abigail Armstrong—may your work as health activists continue to influence how we care for each another in vulnerable moments. To Dr. Pete Anderson and Ian Cion—you routinely take the hardest moments a family can experience and soften the edges. Thank you.

This book benefited greatly from a faculty fellowship leave provided by Ohio University and Steven and Barbara Schoonover who endowed my professorship in health communication. The importance of this professorship and my appreciation for it cannot be overstated. The resources offered by the Schoonover family have allowed me to increase the scope and significance of my work and I remain grateful for their support.

In the course of writing, I was reminded of how very little I know, and remain indebted to those who willingly shared their expertise and time. My father always stressed to me that a sign of intelligence is the ability to surround one's self with people who know more or are better equipped to navigate some settings. To that end, several associates contributed chapters to this volume, and the book is stronger because of everyone's contributions.

I am especially grateful to Scott Titsworth, Bill Rawlins, and Raymie McKerrow for being early readers of chapter drafts. Several other colleagues and friends nourished me with edifying conversations and wit including Gayle McKerrow, Karen Deardorff, Sandy Rawlins, Heather Grove, Jerry and Valerie Miller, Jennifer Bute, Phyllis Japp, Erika Kirby, Laura Ellingson, Barbara Sharf, Jill Yamasaki, Brittany Peterson, Claudia Hale, Anita James, Maggie Quinlan, Stephanie Ruhl, and Marie Ficklin. A special thanks to my friends at Sonic—for Diet Coke and pebble ice.

As always, I am indebted to Angela Willenbring and Paul Carty for their patience and unwavering trust in my vision and capacity to execute the project. The editorial skill of the Kendall Hunt staff has allowed me to transform ideas into a readable text. I am proud to publish this book with the Kendall Hunt masthead. I thank Lisa Villamel and Larry Hamel-Lambert for their work in designing the book jacket.

Above all my debt is to my family. Bev—thank you for always believing in my potential. Scott and Emma—you are my best. I have no words to express what this book owes to you. Thank you for filling my life with love and laughter.

LMH

ABOUT THE CONTRIBUTORS

Pete Anderson (M.D., Mt. Sinai School of Medicine; Ph.D., City University of New York) is the Curtis Distinguished Professor, Division of Pediatrics at the University of Texas MD Anderson Cancer Center, Houston, Texas. He is an expert at treating cancer in young people. His very active clinical practice and research focus on innovative treatments of sarcomas, reduction in the toxicity of cancer treatment, and facilitating a family-centered approach to oncology care.

Michael Broderick (M.A., Ohio University) is a Ph.D. candidate in Communication Studies at Ohio University. He studies organizational and health communication and focuses on issues of power/resistance and how to organize for social change through everyday acts of resistance.

Karen L. Deardorff (Ph.D., Ohio University) is an Instructor in the School of Communication Studies at Ohio University. Guided by feminist and narrative sensibilities, her research focuses on communicative strategies used by women living in poverty to remain resilient in the face of material and resource scarcity.

Laura L. Ellingson (Ph.D., University of South Florida) is a Professor of Communication and Women's & Gender Studies at Santa Clara University. She engages the possibilities of feminist and qualitative methodologies to honor multiple voices in healthcare and in extended family networks.

Patricia Geist-Martin (Ph.D., Purdue University) is a Professor in the School of Communication at San Diego State University where she teaches organizational communication, health communication, ethnographic research methods, and gendering organizational communication. Her research interests focus on narrative and negotiating identity, voice, ideology, and control in organizations, particularly in health and illness. She has published three books and over 60 articles and book chapters covering a wide range of topics related to gender, health, and negotiating identities.

Lynn M. Harter (Ph.D., University of Nebraska) is the Steven and Barbara Schoonover Professor of Health Communication in the School of Communication Studies at Ohio University. Guided by feminist and narrative sensibilities, her scholarship explores the communicative construction of possibilities as individuals organize for survival and social change.

Mark Leeman (Ph.D., Ohio University) is an Assistant Professor of Communication Studies at Northern Kentucky University. He specializes in organizational communication with an emphasis in meaning management that occurs between those in poverty and the middle class, with hopes of bringing better understanding and cooperation across differences.

Timothy McKenna (M.S., Illinois State University) is a doctoral student in the School of Communication Studies at Ohio University. His research focuses on the intersection of difference and socialization in organizations, with an emphasis on the ways narratives empower identity and the stories that create, maintain, and change individuals' lived experience.

Julia Moore (M.A., San Diego State University) is currently pursuing a doctoral degree from the Department of Communication Studies at the University of Nebraska-Lincoln. Her research focuses on gender, sexuality, identity, and the relationship between everyday communication and cultural discourses. A recent focus of her research is on the topic of voluntary childlessness and the identity implications that come with deciding to never have children.

Spencer Patterson (Ph.D., Ohio University) is the acting Chief Executive Officer for CrowdCare Foundation, a 501(c)(3) non-profit organization. His scholarly interests are guided by narrative perspectives and focus on communication training for providers and patients.

Brittany L. Peterson (Ph.D., University of Texas at Austin) is an Assistant Professor in the School of Communication Studies at Ohio University. Her research focuses on challenging and extending traditional constructions of membership in organizations as well as deconstructing the ways in which membership is fundamentally tied to socialization and identification processes.

Margaret M. Quinlan (Ph.D., Ohio University) is an Assistant Professor of Communication and a Core Faculty Member of the Health Psychology Ph.D. Program the University of North Carolina at Charlotte. Her scholarly work explores the organizing of healthcare resources and work opportunities for people with lived differences.

Stephanie M. Ruhl (M.A., Western Michigan University) is a doctoral student in the School of Communication Studies at Ohio University. Guided by aesthetic, narrative, and pragmatic sensibilities, her scholarship explores the communicative experiences of health and healing as individuals create space for the intimate sharing of dialogic relationship.

Barbara F. Sharf (Ph.D., University of Minnesota) is Professor Emerita at Texas A & M University and presently an independent researcher. As a qualitative investigator and scholar of narrative inquiry, she has explored multiple aspects of personal and public communication related to healthcare, illness, and well-being. Her current project concerns the interface between complementary/alternative approaches to health and conventional medical practice.

Amanda Torrens (M.A., Western Michigan University) is a doctoral student in the School of Communication Studies at Ohio University. Her research lies at the intersections of interpersonal communication, health, spirituality/religion, and narrative.

Sam Venable (M.A., Ohio University) is a doctoral student in the School of Communication Studies at Ohio University. He is the Director of Prospect Research and Management at Ohio University. His scholarly interests focus on technology, interpersonal and organizational communication.

Jill Yamasaki (Ph.D., Texas A&M University) is an Assistant Professor of Health Communication in the Valenti School of Communication at the University of Houston. Her scholarship focuses on narrative inquiry and practice in health communication and aging, particularly in the contexts of community and long-term care.

FOREWORD

Pete Anderson, M.D., Ph.D.

Dr. Lynn Harter's *Imagining New Normals…A Narrative Framework for Health Communication* addresses the need for us to develop wisdom in medicine through the use of narratives and storytelling. I am a pediatric oncologist who is on the frontlines of patient care at an MD Anderson Cancer Center. Since Lynn knows we are known for innovation and improving cancer care, we became the primary resource and setting for "the Art of the Possible," one of my first projects with her. In this documentary she and coproducer Casey Hayward capture with words and images the rich narratives that young people have as they seek answers to cancer. Her current effort is a scholarly work that closely examines and privileges a narrative framework because of its capacity to enrich the lives of health professionals, patients, and their families.

We live in a fast-paced era in which information gathering is accelerating, connecting with others through electronic means is quick—sometimes "too easy"—and there is an overabundance of information and advice. In oncology some information is helpful, some not so helpful, and some even useless or harmful. In the high-stakes game of life, how does a patient, family, care provider, or professional sort out this deluge of information and opinions? Despite increasing scientific knowledge and recent evidence-based medicine trends, acquiring knowledge without wisdom is useless. How do we use knowledge wisely?

I think we are hard-wired to learn from stories, not just facts. We learn best from experience and the experience of others. Correct application of that experience is the beginning of wisdom. As a pediatric oncologist I have come to realize that families have a thirst for knowledge about their child's condition and really want to learn how to anticipate and prevent problems and improve health in difficult situations. Lynn's book addresses the importance of narrative as learning tools for physicians, patients, families, and caregivers. Today these narratives are shared with others involved in the healthcare journey in many ways that involve storytelling, including listserv discussion groups, blogs, pictures, movies, caringbridge. org site, carepages, myhelpinghands.org site, e-mails, text messaging, letters, cards, and art projects, to name a few.

The rich context of these narratives is sometimes lost in the busyness of the medicine business. Are we too busy to listen, care, and share properly? It is important to s-l-o-w down and pay attention to our sources of information. On hospital rounds I like to point out to residents, fellows, and nurses, that if you sit down, you will learn a lot more from the patient and their family. Your body language conveys interest and respect for them and a willingness to learn from their narrative. I sometimes will tell the residents "you don't get smart from talking to yourself"; there is something to learn in each encounter. An important contribution of Dr. Harter's book is to show us that if we slow down and listen to these narratives, there is so much to learn. If we apply principles learned from these lessons, that is wisdom in action.

Visual information is also very important in medical communication. For example, I can much more easily explain a plan of care using a calendar—something almost everyone can understand "at-a-glance"—than a "laundry list" of tasks. Sending children to the Wonderful Animals Giving Support (WAGS) program where they get to pet special (and cute) therapy dogs brings smiles to everyone's faces—owners, kids, parents, and dogs alike. I tell residents "if they can play, they are OK." The use of art as experience sharing is also an important part of the book. I personally have seen Ian Cion and his colleague's work at MD Anderson lift the spirits and successfully communicate very meaningful themes such as hope, beauty, and love (see Chapter 2). Art also can be really fun, too!

Lynn's introductory chapters in Parts One and Two show there are an increasing number of new and imaginative ways to collect and share art, pictures, and narratives. We now can use our electronic media devices (pictures, iPhone with facetime, flash drives, iPad, digital movies, laptops, etc.) as means to organize our lives as well as for sharing feelings, emotions, and requests for information and help from others. An unprecedented information exchange has become the new normal. Lynn's book provides real-life examples and meaningful stories of how this is happening.

I am certain readers will find many if not all of these chapters will result in creative thinking and new directions for learning from others and applications of that learning. If we apply some lessons from this book and learn to listen, care, and share, we will not only gain much wisdom, but also pass it forward. Thus, just like the forward observer in the military observation post who can call in help when and where it is needed, we too can become forward observers if we listen, care, and share to make life better for those around us.

FOREWORD

Laura L. Ellingson

While Dr. Pete Anderson's foreword situates Lynn Harter's *Imagining New Normals* within the medical world he so gracefully and courageously inhabits, I offer a complementary perspective as a communication scholar, reflecting on the contribution this book makes to the fields of health communication and engaged/participatory research methodology.

As an editor at the journal *Health Communication*, I encounter a vast range of scholarship, and I can attest that the knowledge in health communication remains overwhelmingly focused on traditional scientific goals of definition, prediction, and control, despite the increase in qualitative research published over the last two decades. Discrete variables, carefully defined, manipulated, and measured (e.g., surveys or scales) render important information, offering a statistical story of experience and often a helpful elucidation of trends. But such approaches necessarily leave out the messy, disordered aspects of reality that cannot be readily contained. Narrative sense-making offers a vital qualitative and critical complement to more rigid approaches to understanding, enlarging not only the aggregate of what we know about healthcare encounters, but also the range of topics in health and illness into which we may inquire (Geist-Martin, Berlin, & Sharf, 2011; Harter, Japp, & Beck, 2005). *Imagining New Normals* is so timely and so beneficial because it provides a narrative framework that will guide scholars who now seek to understand the complexities of communication in a myriad of healthcare settings. Lynn and her collaborators in this volume use narrative sense-making to explore wonderfully complex communication in mobile clinics for underserved people, among senior adults residing in long-term care facilities, and as part of artistic interventions into healthcare. And so many more unruly health communication topics are or could be explored using the narrative logics and modes of inquiry richly illustrated in this volume: end-of-life conversations (Foster, 2006), interdisciplinary collaboration on healthcare teams (Ellingson, 2005), living with inflammatory bowel disease (Defenbaugh, 2011), adolescents' strategies to resist illicit drug use (Hecht & Miller-Day, 2009), and coping with substance addiction (Jodlowski, Sharf, Haidet, Nguyen, & Woodard, 2007), to name just a few.

This narrative framework also contributes to the field of participatory methodology, an interdisciplinary area of research practice that overlaps with qualitative methods, feminist methods, applied research, and engaged scholarship. Participatory research projects seek to share power with participants by refusing to consider them simply sources of data and instead positioning participants as experts in their own lived, embodied experiences who collaborate with researchers to co-create knowledge (e.g., Koch & Kralik, 2011; McIntyre, 2007; McNiff & Whitehead, 2011; Norris, 2010). Lynn and her colleagues demonstrate how narrative and arts-based approaches to studying illness and healthcare benefit those who participate in research while simultaneously yielding meaningful, useful findings. Moreover, readers learn about ways of expressing and sharing findings that go beyond traditional research reports to showcase the advantages of documentary film, photography, theatre and performance, painting and other arts for communicating beyond the written word. Such genres need not be understood as competing or mutually exclusive with journal articles and other scholarly genres. Instead multiple genres enrich the possibilities for knowing about communicating health and illness and for widening the circle of stakeholders involved in dialogues about reinventing healthcare (Ellingson, 2009).

My academic expertise notwithstanding, I also value *Imagining New Normals* on a deeply personal level. I, too, am a member of "the community of pain" (Frank, 1995). I initially lacked the terminology for the sense-making process that began more than two decades ago when I was diagnosed (like Dr. Pete's patients) with osteosarcoma. Since then I have struggled to build and rebuild a coherent narrative of the cancer, treatment, and long-term effects of the treatment on my body and self. As Lynn so skillfully weaves together narrative theory and personal narratives into the study of communication within healthcare encounters, my own story knits together the narrative threads of my professional interest in studying healthcare, my passion for improving the medical system, and my own ongoing, embodied journey as a long-term cancer survivor. The narrative framework in this book helps me reimagine myself because it undoes the false divisions between self and other, healthy and sick, healer and healed, art and science, researcher and researched. Yes, the cancer took up much of my college years, damaged and ultimately destroyed most of my right leg, left me with chronic pain, impaired my mobility, and permanently eviscerated my naive belief in my own invulnerability. But that is not the whole story. Cancer also gifted me with a career focused in health communication research, fueled my passion to be a better teacher and writer, taught me about patience, forged a more compassionate and generous heart within me, and solidified my most valued relationships.

What I learned through surviving cancer and researching health communication parallels the lesson Lynn Harter offers all who read this remarkable work—stories can heal, even when medicine cannot. Lynn's invitation to narrative and aesthetic knowing will offer a jumping-off point for many researchers who are eager to go where few have gone before in making sense of the chaotic experiences of health and illness and, perhaps even more importantly, to making compassionate space for the chaos when it proves untamable.

REFERENCES

Defenbaugh, N.L. (2011). *Dirty tale: A narrative journey of the IBD body.* Creskill, NJ: Hampton Press.

Ellingson, L.L. (2005). *Communicating in the clinic: Negotiating frontstage and backstage teamwork.* Cresskill, NJ: Hampton Press.

Ellingson, L.L. (2009). *Engaging crystallization in qualitative research: An introduction.* Thousand Oaks, CA: Sage.

Foster, E. (2006). *Communicating at the end of life: Finding magic in the mundane.* Mahwah, NJ: Erlbaum.

Frank, A.W. (1995). *The wounded storyteller: Body, illness, and ethics.* Chicago: University of Chicago Press.

Geist-Martin, P., Ray, E.B., & Sharf, B.F. (2011). *Communicating health: Personal, cultural and political complexities.* Long Grove, IL: Waveland Press.

Harter, L.M., Japp, P., & Beck, C. (Eds.). (2005). *Narratives, health, and healing: Communication theory, research, and practice* (pp. 277–294). Mahwah, NJ: Erlbaum.

Hecht, M.L., & Miller-Day, M. (2009). The Drug Resistance Strategies Project: Using narrative theory to enhance adolescents' communication competence. In L. Frey & K. Cissna (Eds.), *Routledge handbook of applied communication* (pp. 535–557). New York: Routledge.

Jodlowski, D., Sharf, B.F., Haidet, P., Nguyen, L.C., & Woodard, L.D. (2007). "Screwed for life": Examining identification and division in addiction narratives. *Communication & Medicine, 4,* 15–26.

Koch, T., & Kralik, D. (2006). *Participatory action research in health care.* Malden, MA: Blackwell.

McIntyre, A. (2008). *Participatory action research.* Thousand Oaks, CA: Sage Publications.

McNiff, J., & Whitehead, J. (2011). *All you need to know about action research* (2nd ed.). Thousand Oaks, CA: Sage.

Norris, J. (2010). *Playbuilding as qualitative research: A participatory arts-based approach.* Walnut Creek, CA: Left Coast Press.

INTRODUCTORY REMARKS: A LETTER TO READERS

Dear Readers:

How can individuals live well in the midst of inescapable illness and suffering? What symbolic and material resources foster resiliency among individuals facing vulnerable life circumstances? How can individuals imagine new normals when illness disrupts their otherwise insulated and comfortable lives? In this book, colleagues and I engage these questions while positioning narrative as central to human survival and social change.

Storytelling reflects the narrative impulse and is a powerful form of experiencing and expressing suffering and loss. Acute and chronic illnesses represent corporeal and social threats to a person's previously imagined lifecourse. Patients, healthcare providers, and activists alike rely on storytelling to make sense of expectations gone away and compose life anew.

The book is composed of three main parts: (1) Foundational Considerations, (2) Storytelling in Diverse Healthcare Contexts, and (3) Future Directions. Chapters in Part One survey narrative roots in health communication scholarship and enlarge the terrain by advancing a decidedly poetic and political standpoint. In Part Two, authors locate narrative sense-making in action by exploring storytelling in clinical interactions, medical school pedagogy, health advocacy organizations, mobile health clinics, complementary and integrative medicine, and long-term care. Chapters in Part Three include autoethnographic accounts and poetic transcriptions—genres of storytelling that I envision as central to the future of narrative theory and practice.

Across chapters, authors tell stories informed by personal experience, research interviews, and public discourse. Presentational formats range from ethnographic portraits to fictional composite narratives. Some individuals schooled in traditional social scientific methods may find it difficult or uncomfortable to make sense of knowledge claims that do not strive for objectivity and generalizability. Even so, some aspects of human experience do not easily lend themselves to conventional research expectations, and dominant writing genres can inadvertently distance authors and audiences. Chapters push the boundaries of mainstream health communication scholarship through nonstandard forms of representation. Authors offer ideas meriting further conversation rather than undebatable conclusions.

As with any story, this publication is partial. I remain convinced that storytelling is a necessary survival strategy as individuals adjust personal expectations and reidentify priorities in the face of once unimaginable circumstances. Indeed it is an ode to human resilience that we can imagine new normals and thrive within changing conditions. Yet, there are moments when individuals and groups ought to challenge a collective normalization of suffering. We should be outraged, for example, that rates of childhood cancer continue to increase in the United States. I regret that the book does not delve more fully into the dark side of storytelling and its capacity to silence rather than liberate. I hope the book, short of being perfect or comprehensive, sparks ongoing dialogue among healthcare activists and care providers, patients and families, and scholars across academic disciplines.

As you read each chapter, I invite you to consider how narrative logics and the practice of storytelling can be leveraged in the service of living well in the midst of inescapable illness, trauma, and disability.

Sincerely,

Lynn M. Harter
Steven and Barbara Schoonover Professor of Health Communication

PART 1 FOUNDATIONAL CONSIDERATIONS

CHAPTER 1

THE POETICS AND POLITICS OF STORYTELLING IN HEALTH CONTEXTS

— LYNN M. HARTER —

When you leave the exam room, it is not just your child's life you are trying to save. You could be trying to save your marriage, and your mortgage. And doctors need to understand that. At the cancer hospital, it's cancer, 24/7. And that is their goal is to fix you, and you want that. But our lives were changed forever with that diagnosis. We refer to it as B.C. and A.C.—before cancer and after cancer. Umm, we were living in a new normal now. But we still had some other stuff that wasn't following us,

it wasn't coming to where we were. So we had to drag it to our new normal. I could leave the house to go to take Abigail to treatment, but the boys would be grasping my leg, saying, "Mommy, please don't leave us, don't go." Ah, Mario and I might be fighting. Or the car might not be running. And we wouldn't know where we were going to get money to fix it. And the doctors would come in the room and say, "Tomorrow, we need to do this and do that." And I am sitting there thinking, "Who is going to watch my boys? And, how am I going to get the money for that?" Was Abigail my number one priority when she had cancer? Yes, of course. But my mortgage didn't let me forget it, my marriage didn't let me forget it, and my boys didn't let me forget them. So, yes, I will bring Abigail back tomorrow, but we need to get a babysitter for my other kids. Cancer is not the only thing happening in our lives. (Rhonda Armstrong-Trevino, Interview)

No one willingly auditions for the role of cancer patient or care provider. Nonetheless, in 2012 the estimated number of new cancer cases in the United States was 1,638,910 (American Cancer Society, 2012). Cancer is a common chronic illness, second only to heart disease and accounting for one in every four deaths. Tumors are born from defective cells no longer resting dormant in the body's immune system. Forty-eight months ago, Abigail and her family found themselves in circumstances anything but ordinary, jagged with impossibility and inconvenience. Bone malignancies stemmed from mesenchymal cells in the growth plates of Abigail's distal femur. In cancer's grip, danger hovered and anxiety increased as she and her family were cast out of everyday roles, grasping for something familiar and safe. As I pen this chapter, Abigail is 17 and in her fifth year of survival. After being diagnosed with osteosarcoma at the age of 12, a dozen rounds of chemotherapy, numerous surgeries, a limb salvage procedure, and staph infection, Abigail's cancer is in remission.

Those with cancer are not the only ones affected, as Rhonda's testimony makes painfully clear. Living with cancer and its treatment requires sustained and coordinated efforts to handle myriad demands that are physical, relational, and financial in nature. Family members, in particular, are swept up in a maelstrom of chaotic life events and role changes—from doting mom of three children to a highly driven advocate consumed with a child's cancer, from counting on mom for warm meals to wondering when she is coming home and in what mood. The stories of their coping strategies (those that work and those that fail) circle around "the cancer story," impacting its meaning and changing its relationship to their own stories. It may seem painfully obvious but is worth emphasizing: Cancer and cancer care are inherently relational. "Our world was turned upside down, flipped over, and deep fried. Everything in the South is deep fried, you know," reflected Rhonda. The experience of vulnerability is a shared one, a relational process constructed within and constrained by the matrix of assumptions, expectations, and values common to institutional and cultural life. Abigail's brothers, Noah and Micah, experienced the disquieting nature of osteosarcoma and its remission alongside Abigail, as did her extended family. Consider Rhonda's reflections:

You wouldn't believe the number of moms I've talked to and their kids are in remission and they are having chest pains and wearing monitors because they think they are having heart attacks. And I'm telling you, I think we have broken hearts. And our hearts are trying to mend. We have broken hearts. I'm having panic attacks because we finally got off that cancer train. It dumped us off and we did not know what to do and where to go when we got to that stop. We didn't know what to do with that. We were still in fight mode and we didn't know what to do next. We were lost. (Rhonda Armstrong-Trevino, Interview)

It may seem strange, then, to say that this book is not about cancer, although many people who populate its pages have experienced its treatment and what remains in the aftermath. This book is about *imagining new normals* in the midst of profound vulnerability, uncertainty, and complexity. Whether through birth, life events, or unfortunate circumstances, humans live with vulnerability. Misfortune is one careless driver away, a distracted turn on the highway. The details and dimensions of grief differ among us, but we all experience suffering and loss. Some ruin we bring to our own door while other crises are unbidden, surprising. A life-threatening illness represents a corporeal and social threat to a person's previously imagined lifecourse, curious in its capacity to change life so quickly and completely. Individuals rely on many things to make sense of expectations gone awry, including storytelling.

Narratives endow disruptions with meaning by organizing events in time and space, developing characters and their relations with one another, and ascertaining causality by plotting otherwise disconnected events. Narratives, thus, represent what Kenneth Burke (1973) might term "equipment for living"—symbolic resources allowing individuals to size up circumstances and *imagine new normals*. As such, stories instruct us about what to notice, and how to judge actions and outcomes. The practice of storytelling reflects the narrative impulse and is a powerful form of experiencing and expressing suffering and loss.

Narrative is at once a phenomenon worthy of study and an orientation toward the study of social phenomenon. As an orientation, a narrative perspective acknowledges storytelling as a legitimate form of reasoning—a way of knowing historically positioned as something "other" than "scientific" logics (Lyotard, 1984). As a social phenomenon, narrative is both a process and textual artifact. I approach narrative from an explicitly broad vantage point, casting a wide net that incorporates autobiographical stories, cultural scripts, institutional plots, and the process of storytelling. I understand narratives as *enactments* of events—texts including characters, content, style, storyline, context, and narrators. I also conceive of narratives as performative *acts* that shape and are shaped by material and corporeal experiences (see also Langellier, 2001; Maclean, 1988). The process of building a house is as interesting as the house itself. As such, I consider both the acts of making stories and the resulting narrative enactments as worthy of consideration.

Photo credit: Rhonda Armstrong

Mario, Rhonda, Abigail, Noah, and Micah

In health contexts, narrating is a relational process that constitutes knowledge of self and others. In the United States, healthcare tends to focus on the individual. Yet, those who are ill do not respond to diagnoses in a vacuum. Individuals like Abigail may experience her own body's response to methotrexate, a commonly used chemotherapy drug; however, cancer and cancer care are inherently relational.

A family's ongoing struggle to deal with a seriously ill member can be understood as the construction of a group story that allows them to cope with changes in identities and relationships brought forth by an illness.

Provider–patient interviews can be understood as the co-construction of narratives, ones that involved individuals use to understand and explain the physical and psychological experiences of the patient. On countless occasions, Abigail narrated her experiences to care providers who reshaped story elements into a medical form, incorporating bits of information gleaned through questions, from examination of Abigail's body and test results. Some healthcare providers see nothing but a tibia or a humerus while others see the humanity in a lesion. From a bone or a cyst, you can build a story about a human being who has interests and values, living in a social order with daily routines and relational rituals.

Narrating is a central feature of communication between care providers and patients, in the relationships realized in health organizations, and in the mediated world of health-related information and entertainment. Advertising, news, popular culture, and social movement rhetoric use discrete stories that, taken collectively, compose a cumulative story about health and illness in our culture, our shared expectations and fears, beliefs in causes, and cures. This book focuses on the role of narratives and storytelling across micro settings (e.g., provider–patient interactions), institutional environments (e.g., cancer clinics), and macro contexts (e.g., public health movements). Importantly, no story is solely personal, organizational, or public. Memoires penned by doctors and patients' autobiographical accounts cannot escape the imprint of institutional interests, nor are they separate from cultural values, beliefs, and expectations.

In the remainder of this chapter, I outline basic features, form, and functions of narrative activity in health contexts. In doing so, I advance a decidedly *poetic* and *political* standpoint. I move between scholarly literature and stories drawn from popular culture, public discourse, and fieldwork during the production of the documentary *The Art of the Possible* (Harter & Hayward, 2010). I envision this chapter as a conversation between theory and life or, at least, between conceptual ideas and the offered stories of life. As with all narratives, readers should assume there are intentional silences, parts of the lived experience that individuals chose not to reveal or editors chose not to publish. Narrators are curators of what they share about themselves even as gatekeepers have power in selecting, representing, and interpreting others' experiences.

— NARRATIVE FEATURES AND FORM —

I just pray that when I get on the elevator that I go from 1 to 7 and we don't stop at 5, because as soon as those doors open, I smell it. It is the smell of fear, of loss of control. Someone told me it is the smell of anesthesia, but it is so much more than that to me. I'm like, "Really, you think it's just the smell of anesthesia?" To me that smell makes me see Abigail being wheeled back for the first time, and I have to let her go and trust in what they are doing in that room. I'm not back there watching them, I have to let my baby go, I have to hand over my baby to them. That is what the smell is to me. Anesthesia, yes. But fear, and vulnerability,

CHAPTER 1 • The Poetics and Politics of Storytelling in Health Contexts *and loss of control. Every time she comes back from surgery, she is different every time. Some-times she has a bone removed, or metal [put] in her leg. And we have to think about what we are going to have to deal with next, and is she going to make it? So that smell is fear, it's the unknown. The loss of control is the biggest for me. Because when my babies have something wrong at school, I am there. We are going to fix this. But I can't fix cancer, I can't fix it. Imag-ine just handing your daughter over to the surgeon and going, "Here, can you fix her, because I can't."* (Rhonda Armstrong-Trevino, Interview)

Tragedy sometimes arrives with a sound. A late night phone call. A ring with a slightly shriller tone to it, one that divides life into before and after. For Rhonda, tragedy has a smell. The olfactory system is an important part of the brain, sending information that governs emotions and behaviors. Individual odor molecules stimulate all sorts of receptors—and memories (see also Ellingson, 2005). Misfortune brought the Armstrong-Trevino family to the fifth floor, up from the echoing concrete garage of a grey building composed of steel and glass, brick and mortar. Here, heartache lurks behind glass doors and thin curtains, amidst the hums from machines and monitors and in air perfumed with the scent of a nameless disinfectant.

Western medicine is well equipped to treat specific maladies with drugs or interventions. Every day its practitioners operate to remove appendices, prescribe penicillin for pneumonia, administer epinephrine for acute allergic reactions, and coordinate multimodality treatment for cancer (i.e., surgery, radiation, chemotherapy). When the surgeon identified Abigail's tumor as malignant on her twelfth birthday, Rhonda recounted, "We got on the cancer train, and we didn't know when we would get off, or where we would be." Abigail found herself at MD Anderson, ranked number one among its peers for its treatment of childhood and adolescent cancer (Murphy et al., 2010) and under the care of Dr. Pete Anderson, a pediatric oncologist specializing in osteosarcoma. Dr. Pete had at his disposal state of the art technology measuring blood pressure, oxygen saturation, and the electrical activity of a heart.

When we think of modern medicine and its remarkable capacities, science is what we envision and all it offers us in the form of ever-enlarging menus of technology. Yet, when you have an ache in your knee that lingers like Abigail did, one that disrupts your daily routines, it is not science you call on for a cure—it is a care provider. The social dimensions of healing are as essential as the scientific. Healthcare involves genetic and cellular interactions as well as human ones. Experience is simulta-neously material and corporeal on the one hand, and instilled with culturally defined meaning on the other (McKerrow, 1998).

My purpose is to interrogate the ways in which health and healing are socially constructed—how our sense of reality is mediated by symbolic expressions. Burke's (1969) theory of symbolic action is familiar to scholars and students in communication studies, rhetoric, sociology, anthropology, psy-chology, and political science. He chose a poetic (often referred to as dramatistic) metaphor for the human condition, a lens that emphasizes people as actors using symbols to shape selves, scenes, and society. His major premise can be summarized as follows: Humans "act," that is, they create social worlds through their use of symbol systems. Society arises in, continues to exist, and shifts through the communication of significant symbols. The choice of symbols to describe human desires, emo-tions, situations, struggles, contexts, and all other psychosocial-material phenomena reveals how those phenomena are understood and how humans will act toward them. Symbolic constructions become our realities, the baselines we take for granted as we maneuver through our worlds of experience.

I am interested in how symbolic acts construct beliefs and inform cultural practices. In taking a discursive turn, I explore how members of a given culture rely on symbolic activities to name, legitimize, and establish meanings for social organization. I focus on a particular type of social construction—narratives—and the process of storytelling in health-related contexts. Over the past decade, scholars and practitioners have positioned narrative activity as central to understanding health and healing (e.g., Frank, 2004, 2010; Harter, Japp, & Beck, 2005; Hurwitz, Greenhalgh, & Skultans, 2004; Mattingly & Garro, 2000; Montgomery, 2006; Sharf & Vanderford, 2003). Indeed, Charon (2006) suggested healthcare would be impossible if not for humans' capacity to order and embody experience in narrative form. Dr. Pete, Abigail's oncologist, stressed, "My patients come to MD Anderson with rich, long narratives full of detail. They come to write a few more chapters and also hope to write a whole new book" (as cited in Harter, Patterson, & Gerbensky-Kerber, 2010, p. 470).

NARRATIVE FEATURES

A defining feature of narrative is what Burke (1969) might label Trouble with a capital T. Life-threatening illnesses disrupt a person's conditioned and typical ways of understanding and inhabiting the world. Humans draw on and create stories to make sense of chaos and their imperfect grasp of the human condition. It is transformation of Trouble with a capital T into narrative plight that makes a well-wrought story so powerful, formidable, and culturally essential (Bruner, 2001). In an essay penned for an English Composition class, Abigail recounted her expectations gone awry:

> *I had pain as I lay on the chilling operating table. I was just now waking up from surgery...It was September 25th, my twelfth birthday. I was having what they called a biopsy. Now that I was awake I could see they put me in a room full of color and the smiling faces of my family. Somehow when I saw them all my pain slowly disappeared. They then sang happy birthday to me as I ate my birthday ice chips. Everything seemed perfect until the doctor came in and pulled me back into reality. As she came in I looked at my mother, something just wasn't right. Her expression was never like I had seen it before...*
>
> *Through this whole time period I was confused, I had no clue what was going on, I couldn't grasp onto what they were telling me, I didn't know what they were saying. The only thing I heard clearly was "Abigail we are going to take good care of you." My life was about to change like never before, my journey started here, and I didn't know what to do besides accept the things that were being thrown at me like a fastball. My doctors explained all the procedures and what would happen with my hair, and they made sure not to leave out what would happen if I didn't do the treatment. All of these things were yet to come, when we were talking with the doctors they wasted no time, it was like they weren't breathing when they spoke. (Abigail Armstrong, Your Storm and My Rainbow, p. 1)*

Every life has its defining moments. Years later, Abigail would look back and realize hers took a swift turn that September. She began her birthday with a child's sense of invincibility. With needles inserted in her arms and in the midst of the steady beats of an EKG, she witnessed her own mother's eyes sharpen with terror. Not yet old enough to drive but wise enough to foresee loss. She left a good bit of her childhood on floor 5.

The story of Abigail and her family, which I have introduced and will continue to share in this chapter, illustrates widely recognized features of the rhetorical form known as a narrative. This account was prompted by disorder—a cancer diagnosis and its ensuing treatment—and the human desire for coherence. The main narrators and protagonists are Abigail and her mother, Rhonda. However, several other characters co-construct, narrate, and develop this account, including Abigail's dad and brothers, healthcare providers, hospital administrators, spiritual advisors, journalists, bloggers, and even researchers like myself. Each narrator connects occurrences into configurations that reveal their significance and are consequential for later action.

Narrative plots are event-centered and sequentially depict human action and agency. The process of emplotment refers to how characters and episodes are rendered significant by way of their configuration in a temporal trajectory (Ricouer, 1981). "It is appropriate to speak of a plot, to call attention to the ordering peculiar to narrative," argued Burrell & Hauerwas (1977). "It is that ordering, that capacity to unfold or develop character, and thus offer insight into the human condition, which recommends narrative as a form of rationality" (p. 130). The sense-making potential of narrative—its knowledge-producing ability—rests in large part with the temporal and causal connections made between seemingly random moments, people, and actions.

Accounting for misfortune is an interpretive practice. A pastor's sermon prompted Rhonda to reconsider her attribution of blame:

> Mario, Abigail, the boys, and I are in church. And the pastor starts talking about the hate in our heart, and he asked us, "Who do you need to forgive? Who do you need to forgive?" And I'm sitting there, and I'm thinking, "Oh my gosh, the pastor is talking to me." So I'm thinking, me and mom are good, me and Mario are good, me and my kids are good, who do I need to forgive? And I just felt this ton of bricks on my shoulder, like an ox being drugged. The pastor said, "You can't take the Lord's supper with hate in your heart, you have to forgive. Who do you need to forgive?" And all of a sudden, I said, "Oh my gosh, I need to forgive cancer. I have to forgive cancer." I felt the bricks starting to lift. I have to forgive cancer. I had turned cancer into a person, and I hated it. I was going to destroy it. I hated it for what it did to my daughter, what it did to my family...And I was fed up. And I wanted to destroy it. And I had turned cancer into a person. I think as soon as I was able to say that and acknowledge it, and realize it, I could let it go. Cancer was not a person that set out to get Abigail. She just got cancer. It didn't say, "I'm going to get her." She just got cancer. And I was free. I was able to forgive it. And the pastor talked about living in your pain, being able to function in your pain. And I was in so much pain, but I wasn't able to function in it. I was able to just take that in and say, "I'm done blaming cancer." I was able to live in the pain better. (Rhonda Armstrong-Trevino, Interview)

In telling stories, Rhonda orders events and how they are perceived and responded to. As this excerpt reveals, narrative sense-making often involves assigning responsibility. A plot weaves together a complex web of characters and events and articulates their contribution to the development and outcome of the story. Opportunities and identities arise for Rhonda, as narrator, and other characters through the telling of particular stories in particular ways. As she attested herself, Rhonda's (re)framing of cause and effect influenced her ability to "live in the pain."

Events lived by characters are located in particular places. Plots take into account the historical and social context in which events occurred. In its capacity to connect scenes, acts, agents, agency, and purpose (see Burke, 1969), narrative theory provides a rich perspective for understanding how context matters. For Burke, scene is the symbolization of time and place, the setting of the act which creates the conditions for social action. He emphasized the importance of scene when he argued, "terrains determine tactics" (p. 12). Narrative scholars focus attention on the setting in which events have transpired, the enveloping circumstances that frame and give meaning to events for narrators. Consider Rhonda's testimony:

> *Dr. Pete suggested doing outpatient chemo, and I said, "Yes!" He cautioned me, "You will have to drive back and forth every day." "I don't care, I will drive back and forth every day." Financially, it helped, because we didn't have to pay for food. We still had to park, but it was five dollars versus twelve dollars for the overnight stay. Definitely, there was a financial difference. Even with gas, it was better financially. The peace of having her at home and being able to be at home with the boys and my husband. To breath our own air and not smell floor 5 and not see so many sick people. And get rest because it is hard to get rest in hospitals. But it does come with anxiety. If that machine started beeping, it was like a fire alarm to me. It would jolt me out of bed. And Abigail was freaking out, "Why is it beeping?" And the nurse is not there to turn off the machine and tell you why it is beeping. So you have to read these codes, and you have to call these people who tell you how to turn it off. And so, it comes with anxiety. We wouldn't let her sleep in her room. She had to sleep on the couch, because our room was right next door. And we had her little porta-potty right by it and a bucket. But she was rarely sick from the chemo from home. She was tired. And she lost all her hair. But she wasn't throwing up. But I loved it. Because I could cook, I could clean. It helped my mom and dad because they didn't have to relieve me with the boys as much. The anxiety is worth it. I would still choose to do it.*

Context matters. Material and social environments are inseparable from how roles are performed. The physical space in which action unfolds (and its symbolic meanings) enlarges or restricts possibilities for participants, process, and outcomes. As situations shift, new stories emerge. Rhonda's meaning-making about Abigail's chemotherapy was fundamentally conditioned by the setting in which it was administered. Their home setting afforded possibilities too often surrendered in medical contexts, but that sense of agency was coupled with increased responsibility for lay caregivers. Meanwhile, Rhonda's testimony reveals how actions can invent, not just respond to, material conditions. A case in point: Family members claimed, marked, and redefined living spaces through buckets, a portable toilet, and medicine dispensers. In doing so, family members shift communal understandings of role performances and storylines appropriate for those scenes (see also Harter, Deardorff, Kenniston, Carmack, & Rattine-Flaherty, 2008).

Notably, narrative scholars' preoccupation with context extends beyond the scene of storied events (i.e., the *lived context* of storied events) to include the setting of the storytelling act itself (i.e., the *living context* of storytelling; see Babrow, Kline, & Rawlins, 2005). Meaning does not exist outside of the occasion giving rise to the storytelling and the interpretive activity of contemplators. Audiences bring their positioned identities and cultural filters to the interpretive process. A contextual understanding of meaning-making acknowledges the *relational*, *conditioned*, and *indeterminate* nature of narrative form.

Abigail's Fish Jumping Out of Water

Photo credit: Rhonda Armstrong

NARRATIVE FORM

> *There were a lot of times when I wanted to be left alone. But I loved painting, and I loved that they [MD Anderson Children's Art Project] gave me that chance. It brought me out of myself I guess. I drew a fish that is jumping out of water and they put it in the calendar. I think June or July. When I drew it, the um fish, I remember getting ready to go to chemo, and I just wanted to be free. I wanted summer to come. So, I drew the jumping fish. That fish was in the water and it was free and that is what I wanted for me.*
>
> *I loved it [MD Anderson Children's Art Project]. I took advantage of it whenever I could. I got closer to art during my cancer experience because in some ways it was all I could do. I had a 12-inch metal rod in my leg and I couldn't be physical or athletic, but it was something I could do sitting down. I wouldn't get too nauseous just moving my hand.*

Focusing attention on experience and interpreting it culminates in *form* (e.g., a newspaper editorial, a diary entry, lyrics, choreographic structures). The process of conferring form is a *poetic* one by which the creator represents experience. An idea (e.g., freedom) felt by a narrator (e.g., Abigail) transformed by materials (e.g., canvas and color) yields a drawing (e.g., the jumping fish). Poets conceive happenings through diverse processes including speaking, writing, painting, singing, dancing, photography, and even quilting. Even so, a linguistic bias characterizes narrative scholarship in the discipline of health communication (for exception see Langellier, 2001; Quinlan & Harter, 2010; Sharf, 1995; Yamasaki, 2010). Riessman (2008) argued, "Words, however, are only one form of communication; other forms (gesture, body movement, sound, images) precede words in human development and continue to communicate meaning through the life course" (p. 141). Storylines can be developed, characters' plights performed, and the particularities of settings conveyed through choreographed movement, music, images, as well as words.

Despite a movement toward understanding the embodied nature of storytelling (e.g., Ellingson, 2005; Hawhee, 2009; Langellier, 2001, 2009), communication scholars understandably gravitate toward language and verbal discourse in their treatment of storytelling. Without discounting the importance of language, health communication scholarship and practice can be enriched by enlarging its sense of form. As argued by Barbara Sharf (2009), "There is a need to be careful about over-privileging the verbal such that other important sensory contributions are not recognized and credited" (p. 136). Narrative scholars can expand their arsenal of rhetorical resources to include numerous narrative forms like Abigail's visual imagery. Her artwork opens up new possibilities for cancer narratives as subtle and multidimensional forms of experience surface that bespeak the power of artful beliefs and practices. This is particularly important when research aims to ensure the active participation of nonacademic persons or include the voices of lay individuals who previously have been denied opportunities to articulate their points of view (Ellingson, 2009).

Over the past decade, we have witnessed an increased openness to diverse narrative texts in academic circles, including literary, visual, poetic, and dramatic expressions. A case in point: When working on a chapter for the second edition of *The Handbook of Health Communication*, colleagues and I were granted the opportunity to explore how one family memorialized a member's cancer experience in the form of a scrapbook that included, among other things, photographic images of medical procedures (e.g., surgery to biopsy a lung). We moved between visual images and spoken and written discourse to understand scrapbookers as memory curators, individuals who create and transmit intergenerational health legacies (see Sharf, Harter, Yamasaki, & Haidet, 2011).

Authors remain constrained by the particularities of any given venue or space (e.g., periodicals limit three-dimensional capacity). Meanwhile, narrators and contemplators must tolerate the unease that can accompany the abandonment of traditional understandings of form. Chapter 2 offers an extended treatment of the storytelling capacities of various aesthetic forms including music, visual imagery, photography, and painting.

Irrespective of the mode of expression, the meaning-making aspect of form is *relational* in nature. From Burke's (1931) perspective, form involves "a communicative relationship between writers and audience, with both parties actively participating" (p. 329). His writings continue to influence scholarly conversations about the narrative forms used by humans to bring order and meaning to their lives. Even so, Burke's early interest with poetic processes and the rhetorical qualities of artistic expression is often lost in contemporary translations. His early articulations positioned *form* as *incipient action* and communication, directing critics' attention to socio-historical realms from which forms arise and actions commence. Ultimately, Burke advanced what he termed a "new poetics" that stretched beyond understanding art as the biographical self-expression of an author/creator to acknowledging its communicative potential to arouse contemplators and conjoin individuals. "I was trying to work out of an esthetic theory that viewed art as self-expression, into an emphasis upon the communicative aspect of art," reflected Burke as he reminisced about his early work, "I was trying to develop a theory of literary form" (1976, p. 62).

Russian literary theorist Mikhael Bakhtin (1990) also offered a relational, or dialogic, understanding of form. Bakhtin understood dialogue as characterized by difference and the acknowledgement and consummation of another. "The aesthetic whole," argued Bakhtin, is "actively produced, both by the author and by the contemplator" (p. 67). From this perspective, both I and the other engender creativity and meaning-making. By extension, narrative form must be consummated by the other to create meaning just as each of us is incomplete without the response of the other (Har-

Photo credit: Rhonda Armstrong

Abigail and Danielle Carlin and Alyssa Carlin

ter & Rawlins, 2011). Books come to life when readers engage them. Plots awaken as characters move and dance about for audience members. As such, stories alter contemplators in ways narrators cannot foresee. For both Burke and Bakhtin, the consummation of any aesthetic effort remains an ongoing relational activity.

Stories don't stand still. Meaning shifts by narrator, setting, audience, and just the passing of years. Events once familiar become strange again as scenes play themselves out afresh over the kitchen table or in the boardroom. Rhonda's reflections on "a day in my life" point to the indeterminate nature of narrative sense-making.

> *The first time I shared my story, I believe I did it for the staff meeting at the Children's Cancer Hospital. I was a wreck. And I was crying, and the audience was crying. Then I've spoken for the Anderson Network, and the Advisory Council of MD Anderson. I went recently to a survivorship conference on adolescent and young adults. And you know, it is a different story now when I tell it. A day in my life now is different. Abigail's getting older. I'm at a different place. The first time, it was really difficult. Now, I'm still passionate, I'm still emotional, but there is more celebration. It is different when I talk today. The story has changed.*

Emotions, values, felt experiences with the world, and narrative accounts do not remain static in a way that allows for certainty. As situations and standpoints shift, new and different accounts and meanings emerge. In the interplay of telling and listening, the question of authorship becomes critical. A relational perspective demands that we move away from a message production standpoint (i.e., narrator as owner of story) and acknowledge the fluid and co-constructed nature of meaning-making (Beck, 2005; Rawlins, 2009).

The multiple and shifting nature of meaning should not be perceived as dismissive of patterned practices, canonical truths, or archetypal characters. The ordering of events within a plot is informed by the cultural repertoire of sedimented stories, recurrent patterns of human symbolizing developed and reinforced by conditions of living. We dramatize, emplot, idealize, and formulize according to convention. Representative anecdotes are narratives that embody, with a particular lucidity, general patterns that recur in countless forms in a given culture (Burke, 1969). For example, in Western cultures, members typically yearn for stories that redeem disruptions in orderly ways. Restitution narratives remind patients and families, among other things, of the efficacy of science and technology (Frank, 1995; Harter & Japp, 2001; Workman, 2001). Although infinite interpretations are present in any form, some possibilities are more plausible and defensible. Value remains in ascertaining intended, preferred, and dominant readings of narrative form, as long as we remember "it's not a project we'll ever complete or get completely right" (Ellis & Bochner, 2000, p. 752).

Communication scholars are uniquely equipped to analyze narrative form, novel and recurring plots, causal connections between actions and outcomes, and archetypal characters. In Table 1.1, I pose questions inspired by narrative theory that are worthy of consideration and serve as a backdrop for the discussion that follows in ensuing chapters.

One caution: Much to the contrary of dominant literature, narratives rarely emerge as self-contained and structured linguistic events (i.e., beginning, climax, conclusion). Stories unfold, in daily living and as elicited during interviews, as fragments not nearly as tidy or coherent as often portrayed in academic theorizing (see critiques by Barge, 2004; Boje, 2001; Manoogian, Harter, & Denham, 2010). A story can come in hints and glances, and remain, in the words of Setterfield (2006), "an impoverished, malnourished little thing" (p. 7). Scholars can resist imposing what Boje termed a "counterfeit coherence" (p. 2) on individuals' accounts while still highlighting concerns of interest to narrative scholars: disruption, time, setting, form, characters and their motives, actions, relations with others, and the functions of storytelling.

— IMAGINING NEW NORMALS —

Though the materials of experience are established, we are poetic in our rearrangement of them. (Burke, 1984, p. 218)

When the continuity of our lives is disrupted, we reach for the comforts of a story. Storytelling and its by-products circulate in society and have varied consequences for individuals and groups. Storytelling matters—it reflects and contributes to cultural idioms, shaping people's thoughts and actions. The heuristic potential of storytelling in health contexts is revealed when patients and families draw on the ordering impulses of narrative to re-envision their lives in the midst of vulnerability, health activists mobilize narratives to personalize and politicize inequities, or a senator draws on the emotional pathos and character-related ethos of personal stories to urge a government committee to shift healthcare resources. When faced with novel, uncertain, and difficult situations, individuals can draw on narrative resources in their surround to (re)act and *imagine new normals.* Too often we wait for life to return to "normal," holding on to what used to be. The challenge is to envision otherwise in light of current exigencies.

Imagining new normals requires an aesthetic spirit. Narrators focus attention on experience and interpret it, creating a representation from raw experience. Storytelling is an aesthetic and knowledge-producing experience insofar as it offers an enlarged sense of possibility, a greater depth of insight, fuller and richer interactions (Harter, Leeman, Norander, Young, & Rawlins, 2008; Harter, Scott, Novak, Leeman, & Morris, 2006). Poets strive to create conditions in which plots resonate with contemplators. "Poetic intensity depends on the writer's skill in creating conditions through which the plot

TABLE 1.1: QUESTIONS INSPIRED BY NARRATIVE THEORY

Characters
- How are characters and actions organized in time and space?
- What archetypal characters live in stories (heroes, antagonists)?
  - Who is chosen?
  - Who is barred?
  - Who is not eligible or qualified to enact certain roles?

Setting/Context
- What is the setting(s) of the actions? What is the setting(s) of the storytelling?
- How do contexts give rise to particular stories?
- How does storytelling reveal conditions of its production?
- What sorts of actions or developments does the setting suggest and/or require?
- What recurrent patterns of human symbolizing are developed and reinforced by conditions of living?
- What narrative conventions are privileged in particular contexts?
- What stories are (re)told in particular contexts until they become taken for granted?

Plot/Arrangement and Timing of Events
- How are the past and future envisioned in light of present circumstances?
- Why is the succession of events configured in this way?
- How did the outcome come about?
- What events and actions contributed to the solution?
- Are there inconsistencies that suggest alternative narratives?
- Where are the gaps in stories? Narrative silences? The unmentioned or unmentionable? Absence of some stories altogether?

Storytelling Activities and Relationships
- Who is narrating?
- Who composes the anticipated audience?
- To whom are stories told?
- How do stories position readers?
- What duties are incurred by virtue of witnessing a story?
- What does the process of narrating do?

Consequences of Narratives
- What does the story accomplish?
- What are the consequences produced by particular stories?
- What social orders are maintained or disrupted through storytelling?
- What subjectivities/identities are called into being by stories?
- What new possibilities do stories introduce for being in this world?

- Under what conditions is storytelling therapeutic?
- How do stories evolve and change over time as various constituencies render their experience in alternate stories?

Purposes/Motivations of Narratives
- What worldviews are reflected in stories?
- What cultural markers of concern are revealed in narratives?
- Whose interests are served (or not) by stories?
- What stories are told to justify actions? Relationships?
- What motives are assigned to characters through storytelling?

and plight of characters have cultural resonance," Harter argued (2009), "at once stirring the reader's sense of the familiar and capacity to break through crusts of convention" (p. 674). Aesthetic impact occurs when storytellers use form to awaken audience members and provoke future action.

Art draws upon past experiences and prepares people for settings and events, or in Burke's words, art functions as equipment for living. "Art forms like 'tragedy' or 'comedy' or 'satire' [can] be treated as equipments for living, that size up situations in various ways and in keeping with corresponding various attitudes" (1973, p. 304). In stories, we discover and identify with people, most flawed and some heroic. When faced with profound ambiguity, we can secure ourselves to a strand of a plot and vicariously test life possibilities. Viewed aesthetically, the poetic mandate of storytelling is what Burke (1931) identified as "the element of self-expression in all human activities" (p. 52).

Likewise, we employ our pliable capacity to imagine when consuming stories. The imagination is a muscular mechanism by which we enter and partake in another's lifeworld. "The boldness of the imagination," argued Charon (2006), "is the courage to relinquish one's own coherent experience of the world for another's unexplored, unplumbed, potentially volatile viewpoint" (p. 112). Narratives transport contemplators into another world, inviting them to stretch their imagination and grasp the losses sustained and blessings incurred by another (Green & Brock, 2000). To exercise our imagination is to affirm our capacity to move beyond the boundaries of our own experiences to appreciate others' representations of reality.

Humans make and witness stories, both of which serve salient *functions* in health-related contexts including (1) transforming self, and (2) transforming society. Like other aesthetic activities, storytelling can constitute a heartening form of *worlding*, described by Harter and Rawlins (2011) as "a collective arrangement of activities and works proposing edifying spaces for the human spirit" (p. 283).

TRANSFORMING SELF

To begin, it takes creativity and strength to imagine a new normal when one's taken-for-granted sense of reality is shattered. Once Abigail began cancer treatment, she realized some of her previous goals were unobtainable.

> *I had promised myself I would try out for the football team in 7th grade. I wanted to suit up, get the ball, run it, and score. That is not my dream anymore. Now, it's their [players] dream. But as a trainer, I get to take care of them and help them. If they get hurt, they come to us, and we get to help.*

I understand Abigail's passion for football, if not her love for the Texas Longhorns. She will never run a wheel route or catch a pass and score six points for her beloved Katy High Tigers. Yet, as a trainer, she collaborates with coaches and other care providers to optimize players' experiences during practice and games. She imagined a new normal.

The suffering and uncertainty accompanying a life-threatening illness like cancer includes a host of traumas—pain, anguish, fear, loss, grief, and in some cases, the destruction of a lucid and meaningful reality. Patients can use narration to craft a sense of who they are in light of bodily malfunctions and changes. Indeed, Arthur Frank (1995) positioned sickness as a summons for stories and suffering individuals as wounded storytellers. Using a term coined by Ronald Dworkin, the *narrative wreck*, Frank argued that illness stories carry "some sense of being shipwrecked by the storm of disease" with repeated storytelling functioning as "repair work on the wreck" (p. 54).

Members of the Armstrong-Trevino family embrace the storm metaphor—it flavors their everyday family conversations, appears in the title of an essay composed by Abigail (i.e., Your Storm and My Rainbow) and in reflections shared by Rhonda.

> *Our CaringBridge website is still there, and I sometimes go on it even now. I found, while we were in the middle of the storm, I needed it [the website] to make sense of the storm. We were in a lot of pain and I needed to learn to live in the pain. I started journaling about the experience, and I uploaded most of my entries. So, updating on the site became a release for me. It became a therapeutic release. Umm. But it also allowed me to spread the word about what was going on with Abigail. And I found when I didn't have anything to update, I had to look for things to put up. And I realized, then, how wonderful it was not to have to update. It was a good sign.* (Rhonda Armstrong-Trevino, Interview)

Abigail working as Katy High Athletic Trainer

Photo credit: Rhonda Armstrong

Abigail and Colt Atwood

Photo credit: Rhonda Armstrong

CaringBridge is one of countless social networking sites dedicated to connecting individuals facing significant health challenges with family and friends. Authors can add health updates and photos "to share their story" just as visitors can respond and leave messages in a guestbook (http://www.caringbridge.org/about). Since the Armstrong-Trevino family created Abigail's website, Rhonda has posted over 170 journal entries and more than 38,000 people have visited the site.[1]

Rhonda's testimony illustrates what countless narrative scholars have argued: Storytelling works simultaneously as an agent of self-discovery and creation, constituting knowledge of self and others. "In order to make sense of our lives and to express ourselves," argued White & Epston (1990), "experience must be 'storied' and it is this storying that determines the meaning ascribed to experience" (pp. 9–10). The act of generating a story can allow narrators to explain circumstances and assert agency when an experience threatens one's sense of control (Kleinmann, 1988; Pennebaker, 2000; Sharf & Vandeford, 2003). As spoken by Kathy Charmaz (1995), "Adaptation to impairment takes people with serious chronic illness on an odyssey of self" (p. 675). Disease and its ensuing sickness contribute to bodily appearance and function, and may require significant revisionings of self and patterns of living. Treatment is nothing more or less than a constant test of character.

Just as stories do not sit still, neither does an individual's sense of self. Storytelling is an identity struggle rather than the act of a self with a fixed essence. Assuming the construction of a self occurs through storytelling, inquiry moves from who I am to when, where, with whom, and how I am (Reissman, 2008). For example, Abigail moves back and forth between rejecting and embracing the label of "cancer survivor" as a primary identifier of selfhood.

> When I came into high school after my 8th grade year, I just wanted to be a kid. I didn't want to be the kid that had cancer. I was trying to get over and past it. After I was in remission and went back to school, a lot of people came up to me and I didn't know what to do with that, how to take that in. So, I was kind of mad a lot. I was confused. But then again, I was really shocked at how many people I affected...After a while I started to appreciate that I had cancer. Now that I think about it and to this day, I am glad that I went through the journey of cancer. I got to meet a lot of new people, I learned a lot of new words. And I got to advocate for myself. And a lot of people think I'm older than 16. So, at times, I kind of like being known as a survivor. It defines me in important ways.

Individuals like Abigail who experience serious illness realize it can have lasting physical and social consequences. Just as hairstyles, attire, and makeup are transitory markers of self, Abigail's 18-inch scar and slight limp marks her physical body with cultural significance.

Throughout her life, Abigail will be faced with identity dilemmas associated with the layered markings of cancer inscribed on her body, some scars visible and others not. As her mother, Rhonda often negotiates these dilemmas with Abigail:

> Abigail started this new training thing at Katy High. She is starting her new life. She is Abigail. Just Abigail. No one really knows her there. She doesn't have the stigma of cancer anymore. So, umm, we go to the high school and we are going to meet the trainer, the head coach, so we park in the handicapped parking. Because I was still there, I was still stuck in the cancer. You deserve handicapped parking. They know that you deserve this. And so I parked there without asking Abigail. And so as I parked there, there were some guys over there, and they were looking at us. And when we got out, I noticed they kept looking at us. And that is

ok, you can look. Just don't say anything. Because you don't know what we're going through, you don't know what the handicap is, just don't say anything. So we go inside and take care of our business and we come out and some of the guys are still standing there. And here comes a Katy High Police Officer and he parks behind me. And I look for a second, and I think, no this is not going to happen, just relax Rhonda. Because I had my edge up. He comes and taps on my window. And I said to myself, "I can't believe this." And he says, "Ma'am, I need to see the drivers license for this handicap placard." And I said, "I'd be glad to show you the license for this handicap placard. But I am offended and appalled that these guys right here thought they needed to call and tell on me because they didn't think we were handicap." And I went through Abigail's medical history again in front of these other guys and I said it loudly because I wanted them to know what they did, and I wanted them to feel bad about what they did. And the police officer tried to calm me down. And he said, "I'm sorry that I offended you. But I'm sure you understand there are people who try to take advantage." And I understand that, I do. And as we were leaving, Abigail turned to me and said, "You know what mom, I want you to stop giving my medical history to people. I don't want everybody to know I had cancer. I'm Abigail, I'm a person, and I don't want cancer to be the only thing that defines me." And I took that in, and I just thought, wow, she just taught me something important. She is amazing.

Ruptures in health expose selves to new dimensions, and Abigail is no exception. Rhonda and Abigail's accounts explain and justify decisions already made and sequester distressing storylines in anticipation of the future.

Narrating one's defining moments can prove helpful in strengthening the teller's capacity to deal with life changes and simultaneously increase audiences' awareness of salient issues. In other words, storytelling can reach beyond the transformation of self to include institutional and social change.

TRANSFORMING SOCIETY

From a Burkean perspective, aesthetic encounters are reflections of and contributors to the cultural idioms shaping citizens' thoughts and actions. "[A] great work, dealing with some hypothetical event remote in history and 'immediacy,' may leave us with a desire for justice," suggested Burke (1931, p. 189). "Art negotiates the conditions under which 'life' or 'aesthetic' value can be understood within a culture. In other words, art filters life through the pieties of human perspectives" (p. 314). Burke's ability to read art and culture ideologically remains one of his greatest legacies (Hawhee, 2009; Swartz, 1996). By recognizing the rhetorical elements of literary forms, Burke urged scholars to *politicize* the *poetic* construction of worldviews giving rise to partial perspectives and resulting in "trained incapacities" (i.e., one's training results in one's incapacity to envision otherwise). In *Permanence and Change* (1984), he foreshadowed how performances emerge as contested terrains characterized by competing discourses, and inspired countless contemporary scholars to explore the emancipatory potential of "counter-narratives"—clusters of histories, anecdotes, and other fragments woven together to disrupt stories of domination (e.g., Lindemann-Nelson, 2001).

Narratives represent a performative strategy with particular significance for vulnerable individuals. During Abigail's treatment, Rhonda realized the power of voicing her experience to raise awareness about inequitable situations. Consider the following example:

Abigail: One of my worst memories was when I was fasting for, I think I had a CT scan, and it was scheduled for like 8:00 at night. And I had to fast all night for it, the night before. And my mom fasted, because she said if I was going to fast, she was going to fast. So we both fasted. And that was too late in the day for a test. For some of these kids, they need to be scheduled first. When you are 3, or 5, you shouldn't have to fast until late in the day. An adult can go a lot longer than a child can. I shouldn't have had to fast all day. That was ridiculous.

Rhonda: I learned quickly to become an advocate for Abigail. I would tell them, "You don't want to see me after I've been fasting all day, so you need to schedule us earlier." And, so, then, they would schedule our appointments for like 6:00 am. And now as a Parent Coordinator I get to advocate for others. This is something that we have changed at the hospital. Our family advisory council changed that. We stressed the importance of getting kids in early.

Two years after Abigail began treatment at MD Anderson, and once her osteosarcoma was in remission, Rhonda was hired as the Parent Coordinator of Family-Centered Care at MD Anderson.

When I asked her why she accepted the position of Parent Coordinator, Rhonda humbly stated, "It's about giving back. It sounds so simple, but really, I just wanted to give back and help others." In her job, Rhonda often relies on personal stories to illustrate health dilemmas and set the stage for collective action.

Any way I could learn from my experience and make it better for others. Even something simple as coffee. When the budget cuts came and everybody was cutting, they took coffee pots out of in-patient floors by the nurses' stations. When Abigail was sick, I could go and get coffee. Other parents could get coffee. And they took those coffee pots out. And this brought me to tears. And people were looking at me funny. But I was like, "You do not get it. This will make a parent snap, taking the coffee pot." It was something so small. "Do you realize, people, that my daughter has maybe been up since 3 in the morning vomiting her guts up, and I haven't left her side. I certainly haven't eaten. So that cup of coffee is my nutrition, it's my way to get out of the room, to get out of the room and breathe different air, say good morning to other people, and then go back. It's more than just coffee." I was livid about the coffee. And everyone knew it. So we found a donor, and we got a coffee pot back on that floor. Somebody through the advanced team [got] an industrial pot and filters. The coffee at one point was coming from [a] gift card [we got] from somebody. So, I would go to Sam's and go get coffee with that gift card. Finally, the power that be in that group, whoever has the money, they starting putting coffee back in the budget again…I care about coffee.

Politically, storytelling can restructure institutional and communal life. Feminist scholars position narratives as central resources in their attempts to raise consciousness about lived inequities (e.g., Clair, Chapman, & Kunkel, 1996; Fixmer & Wood, 2005). Plots connect events and agents of causation in consequential ways, suggesting moral visions for living. In other words, stories have strings attached—they demonstrate what counts and the peril of missing it.

One of Rhonda's first initiatives was to send a notecard to the families of recently diagnosed children and adolescents being treated at MD Anderson. In the card, Rhonda draws on her own experiences in an effort to connect with other families and invite them to contact her with questions and concerns. "My story becomes part of my job. That is why I am here. My daughter had cancer and was treated here. That is why I am here. What could say more than that? So I send notes to all new parents," stressed Rhonda. The Director of Family Centered Care, Patty Wells, positioned Rhonda's personal experiences as central to her contributions as a Parent Coordinator. "The fact that she's a parent with a child undergoing treatment here makes her the expert," stressed Patty. "You take the lead from the patients and parents who are going through the experience. They keep you focused, on target, and working on what really matters" (Overton, 2009, p. 20).

Rhonda shares her story in diverse contexts including hospital administrative meetings, social support groups, and fundraising events. "One thing that I did that helped me, there was a mom on CaringBridge, and she challenged me to write 10 things that my child's cancer gave me," reflected Rhonda. "And so I did that. I wrote 10 things that my child's cancer gave me. And so now I am able to share that when I share my story" (see Table 1.2).

At times, Rhonda and Abigail participate in cancer-related projects together. For example, they reflected on sexuality and cancer as part of a patient education video now posted online (see http://www3.mdanderson.org/streams/FullVideoPlayer.cfm?xml=cfg%2FPE-Sex-Cancer-2-Women--cfg). In April 2011, Rhonda and Abigail participated in a Relay for Life to raise funds for the American Cancer Society. As part of the event, Rhonda joined a group of other women whose children were cancer survivors—Moms on a Mission—that coordinated a relay team whose location for the event was labeled "Cureville, Texas." At this event, Rhonda, Abigail, and other team participants raised over $10,000.

Narrative activity is by no means a panacea for life's difficulties, but it does acknowledge vulnerability and struggle in ways that lie beyond the traditional reach of Western medicine. Storytelling can appraise and challenge entrenched habits that too often diminish rather than dignify the human spirit. An emancipatory intent, of course, is no guarantee of an emancipatory outcome. The process of storytelling in and of itself is not evidence of resistance toward oppressive histories or damaged identities. Indeed, storytelling can distort voices, disconnect individuals, fail to redress forces that shape and constrain human agency, and even justify violence (Bute, Harter, Kirby, & Thompson, 2010; Cole, 2010). Chapter 8 focuses on how storytelling energizes public health movements and activists' efforts while acknowledging the difficulty in contesting social orders and politicizing the personal.

– CONCLUSION –

No life can avoid vulnerability and the consequences of tragedy. We all stumble and slip, not looking for the rocks in the road or noticing the edge of a cliff. Likewise, we are storytellers who give meaningful form to life's disruptions through symbolic acts. Narratives constitute complex and sophisticated knowledge of individuals as well as the socio-cultural contexts in which characters cope with unexpected blows of fate. Some narrative forms are carefully crafted and edited accounts mediated in public spheres, others are informal tales incorporated into ordinary conversations. We engage in storytelling to explain and motivate action in autobiographies and fiction, news and bits of gossip, in courtrooms and boardrooms. The human frailties revealed in storytelling can allow participants to cope with vulnerability, and if necessary mobilize resources when individuals or groups find themselves on the wrong side of a statistic.

TABLE 1.2: TEN THINGS MY DAUGHTER'S CANCER TAUGHT ME

By Rhonda Armstrong Trevino

1. Compassion: I learned to be more compassionated and understanding. I would get so mad when I would go to Wal-Mart with a list of 5 things and go the counter with a basket of 200 things and the person at the register would not speak to me. I thought "how dare they, where is their customer service?" After Abigail was diagnosed, I realized that not everyone was able to be at the hospital with their sick child. They may be working at Wal-Mart to make ends meet.

2. Awareness: I realized that no matter how sick Abigail was, there was always someone sicker. When we were in clinic and we would see all those kids. Some kids had a brain tumor, some had amputations. We always found ourselves saying how very blessed we were.

3. Humor: I developed a sick sense of humor along with Abigail. We would sit in the clinic with some of our cancer friends and talk about how we could use their now metal instead of bone legs to bust out windows if we would fall off a high overpass to our watery grave. We had to find humor in all the pain surrounding us.

4. Realism: I learned no matter how awesome the doctors are at CCH, they could not save everyone. We met so many friends and we lost a lot of them. I never thought I would see so much death in such a short amount of time.

5. Hope: I learned to look for rainbows. We were in the midst of a horrible storm and it was raging in my heart. I needed hope and I found it in what I like to refer to as rainbows. Whether it was in a free parking pass or finding out a very sick friend lived to see another day.

6. Humility: I learned to ask for and accept help. We almost resorted to opening a strictly "cancer credit care" to help pay for parking, gas and food while at the hospital. I was good at complaining to the powers that could be about the outrageous prices, but was not able to ask for help. I learned quickly.

7. Weakness: I learned that as much as I thought I was strong emotionally, I was a wreck. I had to stop going to the hospital for about a month. I could not stand to see another sick child or hear about another one dying. I survived only by the grace of God.

8. Conflict: I finally understood how something like this can rip a marriage apart. I always heard about families divorcing after the death of a child and I just did not get it. Wouldn't their relationship get stronger with that death? Wouldn't they come together and conquer the pain together? Well, it is difficult to manage a child with cancer, 2 healthy kids, and a marriage. My husband saw things in black and white and I saw lots of grey. My husband wanted to just do what the doctors said and I wanted to ask questions and be given choices. Abigail is alive and in remission and my marriage survived too.

9. Knowledge of Strength: I learned that my daughter was stronger than I ever thought she could be. She endured unimaginable pain, uncontrollable vomiting and horrible emotional anguish. She maintained her smile and a positive attitude during her ordeal. She faced not only physical obstacles but emotional obstacles. She faced the GIANT and she WON!

10. Anger: I learned that no matter how many surgeries, chemos or tests Abigail has gone through, I never get used to it. It never gets any easier to see Abigail get rolled back to surgery, to see her port accessed or to anticipate the results of her scans. I still hate cancer and I do not want my daughter to have it.

Moms on a Mission: Val Marshall, Holly Meredith, Rhonda Armstrong, Rhonda Cardenas, and Missy Ramirez

Moms on a Mission flag for Relay for Life

Cureville, Texas sign

– REFERENCES –

American Cancer Society. (2012). *Cancer facts and figures 2012*. Atlanta: American Cancer Society.

Babrow, A., Kline, K., & Rawlins, W.K. (2005). Narrating problems and problematizing narratives: Linking problematic integration and narrative theory in telling stories about our health. In L.M. Harter, P.M. Japp, & C.S. Beck (Eds.), *Narratives, health, and healing* (pp. 31–59). Mahwah, NJ: Erlbaum.

Bakhtin, M.M. (1990). Author and hero in aesthetic activity (V. Liapunov, Trans.). In M. Holquist & V. Liapunov (Eds.), *Art and answerability: Early philosophical works by M.M. Bakhtin* (pp. 4–256). Austin: University of Texas Press.

Barge, J.K. (2004). Antenarrative and managerial practice. *Communication Studies, 55,* 106–127.

Beck, C. (2005). Becoming the story: Narratives as collaborative, social enactments of individual, relational, and public identities. In L.M. Harter, P.M. Japp, & C.S. Beck (Eds.), *Narratives, health, and healing* (pp. 61–82). Mahwah, NJ: Erlbaum.

Boje, D. (2001). *Narrative methods for organizational and communication research.* Thousand Oaks, CA: Sage.

Bruner, J. (2001). Self-making and world-making. In J. Brockmeier & D. Carbaugh (Eds.), *Narrative and identity: Studies in autobiography, self and culture* (pp. 25–38). Philadelphia: John Benjamins.

Burke, K. (1931). *Counter-statement.* Berkeley: University of California Press.

Burke, K. (1969). *A grammar of motives.* Berkeley: University of California Press.

Burke, K. (1973). *Philosophy of literary form: Studies in symbolic action* (3rd ed.). Berkeley: University of California Press.

Burke, K. (1976). The party line. *Quarterly Journal of Speech, 62,* 62–68.

Burke, K. (1984). *Permanence and change* (3rd ed.). Berkeley: University of California Press.

Burrell, B., & Hauerwas, S. (1977). From system to story: An alternative pattern for rationality in ethics. In H.T. Engelhardt, Jr., & D. Callahan (Eds.), *Knowledge, value and belief* (pp. 111–152). New York: Hastings Center.

Bute, J., Harter, L.M., Kirby, E., & Thompson, M. (2010). (Un)politicizing the personal? Storying age-related infertility in public discourses. In S. Hayden & L. O-Brien Hallstein (Eds.), *Contemplating maternity in the era of choice: Explorations into discourses of reproduction.* Lanham, MD: Lexington Books.

Charmaz, K. (1995). The body, identity, and the self: Adapting to impairment. *Sociological Quarterly, 36,* 657–680.

Charon, R. (2006). *Narrative medicine: Honoring the stories of illness.* Oxford, UK: Oxford University Press.

Clair, R.P., Chapman, P.A., & Kunkel, A.W. (1996). Narrative approaches to raising consciousness about sexual harassment: From research to pedagogy and back again. *Journal of Applied Communication Research, 24,* 241–259.

Cole, C.E. (2010). Problematizing therapeutic assumptions about narratives: A case study of storytelling events in a post-conflict context. *Health Communication, 12,* 650-60.

Ellingson, L.L. (2005). *Communicating in the clinic: Negotiating frontstage and backstage teamwork.* Cresskill, NJ: Hampton Press.

Ellingson, L.L. (2009). *Engaging crystallization in qualitative research: An introduction.* Thousand Oaks, CA: Sage.

Ellis, C., & Bochner, A. (2000). Autoethnography, personal narrative, reflexivity. In N.K. Denzin & Y.S. Lincoln (Eds.), *Handbook of qualitative research* (2nd ed., pp. 733–768). Thousand Oaks, CA: Sage.

Fixmer, N., & Wood, J. (2005). The person is still political: Embodied politics in third wave feminism. *Women's Studies in Communication, 28*, 235–257.

Frank, A.W. (1995). *The wounded storyteller: Body, illness, and ethics.* Chicago: University of Chicago Press.

Frank, A.W. (2004). *The renewal of generosity: Illness, medicine, and how to live.* Chicago: University of Chicago Press.

Frank, A.W. (2010). *Letting stories breathe. A socio-narratology.* Chicago: University of Chicago Press.

Green, M., & Brock, T.C. (2000). The role of transportation in the persuasiveness of public narratives. *Journal of Personality and Social Psychology, 79*, 701–721.

Harter, L.M. (2009). Defining moments. *Health Communication, 24*, 674–676.

Harter, L.M., & Hayward, C. (Producers). (2010). *The art of the possible.* Athens: Ohio University Scripps College of Communication.

Harter, L.M., & Japp, P.M. (2001). Technology as the representative anecdote in popular discourses of health and medicine. *Health Communication, 13*, 413–429.

Harter, L.M, & Rawlins, W.K. (2011). The worlding of possibilities in a collaborative art studio: Organizing embodied differences with aesthetic and dialogic sensibilities. In D.K. Mumby (Ed.), *Reframing difference in organizational communication studies: Research, pedagogy, practice* (pp. 267–289). Thousand Oaks, CA: Sage.

Harter, L.M., Deardorff, K., Kenniston, P.J., Carmack, H., & Rattine-Flaherty, E. (2008). Changing lanes and changing lives: The shifting scenes and continuity of care in a mobile health clinic. In H. Zoller & M. Dutta-Bergman (Eds.), *Emerging issues and perspectives in health communication: Interpretive, critical, and cultural approaches to engaged research* (pp. 313–334). Mahwah, NJ: Lawrence Erlbaum Associates.

Harter, L.M., Japp, P.M., & Beck, C.S. (2005). *Vital problematics about narrative theorizing about health and healing.* In L.M. Harter, P.M. Japp, & C.S. Beck (pp. 7–30). Mahwah, NJ: Lawrence Erlbaum.

Harter, L.M., Leeman, M., Norander, S., Young, S., & Rawlins, W.K. (2008). The intermingling of aesthetic and instrumental rationalities in a collaborative art studio for individuals with developmental disabilities. *Management Communication Quarterly, 21*, 423–453.

Harter, L.M., Patterson, S., & Gerbensky-Kerber, A. (2010). Narrating "new normals" in health care contexts. *Management Communication Quarterly, 24*, 465–473.

Harter, L.M., Scott, J., Novak, D., Leeman, M., & Morris, J. (2006). Freedom through flight: Performing a counter-narrative of disability. *Journal of Applied Communication Research, 34*, 3–29.

Hawhee, D. (2009). *Moving bodies: Kenneth Burke at the edges of language.* Columbia: University of South Carolina Press.

Hurwitz, B., Greenhalgh, T., & Skultans, V. (Eds.). (2004). *Narrative research in health and illness.* Oxford, UK: Blackwell Publishing.

Kleinman, A. (1988). *The illness narratives: Suffering, healing, and the human condition.* New York: Basic Books.

Langellier, K.M. (2001). 'You're marked': Breast cancer, tattoo, and the narrative performance of identity. In J. Brockmeier & D. Carbaugh (Eds.), *Narrative and identity: Studies in autobiography, self and culture* (pp. 145–184). Amsterdam: John Benjamins.

Langellier, K.M. (2009). Performing narrative medicine. *Journal of Applied Communication Research, 37*, 151–158.

Lindemann-Nelson, H. (2001). *Damaged identities, narrative repair*. Ithaca, NY: Cornell University Press.

Lyotard, J.F. (1984). *The postmodern condition: A report on knowledge*. Minneapolis: University of Minnesota Press.

Maclean, M. (1988). *Narrative as performance: The Baudelairean experiment*. London & New York: Routledge.

Manoogian, M., Harter, L.M., & Denham, S. (2010). The storied nature of health legacies in the familial experience of type 2 diabetes. *Journal of Family Communication, 10*, 40–56.

Mattingly, C., & Garro, L.C. (Eds.). (2000). *Narrative and the cultural construction of illness and healing*. Berkeley: University of California Press.

McKerrow, R.E. (1998). Corporeality and cultural rhetoric: A site for rhetoric's future. *Southern Communication Journal, 63*, 315–328.

Montgomery, K.M. (2006). *How doctors think: Clinical judgment and the practice of medicine*. Oxford, UK: Oxford University Press.

Murphy, J., McFarlane, E., Olmsted, M.G., Severance, J., Drozd, E.M., Morley, M., & Hill, C. (2010). *U.S. News & World Report 2010/2011 best hospitals rankings methodology*. Research Triangle Park, NC: RTI International.

Overton, J. (September/October, 2009). Family-centered care: Parents and professionals in partnership. *Messenger*, 20–21.

Pennebaker, J. (2000). Telling stories: The health benefits of narrative. *Literature and Medicine, 19*, 3–18.

Quinlan, M.M., & Harter, L.M. (2010). Meaning in motion: The embodied poetics and politics of Dancing Wheels. *Text and Performance Quarterly, 30*, 374–395.

Rawlins, W.K. (2009). *The compass of friendship. Narratives, identities, and dialogues*. Thousand Oaks, CA: Sage.

Ricoeur, P. (1981). Narrative time. In W.J.T. Mitchell (Ed.), *On narrative* (pp. 165–186). Chicago: University of Chicago Press.

Riessman, C.K. (2008). *Narrative methods for the human sciences*. Los Angeles: Sage.

Setterfield, D. (2006). *The thirteenth tale*. New York: Washington Square Press.

Sharf, B.F. (1995). Poster art as women's rhetoric: Raising awareness about breast cancer. *Literature and Medicine, 14*, 72–86.

Sharf, B.F. (2009). Observations from the outside in: Narratives of illness, healing, and mortality in everyday life. *Journal of Applied Communication Research, 37*, 132–139.

Sharf, B.F., & Vanderford, M.L. (2003). Illness narratives and the social construction of health. In T.L. Thompson, A.M. Dorsey, K.I. Miller, & R. Parrott (Eds.), *Handbook of health communication* (pp. 9–34). Mahwah, NJ: Lawrence Erlbaum Associates.

Sharf, B.F., Harter, L.M., Yamasaki, J., & Haidet, P. (2011). Narrative turns epics: Continuing developments in health narrative scholarship. In T. Thompson, R. Parrott, & J. Nussbaum (Eds.), *Handbook of health communication* (2nd ed., pp. 36–51). Mahwah, NJ: Routledge.

Swartz, O. (1996). Kenneth Burke's theory of form: Rhetoric, art, and cultural analysis. *Southern Communication Journal, 61*, 312–321.

White, M., & Epston, D. (1990). *Narrative means to therapeutic ends*. New York: W. W. Norton.
Workman, T.A. (2001). Finding the meanings of college drinking: An analysis of fraternity drinking stories. *Health Communication, 13,* 427–447.
Yamasaki, J. (2010). Picturing late life in focus. *Health Communication, 25,* 290–292.

— ENDNOTES —

1. Abigail's CaringBridge website: http://www.caringbridge.org/visit/abigailarmstrong/mystory

CHAPTER 2

THE STORYTELLING CAPACITIES OF ARTS PROGRAMMING IN HEALTHCARE CONTEXTS

— LYNN M. HARTER, MARGARET M. QUINLAN, AND STEPHANIE RUHL —

Selena and Alex were among a group of adolescents and young adults gathered around a table in the Robin Bush Clinic at MD Anderson Children's Cancer Hospital. With the use of glitter pens, markers, and colored pencils they were adding texture and color to flower petals cut from cardstock. "What was the most important thing you learned in basic training?" asked Selena. Alex paused briefly before responding, "That incoming fire always has the right of way!"

Alex was a U.S. Air Force Combat Controller (CCT) deployed in Afghanistan when he was diagnosed with leukemia. Among other skills, he is equipped to assist covert groups of Army Rangers, coordinating air support for on-the-ground troops, or in his words, "I am trained to be the eyes and ears on the ground for the Air Force." He traded in his Air Force blues for a hospital gown upon diagnosis, an M-9 Berretta semiautomatic pistol for a chemotherapy cocktail. Life began anew in a fleeting moment, recasting Alex in a different story. The wars and weapons have changed, yet some feelings remain the same—the jagged shards of fear and desperation, the determined bravery and courage. If his innocence was not lost during basic training and on the battlefield, it most surely was in treatment. Insurgent forces generally can't be swayed by pleas, reason, temper, or threats. Neither can cancer.

The pills and procedures of medicine too often overshadow ordinary life. There is always another appointment to be met, another symptom presenting, another insurance claim to file. But today, for 30 minutes, Alex's world did not revolve around his latest blood counts. A brief respite from a brutal reality. While waiting for his outpatient appointment, he joined Ian Cion, Artist in Residence at MD Anderson Children's Cancer Hospital, and other patients and family members in artful activity. With a quiet steadiness, Alex swirled hues of blue and gray on his flower petals. With competent and practiced hands, Ian taught Alex how to fasten the petals together with wire and beads. As they stood back to admire the finished piece, Ian reflected, "Wow, this could be the official flower of the Air Force!" Indeed, the flower resembled the blue cloth and silver metallic piping of the dress uniforms worn by Air Force personnel (see accompanying photo).

Throughout the morning, I was reminded of John Dewey's (1980/1934) metaphor of art as conversation. For Dewey, the rhetorical power of art is not tied to the private world of the artist. It is the relational nature of an aesthetic encounter that renders it communicative. With Ian's guidance, participants offered creative expressions and engaged with others through art. Alex's flower conveyed his point of view. Meanwhile, the process of its production spurred interaction, storytelling about battles waged across the borders of nations and within one's own body. (Lynn's fieldnotes)

Photo credit: Ian Cion

Alex's flower

Medical technologies render the human body seemingly transparent. Complete blood counts (CBCs) determine amounts of red and white blood cells, hemoglobin, and platelets. Bone marrow aspirations remove cells for biopsy. Lumbar punctures collect fluid surrounding the spinal cord. Collectively these technologies detect the presence or absence of leukemia cells. Even so, Alex's experience cannot be visualized fully through pathology reports. By focusing primarily on what machines and tests reveal, providers sometimes miss the less visible implications (van Dijck, 2005). Artful encounters can enlarge the scope of medicine to acknowledge and respect a person's lifestory. How will leukemia impact Alex's military career? Will his battle against cancer prevent him from returning to active duty as a combat controller? What impact will chemotherapy have on his ability to father children in the future? Artists do not eliminate the uncertainties surrounding cancer and its treatment. Still, they answer suffering in ways that lie beyond the traditional reach of biomedicine.

What is the role of the artist in therapeutic contexts? The term "therapy" derives from the Greek word *therapeia*—"to be attentive to" another (Stuckley & Nobel, 2010, p. 254). In the case of leukemia, attention to a patient's plight typically involves multimodality treatments like chemotherapy, immunotherapy, and/or stem cell or bone marrow transplants. Artists draw on different strengths and techniques to attend to and join with another who suffers. This *attentiveness* and *joining* reflects Dewey's (1980) argument that the "real work of an artist is to build up an experience that is coherent in perception while moving with constant change in its development" (p. 53). In therapeutic roles, artists use various modalities—pencil and paper, photography, music—for diagnostic, recreational, and/or palliative purposes (see Malchiodi, 2003 for an overview). Artists' creative use of these modalities makes possible the simultaneous affirmation of feelings and management of the uncertainties, developments, and changes inherent in the experiences of patients, family members, and care providers. In some cases, artists have clearly articulated goals that guide their encounters with patients (e.g., strengthen muscles through fine art techniques) even as unanticipated outcomes organically emerge through interactions (e.g., stress and anxiety reduction) (e.g., Staricoff, 2001). The *State of the Field Report* published by the Society for Arts in Healthcare (2009) suggests an extraordinary range of clinical possibilities for creative programming with applications for diverse health issues including post-traumatic stress disorder, autism, mental illness, child and adult oncology, and neurological disorders. It is not surprising that nearly half of healthcare institutions in the United States report having arts programming.

How is healing understood from the perspective of the artist? What images of care emerge when guided by the expressive arts? What does the appearance of art therapy in contemporary healthcare reveal about the changing relationship of medicine to society? In this chapter we engage these questions and explore the narrative nature of artful encounters in medicine. Drawing from fieldwork experiences, we profile two initiatives: (1) the Arts in Medicine Program at MD Anderson Cancer Center, and (2) DooR to DooR. Ian Cion is Director of the Arts in Medicine Program (see http://www.mdanderson.org/patient-and-cancer-information/care-centers-and-clinics/childrens-cancer-hospital/support-programs/children-s-cancer-hospital-support-programs-arts-in-medicine.html). Ian provides personalized art programming to individuals and coordinates studio groups allowing patients to connect with similarly situated individuals and families. DooR to DooR, founded and coordinated by Joy Javits, brings professional performing, literary and visual artists to inpatient and outpatient settings at the University of North Carolina (UNC) Hospitals (http://www.doorto-doornc.com). In any given year, over 200 professional performers and visual artists engage patients, staff, and family in public spaces and private rooms at UNC hospitals.

Photo credit: Karen Elizabeth Frank

Joy Javits, D2D[1]

The initiatives we profile differ in size, scope, location, and funding, yet they both demonstrate the role of artist in addressing the psychosocial needs of patients, liberating the human spirit through the arts, and affirming collective experience. We weave between our experiences with the Arts in Medicine Program (AIM) and DooR to DooR (D2D) to develop an understanding of artful practices as knowledge-producing resources for organizations responsible for the care of individuals facing life-changing or terminal illnesses. First, we emphasize the rhetorical capacities of art modalities. By fostering creative *expression* among patients, art-making allows individuals to *engage* with fellow sufferers, family, and friends. Second, insofar as activities allow individuals to *envision* otherwise, patients can *transcend* existing circumstances and imagine new normals. Art-related encounters in clinical settings can function palliatively by alleviating various types of suffering experienced by patients, family members, and care providers, making circumstances more bearable and providing solace.

– EXPRESSION OF SELF <–> ENGAGEMENT WITH OTHERS –

Illness unfolds in stories. Indeed, the central events of healthcare are the giving and receiving of accounts of self (see Chapters 1 and 3). Yet, the scientific acumen of biomedicine, among other characteristics, can create chasms between providers, patients, and families (Charon, 2009). These chasms are numerous and complicated, existing among the multiple standpoints of those affected by and involved with interdisciplinary approaches to care. Although such barriers may seem insurmountable, artists offer a different perspective and skill set that can transcend these chasms of care. From this perspective, art "breaks through barriers that divide human beings, which are impermeable in ordinary association" (Dewey, 1980, p. 254). Joy Javits, founder and director of D2D, stressed:

> *Artists tend to have another way of looking at things. And to include their thoughts,*
> *observations, intuition, it seems so adventurous, and yet logical to me...I would love to get*
> *a group of artists and scientists, or doctors, all those varieties of people that treat people,*

together. A group that would brainstorm about how to heal. You know, what else can you do? Maybe together they could dream ways. You know, doctors, I feel sorry for doctors. They really—they have surgery and they have drugs. That's it. I think artists, their voice should be there too.

Oncologists and surgeons develop intimate knowledge of patients' bodies as they *face illness*. As part of interdisciplinary health teams, artists can help patients *face life*. When the body and self is at stake, patients need attention to both the corporeal nature of abnormalities and their personhood—who they were, are, and can become through relations with others. In this section, we explore the capacity of art-related encounters to foster self-expression and relational connections.

EXPRESSION OF SELF

How is healing understood from the perspective of the artist? For Ian, "To heal is not only to repair, but to create anew." Art therapy in general is based on the idea that the creative process fosters healing through self-discovery, expression, and transformation (Malchiodi, 2003). In this way, artists perform narrative care, described by Kenyon, Randall, and Bohlmeijer (2011) as "acknowledging and respecting a person's lifestory" (p. xv). Although the biographical nature of artful practices is evident outside the realm of medicine, the narrative capacity of art is especially significant for patients whose lives have been altered by severe chronic or acute disease and disability. Art-related encounters can elicit or restore feelings for patients while also developing the capacity to feel among others, creating a shared comprehension of illness.

Making art is a human act of creating meaning out of formless materials. As such, it can be a powerful vehicle for expression. Importantly, the arts include a range of modalities for biographical performance. Some individuals may have limited language skills or impaired speech, and in such cases the arts offer diverse media for expression (e.g., Harter, Scott, Novak, Leeman, & Morris, 2006). The visual arts, for example, foster nonverbal communication, often bringing order and clarity to poorly understood feelings or experiences that may be difficult or too painful to put into words (Rollins, 2005). Visual narratives introduce elements not always represented in verbal tellings, rendering experience "seeable" if not "sayable" (Reissman, 2008).

For several months, Ian worked with Shelby, a 16-year-old patient then being treated at MD Anderson Cancer Center. In an effort to help Shelby develop meaningful relationships with individuals beyond her family, Dr. Martha Askins, a clinical psychologist at MD Anderson, solicited the assistance of Ian. "Part of our therapeutic goal," reflected Ian, "was that I would become another person that she could interact with comfortably." In reflecting on why she referred Shelby to Ian, Dr. Askins suggested:

I thought maybe getting her engaged through a more nonverbal modality would build on her strengths. She [Shelby] has this great wit. She comes out with these one-liners. She has created these riddles about the 50 states…So when I heard about the riddles she came up with, I wondered if she might like to work with Ian to illustrate them in a book. Thinking of it therapeutically, I thought to marry something that she is really good at, her riddles, her sense of humor, with something she could create that would create confidence for her. I thought it could be a way to get her to start opening up.

Over a period of several months, Ian met with Shelby to develop and illustrate a book inspired by her riddles (see accompanying photo). As with any good story, Shelby created a cast of characters engaged in adventures full of peril and danger. Across riddles, her characters came to life and experienced noble sacrifices, miraculous restorations, tragic separations, and reunions. For example, in the Ala-BAM-a riddle, an ostrich was injured in a water balloon accident. The ostrich then sought help in South CARE-olina (see illustrations below). For each riddle, Ian and Shelby sketched accompanying images, and then digitized and colored them on a computer.

Ian and Shelby

Shelby's illustrated riddle of South CARE-olina and Ala-BAM-a

As we pen this chapter, Shelby's family and Ian are working to publish the book. In reflecting on the experience, Ian stressed:

> *When I first started working with her [Shelby] she wouldn't talk. Now, she is talking with me with no inhibitions. And, I am so pleased with how comfortable she has become. It was a*

great transformation. I'm sure she is still going to be dealing with her shyness for some time. It's not something you easily overcome. But certainly she has overcome it with me...Shelby is really proud of this book. Everyone is asking, "When is the book going to be done?" He [her Dad] is hoping that this will boost her self-esteem and that will translate into other areas of her life and in her relationships with others.

Ian structured an environment that fostered inventive expression. Meanwhile, the creative product—the illustrated book of riddles—invites contemplators to connect with Shelby and potentially rethink assumptions about her. One person draws, another witnesses, and in the interchange meaning is born. By creating space for Shelby to communicate through the visual arts, Ian opened an alternative way for her to relate with others, inviting her to move from what Kenneth Gergen (2009) might call "individual being" to "relational being" (p. 32).

Given the temporal rhythms of clinics some artists turn to music as an aesthetic mode. Janet Stolp, a singer and songwriter who works with D2D, stressed, "Music is the universal language and sometimes it's the only way to communicate or give language to a feeling or experience, especially when there is little time in a short visit." In sum, meaning can emerge through visual imagery, motion, and rhythm even as it is negotiated in language (see also Quinlan, 2010; Quinlan & Harter, 2010; Sharf, 2009). Characters' plights can be performed and defining moments clarified as artists connect with patients and families through painting, sculpting, singing, talking, and writing.

Photo credit: Joy Javits

Jonathan Byrd singing with D2D

Narrative sense-making is central to art therapy initiatives in at least three ways. First, in some initiatives, individuals tell stories *through* art. Patients and entire families are encouraged by art therapists to develop a narrative conversation using expressive arts such as drawing or painting, sculpture, and role play (see Freeman, Epston, & Lobovits, 1997). Ian invites participants like Shelby and Alex to give meaningful form to their experiences, what Burke (1968) described as "the element of self-expression in all human activities" (p. 52). As a facilitator and collaborator, Ian makes the aesthetic process possible by organizing materials (e.g., canvases, paint). He engages in conversation with them about particular concepts and mediums participants wish to explore (e.g., painting a horse), offers suggestions and affirms choices (e.g., colors that enhance images), and demonstrates techniques (e.g., how to draw a lotus flower).

For individuals with fine gross motor limitations, Ian engages in a process that he and Dr. Askins call patient-directed art. Dr. Askins offered the following description:

> So we have had a lot of experiences where we have children with quadriplegia or neuropathy or amputation. And it might be amputation of their dominant hand. So, in the art process, we allow them to do as much as they can do, and then we help them to actualize what it is they want it to become or do. We can ask them questions, we can listen to their words, and sometimes we are able to be their hands, or we give them choices to assist them. We can help them _realize a scene_ that they had in their mind, but we have helped them by facilitating that process or executing part of the process.

Patients' disabilities range from minimal to profound in terms of the consequences for art-related activity. Ian responds to the individualized needs of artists so they can tell a story through patient-directed art.

Second, participants can <u>tell a story _about_ art</u>. Natalie Gilbert, a piano player associated with D2D, noted, "I am most moved when patients [are] singing along with a tune they recognize and then begin storytelling about its significance in their lives. This has happened many times." As Natalie attested, music can spur conversation among participants who bring their own memories to the melodies and lyrics. Dawn McDaniel Graff, another pianist affiliated with D2D, agreed and emphasized the music can help "them [patients] relive positive memories." Natalie and Dawn described encounters in which stories about a particular art form (e.g., a song) organically emerged as patients relived memorable moments. Their testimonies illustrate what neuroscientists have argued—music is a language of memory. In brain scans of stroke patients, music has been shown to animate part of the brain—specifically, the medial prefrontal cortex (Omar et al., 2011). The intensity and release patterns in music trigger memories that play in patients' minds. They can see people, places, and incidents. The strongest responses to music—the ones eliciting vivid memories—are connected to the greatest activity on brain scans.

Natalie and Dawn described unscripted moments when patients told stories about particular art forms (i.e., songs). In other cases, art therapists are intentional in their efforts to have patients interpret art forms (see Kaplan, 2003; Riley & Malchiodi, 2003). Sometimes art therapists seek to gain diagnostic insight into momentary conditions or permanent dispositions from the patients' aesthetic expressions. For example, a patient's visual imagery can serve as an anchor for therapeutic dialogue, enhancing the verbal exchange between the patient and the therapist (Stuckley & Nobel, 2010). The content and scope of a patient's artwork—colors, patterns, and subjects—coupled with his or her verbal expressions offer therapists a multidimensional view of a patient's lifeworld, problems, conflict, potentials, and directions.

Third and finally, participants can <u>tell stories while engaged in art-making</u>. In this way, storytelling springs from art. Ian describes his work as "leading with art." By leading with art, he grants authority to participants' voices, creating an egalitarian space in which patients and families can exert control over what they share about their lives and when they share it. In order to provide a nuanced interpretation of what it means to lead with art, we offer an extended personal definition from Ian:

I start with art, and use that to encourage storytelling. What I mean is this. When doctors come in a patient's room, they have a certain authority that is like life or death, and the patients have a visceral physical response to that presence that is connected to fear, connected to anxiety. And even when that presence is there to relieve suffering, it is hard to imagine that ....They have to rationalize that. But when you walk in as an artist, when I walk in, they know, even if they have never met me, they see my cart or all this stuff and they are curious. I look different. There is a certain immediate response to my presence that is different. It is relaxing. Now, there are plenty of doctors and nurses that develop relationships with patients where when they walk in the patients are happy to see them. They are gentle. They are thoughtful. But for me, I have the benefit of that from the start, because I start with art. I lead with art first. That is a benefit of leading with art, going in and leading with it. Now once that is established—that what we are here to do is art—then deeper interactions can come into play naturally without being forced or coerced or extracted. They can come out in their own way and in their own time, in whatever way is comfortable for the patient. But that requires a time commitment. That is why when I go to patients I will sit with them, for as long as it takes. For an hour, 2 hours, 3 hours. I will be with them. And I won't be idle while they are making something. I won't be looking over their shoulder. I am going to sit with them, right along with them, I am going to make stuff. And periodically I can assist them when they need it, or I'll set up a project that is going to need multiple hands to achieve the goal so I'll do a part and they'll do a part and they will know we are working together towards this common goal. But even if it is an individual thing, I will draw a picture too. It can be off-putting to just watch them while they are doing something, it feels like they are under observation. But if you are just sitting with them, and you are not staring at them, if your hands are moving alongside theirs, that physical dynamic between you is equal and that is when they don't feel like they are under a microscope, and I think that is when it is easier to talk and create new narrative cycles that aren't medically-based. Creating an egalitarian space between you and the patient, where you are actually in this thing together, you are committed to the challenge of creativity together.

Photo credit: Lynn M. Harter

Ian making art with Mariel Almendras

When Ian visits kids in their hospital rooms, he brings art materials and an invitation to create instead of bringing needles or pills to swallow. By leading with art, Ian creates and sustains an environment that enables, but doesn't demand, conversation. The vignette at the beginning of this chapter illustrates the power of leading with art. Ian did not ask Alex to tell stories about his experiences as a combat controller—they organically emerged as a group of adolescents and young adults were painting flowers. Art-making can open up dialogue that otherwise might remain dormant, and in Ian's words, "create new narrative cycles."

ENGAGEMENT WITH OTHERS

Importantly, stories told through art, about art, and while making art connect authors and contemplators. In this way, artful *expressions* provide a scaffold of sorts for the achievement of other goals, including participants' *engagement with others*. Although health crises may represent an occasion for communion, illness and its treatment can be quite isolating. During treatment individuals may be separated physically and/or emotionally from their typical surrounds and primary social networks. "It is hard for some of these kids to reach out to their communities because they don't want people feeling bad for them, or they don't want people worrying about them," stressed Ian. "Or maybe they don't want people to see them when their bodies change because of treatment. So this disease [cancer], it can close them off to community."

By design, artful encounters are generative processes, fostering new and enriching potentials through human connection. Helen Wolfson, a musician with D2D, stressed:

> For me, the best thing about DooR to DooR is that it brings human contact and things of beauty to people who are in a position where their illness is often using all the oxygen of their lives, so to speak. When I play for a patient, I am speaking to his or her humanity.

George Winston, a pianist and guitarist for D2D, concurred, and suggested that musical encounters can move patients "from loneliness to community." Sharing an aesthetic experience creates connections between self and others. George and Helen and other artists affiliated with D2D

Photo credit: Robert Ray

Helen Wolfson playing the hammer dulcimer

Photo credit Joy Javits

Steven Fishman singing songs from the 1920s, 1930s, and 1940s

literally bring music *door to door*, and in doing so disrupt the physical and social isolation too often experienced by patients and families.

Ian also strives to build relational connections, what Putnam (2000) might term "social capital." He is emphatic about his primary mission: "I want to build relationships with patients and families through art. So it goes beyond art appreciation. It goes into the realm of shared experience." Ian and the affiliates of AIM and D2D realize in practice what many philosophers have argued: Art can be harnessed to develop richer and fuller relational and institutional life (see Burke, 1968; Bakhtin, 1990; Dewey, 1980). Through art, they are proposing and shaping the worlds people inhabit together.

Communities composed of vulnerable populations are fragile, though, and fraught with risk (Adelman & Frey, 1997). Consider Ian's reflections:

> *This is a community characterized by loss. I feel like, as a caregiver, one of the challenges of this situation, of this methodology, is I see the value of community and the value of connecting individuals, and fostering relationships through art. And I believe in that. Fostering relationships between families through groups is important. There is a genuine value in that. But it comes with risks. And of course this is part of the broader context of the hospital anyway. I'm operating within this context of risk. So I am working with kids who are getting close to one another who are fragile. And they are not always going to experience an outcome like remission. So for kids who are here for a long time, they are potentially making friends with other kids who might not make it. And when that happens, then there is a heightened sense of their own vulnerability, in addition to the loss of a friend. And I am sensitive to that. It's an emotional challenge.*

Ian works with individuals living precarious lives, facing extreme physical illness and its consequences, and coping with recurring loss and survivor's guilt when friends pass away. Fear is inevitable, but so too is resilience. Like Adelman and Frey (1997) we suspect it is the ever-present crisis of human loss and suffering that inspires the profound need for connection in ways that may otherwise elude us in the course of daily living.

Art is a way to engage with others and spur moments of dialogue between patients, hospital staff, artists, and family members. As we acknowledge this, we would like to point out that not all art needs to be interactive; there are times when patients and family members may benefit from just listening, being present, or "taking in" an artful performance. Stephanie recognizes these benefits for both herself and her grandmother as they face life following her grandfather's diagnosis and rapid progression of Alzheimer's disease. In reflection of her most recent visit with her grandparents, she noted:

> *Each day, before Grandma begins her 8 a.m. to 8 p.m. routine of sitting with Grandpa, she spends an hour alone, or with me when I am able to be there, in the dining hall where she slowly drinks her decaf coffee and eats her onion and cheese omelet (or cinnamon roll on Saturdays). As she sits, the sound of old hymns, melodies that her own fingers have created countless times, play from the automated piano that she and Grandpa helped to purchase for the facility years before it would serve an integral, daily role in Grandma's healing process. The piano offers her the company of vivid memories. It's magical, as if her lifestory were in those keys. Each time I visit and accompany her to breakfast, she tells stories of her marriage and we reminisce, we laugh, and we cry. The sound of the piano keys are a necessary background*

for our stories, evoking feelings that we both keep suppressed and creating a space for us to si-multaneously experience vulnerability and strength in our connection and shared experience.

– ENVISION <–> TRANSCEND <–> TRANSFORM –

During our first art session, Maria told me about her love of horses and showed me a pho-tograph of her horse. As her treatment prohibited her from coming in contact with her horse, she was feeling a real sense of loss and greatly missed both the companionship and the respon-sibilities. With this in mind, Maria and I began a series of drawings based on and inspired by the idea of eventually body-painting one of her horses. By setting a large-scale, long-term goal and establishing time each week to work towards this goal, the Arts in Medicine Program served as an integral part of making Maria's experience at MD Anderson a positive one. Over the course of the 3-month project, even her doctors began to notice a difference in how she coped with her treatment. One of the objectives of our program is to implement art projects that are grand in scale so that we can help expand patients' understanding of what is possible for them to accomplish, both as artists and as individuals. I have shown other patients photos and video footage of Maria's horse. When they see the scope of her project, it opens up the possi-bilities for what we can create in collaboration going forward. (http://www2.mdanderson. org/cancerwise/2010/10/the-dream-horse-project.html)

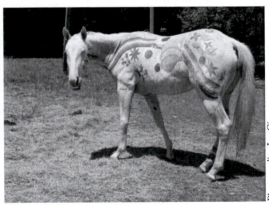

Photo credits: Ian Cion

Maria painting her horse   *Painted horse*

Central Texas is home to countless ranches and breeders of Palamino, Appaloosa, and Thorough-bred horses. Multimodality therapies, bone marrow aspirations, and catheters separated Marie from her Arabian horse. While building her immune system in the aftermath of a stem cell transplant, Maria and Ian created art inspired by Maria's love of horses. In reflecting on the project, Ian stressed:

For Maria, her horse was the thing she felt the greatest sense of loss around. Not being able to be with her horses. That was her life, and she missed that tremendously, and so, she started drawing pictures of her horse, and at one point, I just said, "Well maybe we can paint your horse sometime." So we started working towards that. And she achieved that. She was able to get her white cells up. (Ian, Interview)

Irrespective of one's physical condition, struggle is an anchor of aesthetic processes. Exercising one's imagination requires courage. For Ian, "creativity requires a certain bravery, a willingness to face a blank page, to face the unknown, and to proceed. The fundamental purpose of our endeavor is to ignite and help sustain this sense of bravery." Ian formed AIM from his belief that the courage required in art-making could help both patients and families cope with extreme physical illness, bodily trauma, or invasive medical procedures. To imagine is to *envision otherwise* (Dewey, 1980). From this perspective, aesthetic experiences are knowledge-producing resources allowing participants to envision a future different from the habituated present. A case in point: The Dream Horse Project allowed Maria and her family to find strength and develop determination in the face of human frailty. In Maria's words, "Art helps a lot. It helps me to get away from things. I get my mind off of knowing what they are going to do."

ENVISIONING OTHERWISE

The Dream Horse Project is one of many that bespeaks the power of artful beliefs and practices. To exercise our creativity is to affirm our capacity to move beyond the boundaries of our own bodies and truths and fashion previously unimagined possibilities. Through artful practices, AIM actualizes contemplative spaces for inventing other worlds. Artists working in therapeutic contexts open up new possibilities for individuals facing life-changing and/or terminal illnesses. By tapping into participants' imagination, Ian helps participants to break away from what is supposedly rigid or fixed and carve out new orders. The capacity to re-author one's lifestory is critical for people confronting serious, life-threatening illnesses. Art provides an expressive medium for transforming perceptions into a new story and a new sense of self (Malchiodi, 2003).

Reauthoring of a life can take numerous forms including the development of new outlooks, revisions in the way one lives, or resolutions to personal struggles. Diverse sources provide inspiration for Ian's projects. Generally, he follows the lead of patients and tailors projects to address their needs and interests. The Dream Horse Project was extremely personal for Maria, arising from her sense of loss. That said, the project evolved in an organic fashion to include other patients and families and in light of the metaphorical power of animals and nature.

Ian finds certain concepts and approaches helpful in responding to the needs of individuals and groups. "There is a real marriage of an aesthetic decision and a wellness decision," stressed Ian, in describing his emphasis on the metaphorical power of animals and nature.

There is a certain metaphorical power, a connection to the natural world. The vitality of nature. And then there is a celebration of rivaling and exceeding nature. Not in a typical way in terms of overpowering nature in terms of strength, but really in a sense of rivaling it in terms of beauty. So there are things that we think could be beneficial to the well-being of patients that are really aesthetic decisions, why we choose to make what we make.

What started as a personal journey for Maria and her family developed into a collaboratively composed digital mural of horses that included the work of more than 75 other artists.

Why horses? Ian's primary goal is to provide creative opportunities for participants to cope with their physical realities while connecting with others.

> *Horses are about connections. Maria helped me more fully realize this. With horses there is a sense of kinship, a sense of connectedness, a sense of fellowship. There is a generosity about horses. An animal so great, yet so humble. Something so powerful like a horse is willing to be led. Something so majestic will be a beast of burden for man. That horses are willing to partner with man in the way they do, that is amazing. The horse is an animal that gives that to people. And it allows us to build a connection to the natural world, build an allegiance to the natural world. Nature is the antithesis of the sterile world of cancer. There is something powerful about reconnecting kids to nature. Horses become a bridge between humans and the natural world.*

The aesthetic focus on horses was connected to Maria's original work but evolved into a therapeutic project involving kids of all ages. Over 3 months, patients and family members used different mediums to create art. Participants' creations were then digitally superimposed in collage fashion on lifesize horses.

Photo credits: Ian Cion

Julia and Jenna Cobb

The horse mural was named "Light. Hope. Wonder." by three active participants in the project. Julia Cobb, a patient at MD Anderson, and her sister Jenna and brother Jonathan composed art included in the mural—and cut the ribbons at the unveiling ceremony on July 26, 2012. In reflecting on the name of the mural, Ian stressed:

> *These kids are going through major life upheaval. All of them are. But they are so supportive of each other, and they are maintaining that childlike wonder, and they maintain a light and hope. These words embody what we are trying to do. This is what we want patients and others to remember, even in this context. We are in the midst of upheaval, and we are surrounded by loss and trauma, day in and day out. It is truly a difficult situation.*

The mural is publicly displayed at the entrance to MD Anderson and stands approximately 100 feet wide and 8 feet high. The mural certainly beautifies the space it inhabits. But it also engages everyone who enters the hospital. "The mural is located at the main entrance to the hospital," reflects Ian. "Everyone that comes in will pass it. And if it does what it is designed to do, it will affect how they walk through those doors. And the kids who made it, they knew that their artwork was going to have a positive effect on others."

Light. Hope. Wonder. mural

Photo credit: Ian Cion

The Tree of Life Project also illustrates Ian's intentional marrying of aesthetic and wellness decisions. For 9 months, Ian facilitated the creation of a collaborative art installation, the center of which is a lifesize willow tree composed of participants' artwork. The tree stands 10 feet tall. Its trunk and limbs are composed of strips of material decorated by artists. In the garden is a giant peacock, its long tail made from strings of beads hand-strung by patients and family members. The tree is situated within a garden of handmade plants and flowers, including the flower created by Alex. Birds, dragonflies, fish, and butterflies are included in the art exhibit, unveiled at MD Anderson's Cancer Survivor Day held on September 10, 2011, at the John P. McGovern Health and Medical Science Museum in Houston, Texas. Over 350 patients and family members contributed to the creation of the tree.

> So, the Tree of Life project is an example. I wanted the Tree of Life to be fantastical, to be whimsical. The idea is that if I can get them to experience making something that was better than what they thought they were going to make, beyond their expectations, then they could translate that over to their sense of an ability to deal with their physical reality.

Photo credit: Ian Cion

Tree of Life exhibition

The decision to compose the Tree of Life Project reflects Ian's philosophy of connecting aesthetic and wellness decisions:

> *Going through the cancer experience, you can feel disconnected from the natural world, or even that you are at odds with it because you are fighting the disease. In the Tree of Life Project, the patients have a chance to reconnect with the vitality of nature, to be reminded that they are a vital part of it.*

At the same time, the project remained nimble enough to allow individuals to enter and offer unique contributions. "Kids can choose what they want to do. They can jump in and work on the project in a way that is tailored to them," stressed Ian. For example, during one of Lynn's visits, Ian worked with Marial to compose a lotus flower in a pond of water. Marial's contribution to the project was different from Arnetta, a young woman who strung beads for the peacock's tail.

Photo credit: Lynn M. Harter

Marial's lotus flower

Although people with cancer react to the impact of illness in a variety of ways, they all face unknowns of the disease, loss of control, and the need to readjust life accordingly. By its very nature, art expression can assist individuals in suspending current thinking and considering alternatives. Envisioning otherwise is the first step in transcending and/or transforming their symbolic, material, and corporeal realities.

TRANSCENDING AND TRANSFORMING REALITIES

Joy, Mother Goose, and I [Maggie] rode the elevator over to the children's cancer floor. We walked up to the big doors and were greeted by a nurse who said "You're back!" We smiled. Joy asked, "Do you think there is anyone who would be interested in hearing nursery rhymes?" "Hmmmm," the nurse said, and then consulted two other nurses. "Rooms 2, 4, and 7, but not 16. You can try room 9, but he just had a birthday so he may not be into it." Joy, Mother Goose, and I washed our hands by the sink near the nurses' station. My eyes were drawn to the room where I could hear a baby crying. We walked over and peaked in through a window. A nurse said, "He's been crying all day." He was in his crib crying and playing with his toys. "He isn't even a year," said the nurse. He had a bald head, I wasn't sure if from the medication or just because he is a baby. The nurse said, "Would you like me to go in and hold him?" I knew we wouldn't be able to go in the room because he was on a "drip." The nurse put her gown on and picked him up out of the crib and walked him over to the door. Tears were coming down his cheeks and he tightly held on to the nurse and didn't look over at Mother Goose. Joy and I stood a couple feet away while Mother Goose started to talk to him. She said, "Hello, I am Mother Goose. I am over 500 years old. Will you help me remember my song?" In a high-pitched voice she said, "The itzy bitsy spider, went up the waterspout. Down came the rain and… oh silly me, I have forgotten my own lyrics." She looked at her stuffed goose and said, "Dear goose, please help me remember my lines. Let's start again. The itzy bitsy spider, went up the waterspout. Down came the rain and washed the spider out. Ah, that is better." I know there is more she said to the boy who squinted and furled his eyebrows at her. And then he tilted his as she asked, "Can you help me remember my song? I know it goes something like this: Out came the sun and dried up all the rain. And the itsy bitsy spider…I know I almost have it—nurse and you help me." The nurse smiled and sang into the boy's ear, "Went up the spout again." "Oh now I remember the whole song! Thank you for all your help." The nurse asked, "Can you sing it again?" "Oh sure, but only with your help." The nurse, Mother Goose, myself, and the other two nurses at the station began to sing from the top. By this point, tears had stopped rolling down his chubby cheeks. Mother Goose thanked him for his help and wished him well. We moved two rooms down as the nurse put him back in his crib. Mother Goose began to sing Humpty Dumpty with another little boy. A few minutes into her performance, I could hear the little boy fussing again and then the crying began. Mother Goose looked at Joy and I. My stomach dropped. After she finished singing Humpty Dumpty, she went right back to the little boy and said, "I need some more help from you. Do you know Pat-a-Cake, Pat-a-Cake?" The nurse went over and picked him up again. And from the door, Mother Goose and the little boy did Pat-a-Cake, Pat-a-Cake. Their hands didn't touch. The little boy didn't say a word, but did the gestures to Mother Goose while in the nurse's arms. He no longer had tears in his eyes, but I sure did. At that moment, I didn't need science or medicine to "prove" art heals. I witnessed it. (Maggie, Fieldnotes)

Photo credit: George Remington Photography

Dr. Laura "Lulu" Royster, aka Mother Goose

Maggie's experiences in the field with D2D confirm what many participating artists shared: writing, singing, and even drumming can offer a respite from the corporeal realities of serious illness. In reflecting on poems authored by hospitalized children, Joy argued, "They did express through the poem things that, you know, I don't think their doctors had known, about expanding, and flying, and getting released from their body." Callie, a musician associated with D2D, noted that working in the burn unit is particularly rewarding for her. "I know that the burn patients usually stay in the hospital for a long time. Music is a vehicle that takes them to a different place. When a patient joins me in song, it's as if we're on the same river together." As suggested by Joy and Callie, the creative process can be profoundly normalizing for those undergoing medical treatment, allowing individuals to transcend perceived limits and to escape the brutal realities of treatment.

Hospital and outpatient settings can be sources of distress to an ill person and his or her family. Though naming a condition and beginning treatment can reduce uncertainty and offer hope, the medical environment itself can feel quite foreign. Participating in art-making can transform patients' and families' understandings of place. "Art helps the kids see the hospital as something larger than just the blood draws," stressed Martha. "The hospital becomes a place where people are interested in their well-being, both medically and emotionally." Mariel's mom, Emmeline, concurred:

> *Art makes her forget, forget that she has cancer. It makes her feel like a normal child. And that normalcy is so hard when your child is sick, it is hard to live a normal lifestyle. But when she does art she is just a child again. She forgets she is in a hospital. Like today, it was so nice to see the change in her mood from the time when Ian came in. Before Ian came in, people were coming in every 30 minutes, wanting to take her blood pressure and stuff. And she was just grumpy. I think she was about to say, "Just leave me alone!" So, it makes her day really. It is something she looks forward to. The hospital isn't just a scary place. Although it is still scary.*

Treatment of serious illness often forces individuals to negotiate and survive in spatial domains that, by design, are organized around technology and sterility. In reflecting on D2D music programs, Steve stressed, "For staff it brings a lightness, a different spirit to the floor." Both Emmeline and

46   CHAPTER 2 • The Storytelling Capacities of Arts Programming in Healthcare Contexts

Steve emphasized the capacity of artful practices to transform and enlarge the meaning of place—for patients, family, and staff alike. As suggested in Chapter 1, individuals can redefine the meaning of spaces through material artifacts (e.g., musical instruments, art supplies) and activities (e.g., singing, painting, sculpting). Artists, by virtue of their vocation, disrupt the accumulated experiences and expectations of people who have been served by, worked in, or imagined practices occurring inside their host medical environments. As such, they remind us that any space is contested terrain, the meaning of which is fluid rather than fixed. We argue that the success of art therapy programs rest in part in their capacity to transform meanings of space.

Art therapists, in their finest moments, enable patients to envision previously unimagined possibilities, redefining experience and space. Many artists also have explicit palliative goals. Consider Ian's argument:

> There is another aspect of the imagination that Martha and I are really focused on, and that is using the imagination to address immediate physical pain and fear, using storytelling as a vehicle for addressing pain and fear. And so, in addition, this becomes a kind of metaphorical use of art where you may say, "You can see how this could allow them to see how they could do more," because of course it has that value. But it also has that direct, on the floor value, where you walk into patients' rooms and they are in pain and they have tried a lot of different things to alleviate that pain and none of that has worked, and at that juncture, the toolkit we are bringing is dependent on, can they make art at that time? Are they physically up to it? And sometimes they are. And at those times, if they start making things, they can at least get their mind off, you know, their headache or stomachache or whatever might be bothering them.

What is the goal of therapy? How do we know if therapy is beneficial? What counts as "success" is socially constructed. That is, therapeutic success is defined and legitimized by members of a given culture (Gergen, 2009). As indicated at the beginning of this chapter, nearly half of U.S. hospitals and clinics now integrate some form of art programming. By sponsoring art programs, institutions grant art therapists legitimacy as healers and invite the public to respond positively. Without recognition by medical communities, artists' claims to offer help might lack the power to render them effective in defining human problems or treating them. Meanwhile, the evidenced-based nature of medicine will likely fuel ongoing investigation about the "effectiveness" of art therapy. Although we understand and applaud such efforts, we are reminded of Gergen's caution that the unfettered search for and faith in evidence-based medicine can inadvertently limit access to valuable assistance to those seeking help.

– CONCLUSION –

Serious illness and the severity of measures taken to remedy it invite worry, despair, and sometimes hopelessness. Individuals who enter clinical settings may be hesitant, guarded, and disconnected from their relational networks. Social capital—networks of relationships characterized by trustworthiness and reciprocity—is typically understood and developed through the shared grammars of spoken and written language (Harter, Leeman, Norander, Young, & Rawlins, 2008; Quinlan, 2010). However, communication through symbols is not limited to words. Although some individuals open up and engage actively in verbal conversation, others prefer to express themselves through nonverbal modalities.

Recognizing this, Ian, Joy, and the artists affiliated with AIM and D2D engage a broad repertoire of participants' sensory experiences through artful practices. When patients, family members, and care providers feel out of control and withdraw from social interaction, artful practices offer opportunities for self-expression and engagement with others, inspire participants to envision otherwise, and transcend or transform their symbolic, material, and corporeal realities.

How are we to understand the healing relationship between the art therapist and patient, its potential, and its efficacy? Certainly, artists invite a different (but complementary) form of provider–patient coordination in comparison to medical doctors, surgeons, and specialists. Gergen (2009) offered a benchmark for therapy that includes but extends beyond aesthetic realms: "The primary question, then, is whether the process of client/therapist coordination can contribute to a transformation in relationships of extended consequence" (p. 282). From this perspective, therapy emerges in and through a matrix of relationships. Artistic engagement, and the relationships built in the process of creating, guide individuals in a "growing life," one in which "recovery is never mere return to a prior state, for it is enriched by the state of disparity and resistance through which it has successfully passed" (Dewey, 1980, p. 13). The artists of AIM and D2D offer us images of generative activity that restores, enhances, and transforms the relational life of patients and families.

Ultimately, forms of therapy achieve credibility through social practice and convention. The U.S. healthcare system is characterized by the use of evidence-based practices. As such, the efficacy of any treatment or procedure is typically established through scientific research. It remains difficult to measure quantitatively emotions such as loneliness, fear, joy, and relief. Even so, paralleling the evidence-based movement in the larger healthcare environment, research about art therapy is being conducted across disciplines with findings published in academic journals (see Society for the Arts in Healthcare, 2009, for an overview).

The benefits of arts programming is not limited to patients and families. The lives of artists who work in therapeutic contexts also are enriched through artful encounters. We close with personal reflections from Ian and Jonathan Byrd, a D2D performer. These testimonies illustrate the transformative power of art for the therapists themselves.

> I think the crux of it for me is, I feel more and more responsible for self-improvement. I feel greater and greater responsibility to refine my capacity for caring and tenderness and thoughtfulness. And catch myself in all those moments in my life when I am not living up to where I am when I am with the patients. Because what I notice when I am here and I am on the floor and I am working with patients and families, because their situation is so extreme, it is very easy for me to be totally present with them and totally caring and good to them. And then I can walk down the hall and not necessarily have that same level of patience and compassion with a colleague. And I can go home and not necessarily have that same level of patience with my kids. So a personal lesson in this for me is when you are confronted with this reality, you really appreciate the brevity of life, the fragility of life. You appreciate the splendor of family and love and the power of our hearts and minds to deal with suffering. And I am so in the middle of it. That is life. And yet there are times in my life when I am not that present. But I want to be. So that is the big lesson for me. And I can't go to a mountaintop for this. I have to go right into the middle of pain and loss and yet still maintain a true openness and sense of joy, not only for my own well-being but for the well-being of those around me. (Ian, Interview)

Excerpt from The Toughest Gig by Jonathan Byrd, a performer with D2D:

She was beautiful. Even though treatment had robbed her of her hair, it was obvious from her delicate cheekbones, olive skin, and perfect teeth that she had been a very pretty young woman. Her closed eyes were frozen in the grimace of slow, lasting pain. She was also disconnected from oxygen, IVs, and monitors—literally, her last connections to this world. I wondered what kind of tough decisions her mother had made in the previous days.

Emotionally unready to sing, I decided to play a melody, "Home Sweet Home," a simple tune from the 1800s with a fitting title for the final journey. We were forbidden to get close to very ill patients, but I got as close as I could without touching her and began to play slowly, unsure whether she could even hear me. The young lady curled up into a fetal position and began to rock back and forth. She could hear me.

Everything that I had ever thought was important to me faded from existence. For the first time in my life, I knew what it felt like to be a shaman, a priest, a messenger of God, summoning up all the joy, beauty, and humanity that I could manage and bringing it to people who needed it more than anyone else in the world. I was smiling and crying at the same time.

No higher honor could be bestowed on any musician; no tougher gig ever existed. On a beautiful spring morning, I left that room, carrying a lesson in the power of music. Now, even when I'm playing to a crowded bar or a coffeehouse, I try to remember that I have no idea what someone in that room is going through. Perhaps a mother is there, just back from sitting in the hospital with her beautiful, dying daughter.

Music can be great fun for a night out on the town, but it can also be like water for a lost soul, wandering in a desert of heartache. About once a month, I return to the hospital to visit patients and share the gift of music. I'll never forget the last musical rites of that beautiful young woman and one of the greatest rewards of my career.

– REFERENCES –

Adelman, M.B., & Frey, L.R. (1997). *The fragile community: Living together with AIDS*. Mahwah, NJ: Lawrence Erlbaum Associates.

Bakhtin, M.M. (M. Holquist & V. Liapunov, Trans.). (1990). *Art and answerability*. Austin: University of Texas Press.

Burke, K. (1968/1931). *Counter-statement*. Berkeley: University of California Press.

Charon, R. (2009). Narrative medicine as witness for the self-telling body. *Journal of Applied Communication Research, 37*, 118–130.

Dewey, J. (1980/1934). *Art as experience*. New York: Capricorn Books.

Freeman, J.C., Epston, D., & Lobovits, D. (1997). *Playful approaches to serious problems: Narrative therapy with children and their families*. New York: W. W. Norton & Co.

Gergen, K.J. (2009). *Relational being: Beyond self and community*. New York: Oxford University Press, Inc.

Harter, L.M., Leeman, M., Norander, S., Young, S.L., & Rawlins, W.K. (2008). The intermingling of aesthetic sensibilities and instrumental rationalities in a collaborative arts studio. *Management Communication Quarterly, 21(4)*, 423–453.

Harter, L.M., Scott, J.S., Novak, D.K., Leeman, M.A., & Morris, J. (2006). Freedom through flight: Performing a counter-narrative of disability. *Journal of Applied Communication Research, 4*, 3–29.

Kaplan, F.K. (2003). Art-based assessments. In C. Malchiodi (Ed.), *Handbook of art therapy* (pp. 25–36). New York: The Guilford Press.

Kenyon, G., Randall, W.L., & Bohlmeijer, E. (2011). Preface. In G. Kenyon, E. Bohlmeijer, & W.L. Randall (Eds.), *Storying later life: Issues, investigations, and interventions in narrative gerontology* (pp. xiii–xviii). New York: Oxford University Press.

Malchiodi, C.A. (2003). *Handbook of art therapy.* New York: The Guilford Press.

Omar, R., Henley, S., Bartlett, J.W., Hailston, J.C., Gordon, E., Sauter, D., Frost, C., Scott, S., & Warren, J.D. (2011). The structural neuroanatomy of music emotion recognition: Evidence from frontotemporal lobar degeneration. *NeuroImage, 56*, 1814–1821.

Putnam, R.D. (2000). *Bowling alone: The collapse and revival of American community.* New York: Simon and Schuster.

Quinlan, M.M. (2010). Fostering connections among diverse individuals through multi-sensorial storytelling. *Health Communication, 25*, 91–93.

Quinlan, M.M., & Harter, L.M. (2010). Meaning in motion: The embodied poetics and politics of Dancing Wheels. *Text & Performance Quarterly, 30*, 374–395.

Riessman, C.K. (2008). *Narrative methods for the human sciences.* Thousand Oaks, CA: Sage.

Riley, S., & Malchiodi, C.A. (2003). Solution-focused and narrative approaches. In A.C. Malchiodi (Ed.), *Handbook of art therapy* (pp. 82–92). New York: The Guilford Press.

Rollins, J.A. (2005). Tell me about it: Drawing as a communication tool for children with cancer. *Journal of Pediatric Oncology Nursing, 22(4)*, 203–221.

Sharf, B. (2009). Observation from outside in: Narratives of illness, healing and morality in everyday life. *Journal of Applied Communication Research, 37*, 132–139.

Sharf, B., Harter, L.M., Yamasaki, J., & Haidet, P. (2011). Narrative turns epic: Continuing developments in health narrative scholarship. In T. Thompson, R. Parrott, & J. Nussbaum (Eds.), *Handbook of Health Communication* (2nd ed., pp. 36–51). Mahwah, NJ: Routledge.

Staricoff, R.L., Duncan, J., Wright, M., Loppert, S., & Scott, J. (2001). A study of the effects of visual and performing arts in healthcare. *Hospital Development, 32*, 25–28.

State of the Field Committee. (2009). *State of the field report: Arts in healthcare 2009.* Washington, DC: Society for the Arts in Healthcare.

Stuckley, H.L., & Nobel, J. (2010). The connection between art, healing, and public health: A review of current literature. *American Journal of Public Health, 100*, 254–263.

van Dijck, J. (2005). *The transparent body: A cultural analysis of medical imaging.* Seattle: University of Washington Press.

— ENDNOTES —

[1]   The supplies on her cart are part of a LiveSTRONG grant she received as an artist. The LiveSTRONG grant is not a part of DooR to DooR, but meant to support Joy's personal artwork in hospitals.

PART 2

STORYTELLING IN DIVERSE HEALTHCARE CONTEXTS

CHAPTER 3

EMBRACING NARRATIVE LOGICS AND ENLARGING CLINICAL INTERACTIONS

– LYNN M. HARTER –

The camera focuses on a teenager sporting a white and black headscarf and match-ing attire. At first glance, Christine might be a typical high school sophomore, and, in another time and place, doing ordinary things in ordinary fashion. If viewers pay close attention, though, they glimpse shadows that trouble her eyes, a vortex of emotions and "what–ifs" that makeup can't conceal.

To save her life, parts of Christine had to die. That's the purpose of chemotherapy—to wipe out cancerous cells. The central line beneath Christine's collarbone, barely visible on-screen, is a port that simultaneously serves as an entry point for multiple medications and a potent reminder of the cruel and capricious nature of cancer. Reshuffling of a life. Lost innocence. Osteosarcoma is not a wall one can easily climb over, tunnel under, or knock down.

As the camera spans the room, Christine's parents, Barb and Steve, come into view. The Lunsford family sits in an exam room in the outpatient oncology unit at the University of Texas MD Anderson Cancer Center. A dense mass presenting on Christine's latest computerized axial tomography (CT) scan brought her family from their farm in Virginia to the Children's Cancer Hospital in Houston. As characters in this documentary, the Lunsford family draws audiences into their plight, adding public scope to their private fear and grief.

"Would you like to listen to the dictation process? It's your choice," asks Dr. Pete Anderson, inviting Christine and her parents to enter a process typically reserved for authorized medical personnel. They nod in unison, and Dr. Pete picks up the phone and begins dictation. The human capacity for burden is far more pliable than most of us ever imagine.

"You shouldn't be afraid of what you are going to say in front of a family, because you are organizing their care. You better know what you are doing," stresses Dr. Pete in a voice-over layered upon video footage documenting a routine clinical process (i.e., clinical dictations) performed in a novel way (i.e., with patients and family members present). The Lunsfords attentively listen to Dr. Pete's review of the chief complaint and presenting symptoms, interpretations of her recent scans, and Christine's love of horses. Dr. Pete periodically stops to ask questions (e.g., perceived level of pain?) and address their concerns about next steps in the clinical trial (e.g., how will you communicate with our referring physician?).

The setting shifts to the office of Patty Wells, R.N., Director of Family-Centered Care at the Children's Cancer Hospital. "Sharing information is a hallmark of family-centered care," stresses Patty. "There is no reason why any child or family, no matter the diagnosis, shouldn't be able to go away from each clinic visit with a summary of what is going on, resource information, and contact information so the family has it in their hands. So, I believe it's really applicable not just for cancer, but across the board."

As this action sequence concludes, Maritza Salazar, an oncology nurse, emphasizes, "Being transparent about what you are doing with your patient and when you plan on doing it, and just putting it out there is huge for nursing, for allied health, and for any other consulting physicians that we have." (The Art of the Possible, Harter & Hayward, 2010)[1]

Who and what are being framed in this storyline, and in what settings? What actions are justified, and in what conditions are they possible? Which social orders are maintained or disrupted? As one of the producers of *The Art of the Possible*, I hope audiences pause to consider these questions. Narrators often tell a story with a preferred reading in mind, and even assume some interpretations are more reasonable than others (Eco, 1994). Yet, as argued in Chapter 1, the poetic and political potential of storytelling does not rest solely in its performance. "The meaning of a narrative—a novel, a textbook, a joke—arises from and is created by the meeting between teller and listener" (Charon, 2006, p. 52). From this perspective, *The Art of the Possible* is a living text, a zone of indeterminacy in which contemplators co-author its meaning. Action sequences remain alive and gain traction as viewers enter the story and engage, enlarge, or edit it to make sense of their own lives.

Of particular interest in this storyline is the location (i.e., exam room) in which action unfolds (i.e., medical dictation) and the roles performed by characters (i.e., Dr. Pete, Christine, and her parents). Medical charts—textual representations of social events—remain a staple form of communication in healthcare contexts, serving as a conduit for sharing information among numerous health professionals whose offices may be located in a variety of areas or who may work separate shifts, billing clerks and third-party payers, and even representatives in legal departments. The form of clinical dictations has shifted considerably in the past decade. Once abbreviated handwritten notes placed in a patient's record are now typically digitally composed. Meanwhile, filing cabinets are being replaced by online storage and retrieval services (see Steinbrook, 2008, for an overview). Although many physicians and clinics still maintain paper charts, the desire for and accessibility of electronic medical records (EMRs) is increasing, and in fact represents a rapidly growing industry populated by web services like Google Health and Microsoft HealthVault. In spite of these shifts, the dictation process itself still occurs typically in backstage clinical environments accessible only to health professionals. Drawing from the work of Goffman (1959), I use the term *backstage* in reference to staff-only areas of health settings where preparation for and documentation of patient visits are done (see also Ellingson, 2005; Morgan & Krone, 2001; Morgan-Witte, 2005). Healthcare administrators and care providers control backstage settings, marking areas in which patients can and cannot go and controlling the amount of information readily accessible to them.

Medical records are authoritative accounts that transform events into an ordered and official story including progress notes about the chief complaint, laboratory and imaging test results, prescriptions, and treatment plans (Poirier et al., 1992). As with any organizational document, the creation of medical records is governed by rules—both formal and hidden—that shape who can talk about what in what ways, when, and where. Dr. Pete shifts protocol by inviting patients and families to observe the dictation process, ask questions, and contribute additional information. In reflecting on his process, Dr. Pete suggests:

> *My dictations will be better if patients are in the room. And it can be a fun process. I usually start with a story shared by the patient, something good in his or her life. If patients are in the room, I also can pause, ask questions, clarify treatment protocols, and ensure we are all on the same page. It may sound counterintuitive, but it is more efficient to do dictations with patients.*

Dr. Pete's approach has profound implications for who is given authority to speak, whose narrative accounts are endorsed, and what information is considered relevant. Christine's equestrian aspirations may be of little concern to a billing clerk, but are acknowledged by Dr. Pete as relevant to how treatment fits into Christine's broader life vision—how she imagines her *new normal*. Patients may or may not choose to participate in this activity, but the invitation itself offers (1) a level of transparency and (2) responsiveness to patients' broader life circumstances sought by advocates (e.g., Cohen, 2010; Haidet, 2007; Sharf, 2009).

Patients like Christine enter healthcare organizations without the option of sending back a life circumstance that just doesn't fit, and health professionals are summoned to care for them. I offer the opening vignette and brief analysis as an entry point for a broader conversation about how people relate and coordinate activities in healthcare organizations. First, I articulate a social constructionist perspective to emphasize how communication creates structures that constitute organizations and how, in turn, those structures shape the nature and flow of communication within. I then explore the narrative nature of healthcare and the benefits of *explicating embracing* narrative logics in order to humanize medicine.

— ORGANIZING HEALTHCARE: A SOCIAL CONSTRUCTIONIST PERSPECTIVE —

I view organizations as composed of ordered and purposeful interaction among people and embedded in broader environments consisting of other organizations and varied social, economic, and political forces. People coordinate their interactions with goals in mind and as shaped by organizational and public cultures—rules, resources, and sets of social practices patterned across time and space and layered to form institutions (Giddens, 1984).

The terrain of the U.S. health system is in constant transformation. Contexts of care take diverse form and shift in response to economic contingencies, healthcare reform, and consumerist demands. Healthcare organizations provide preventative, curative, and palliative care and include traditional contexts like hospitals and physician offices, community-based environments like mobile health clinics, complementary and integrative medicine (CAM) settings, and long-term facilities that provide care to individuals with health needs due to factors such as age or disability (see Apker, 2011, for an overview). None of these organizations exist in isolation; in fact, they operate interdependently in a healthcare industry comprised of more than 200 occupations and representing one of the largest employment sectors in the United States (Sultz & Young, 2009). This chapter focuses on relational interactions in traditional healthcare organizations. Chapters 5, 6, and 7 focus on community-based settings, long-term care facilities, and integrative medicine, respectively.

The importance of communication in healthcare organizations extends beyond the flow of messages across channels. I adopt a social constructionist perspective to emphasize the constitutive role of communication in organizing around health. A social constructionist lens accentuates the centrality of language and other symbol systems, and stresses the significance of social interaction in organizing (see also Chapter 1; Allen, 2005; Cooren, Taylor, & Van Every, 2006; Fairhurst & Putnam, 2004). Human action and interaction generate shared understandings of roles and situations—that is, the who, what, where, when, and how of clinical dictations. Patterns of symbolic activity reproduce rituals and routines in regular fashion to the point that a system might appear static, worldviews fossilized, scripts institutionalized, and the imagination "bureaucratized" (Goffman, 1959, p. 56). Even so, humans have the capacity, in Giddens' (1984) words, to "reflexively monitor" their actions and their surround, improvise, and effect change. For example, clinical dictations can be moved to the front stage of care and include the voice of patients and families.

Because narratives are central to how we bring order and meaning to our lives, they remain a principal symbolic form through which organizational practices and patterns are reproduced and resisted. "In organizations," argued Boje (2001), "storytelling is the preferred sense-making currency of human relationships among internal and external stakeholders" (p. 106). Storytelling is a socially symbolic act in a double sense in that it (1) takes on meaning in social contexts, and (2) 'ays a significant role in the construction of social contexts as sites of meaning within which social ʳs are implicated (Mumby, 1987a). Institutional settings supply the narrative auspices through selves come to be articulated. At the same time, individual and institutional stories reflect and `at the very least contribute to, broader socioeconomic and political conditions as they are ʰrough master narratives.

The portrayal of medicine in prime-time medical dramas, a staple of U.S. popular culture, illustrates how no narrative is solely personal, organizational, or public. Dominant storylines and anecdotes about alternative practices of healthcare (e.g., a physician telling a patient the only thing herbs are good for is cooking) reinforce a master narrative that positions technology as progress (Harter & Japp, 2001). In the United States, the technological orientation is encapsulated in the metaphor of "body as machine," a way of perceiving and defining illness as a malfunction of one of the "parts," and health and restoration of it as part of the "working order." What is at stake in this narrative process? Consider Mumby's (1987b) argument:

> Narratives do not simply inform organization members about the values, practices, and traditions to which their organization is committed. Rather, they help to constitute the organizational consciousness of social actors by articulating and embodying a particular reality. (p. 125)

Narrative practices reflect and establish power relations in a wide range of institutions. The master narrative of "technology as progress" incorporates a terminology or language, legitimates a corps of professionals and practitioners, establishes hierarchies among those legitimated, and financially supports and maintains some administrative structures and processes at the expense of others. A case in point: While complementary and integrative medical (CIM) practices may improve health, reduce disease, and reduce healthcare costs, countless conventional scientists still question its legitimacy and some third-party payers remain reluctant to cover its costs (see Chapter 7; Geist-Martin, Berlin-Ray, & Sharf, 2011).

In the next section, I focus on narrative acts and enactments in traditional healthcare organizations. Medicine not only calls upon and uses storytelling but also embodies it by its very nature. Yet, narrative logics often get minimized (or lost completely) amid the scientific and instrumental rationalities of medicine.

– HUMANIZING MEDICINE –

Healthcare would be impossible if not for participants' capacities to order and represent experience in narrative form. As argued in Chapter 1, narratives endow experience with meaning by temporally organizing events, distinguishing characters and their relationships, and ascertaining causality by connecting events. There is little in the practice of medicine that does not have narrative features. Patients narrate their chief complaints, residents and interns present cases in storied form, family members recount intergenerational health legacies, and coroners lament loss in the form of death notes. I first explore the narrative nature of medicine then highlight practices that explicitly embrace narrative logics.

THE NARRATIVE NATURE OF MEDICINE

Clinical practice itself is indelibly stamped with the crafting and consuming of stories. Healthcare providers rely on narrative activity to gather information, keep records, make therapeutic decisions, build relationships with patients, and respond to their concerns. To begin, patients tell providers stories about their maladies, pared-down autobiographical accounts chronicling illness and revealing lay beliefs about cause and effect. A symptom or disease is an event befalling a patient, sometimes caused by something identifiable, at a particular point in time and space and as narrated from a particular point of view.

Consider the case of Anne, a 24-year-old participant in a study of intergenerational diabetes in rural Appalachia (Manoogian, Harter, & Denham, 2010). During a routine physical, she complained of frequent urination coupled with an unusual thirst and extreme hunger. Diabetes populates her family history, and the broader region in which she lives is characterized by disproportionate rates of diabetes. Numerous care providers consumed Anne's account, interrogating and expanding it where necessary. "Have you experienced recurring skin infections?" "Have you noticed blurred vision?" "Have you experienced any numbness or tingling in your feet?" These are questions a provider might have asked to ascertain whether or not Anne's body was producing enough insulin. Ultimately, Anne's doctor positioned her account within a larger biomedical story, what Sanders (2009) described as an *illness script* (e.g., Type 2 Diabetes Mellitus).

Care providers are faced with another narrative challenge: how to help families comprehend tests they don't understand and results that disrupt their envisioned futures. For example, most individuals are unaware that the presence of ketones in one's urine is a sign that the body is using fat for energy instead of using glucose (American Diabetes Association, 2012). Meanwhile, patients may not know how to measure or manage their blood glucose levels. Today, Anne continues to seek assistance from providers about appropriate interventions and lifestyle changes. Providers must position patients like Anne within an intelligible therapeutic trajectory—"*create sense* out of situations" (Mattingly, 1994, p. 812; emphasis in original). Mattingly went on to argue:

> *Therapeutic success depends in part upon the therapist's ability to set a story in motion which is meaningful to the patient as well as to herself. One could say that the therapist's clinical task is to create a therapeutic plot which compels a patient to see therapy as integral to healing. (p. 814)*

In sum, providers *make sense* of a patient's ordering of illness details by locating it in a larger narrative taxonomy of similar cases and, in so doing, recast experience in ways that *create sense* and, hopefully, desirable turning points in the story (see also Garro & Mattingly, 2000; Greenhalgh & Hurwitz, 1999; Hunter, 1991).

Extraordinary care providers are endowed with the gift of plot—they understand how clinical practice relies on narrative activity to diagnosis disease, facilitate treatment, build relationships with patients, and probe the meaning of illness in the contexts of patients' unfolding lives (Montello, 1997). When faced with a diagnosis of T2DM, Anne had to remap her social existence. Along with changes in her dietary routines and daily blood checks, Anne's sense of self shifted with the duties imposed by disease management. In this way, Anne's body, when it could no longer produce or process insulin, set in motion the need for new stories. People like Anne must learn to think differently about their postdiagnosis worlds and construct new relationships in those worlds. By default or choice, providers come coauthors of and characters in their patients' lifestories (Rawlins, 2005, 2009).

Diagnostic and treatment processes, then, are narratively inflected enterprises. Medicine has een without these narrative features or concerns. Until recently, however, narrative logics acknowledged as necessary components of healing relationships (see critiques by Eggly, omery, 2006; Zaner, 2009). The almost unquestioned assumption that medicine is a science deters attention away from interpretive logics that providers rely on in their care of individual patients. This is not surprising given that practitioners and scholars alike typically relegate storytelling to life spheres of consumption and leisure. Culturally determined and arbitrary binaries (art/science, emotion/instrumental reason, leisure/labor) remain deeply rooted in modern Western cultures (Ellingson, 2009). Although such paired terms do not reflect inherent realities, they are expressions and justifications of transformations associated with modernity whose lingering presence is felt in contemporary health organizations.

Providers and patients alike rely on instrumental rationality and administrative structures for routine tasks and third-party payer financing of care (duGay, 2000). Meanwhile, society writ large benefits from scientific research and technology-driven treatment regimens. Yet, scientific and instrumental rationalities are limited conceptions of reason. When experience is isolated from the human conditions from which it arises and the consequences it engenders, its meaning and significance are cut off from social experience (Dewey, 1980).

Amidst ever-enlarging menus of medical technologies in bureaucratic systems, the craft of storytelling may seem out of place. In fact, Dr. Jack Coulehan of Brook University Hospital in New York, during an interview with Daniel Pink (2005), argued that "medicine sees anecdote as the lowest form of science" (p. 150). Without a doubt, anatomical knowledge of the body remains essential for practicing medicine. Healthcare providers appropriate and establish legitimacy from such knowledge-intensive discourse (Barbour, 2010). Even so, the interpretive challenge of clinical work is to ascertain the thoroughly contextual and contingent nature of experience. The social meanings of symptoms can complicate even a straightforward diagnosis. Narrative activity provides situational meaning and perspective for a patient's predicament, sense-making that providers can draw on to understand the patient's plight.

What is at stake if narrative logics are dismissed as irrelevant to clinical interactions? The instrumental and scientific logics of mainstream medicine too often render invisible what Mishler (1984) termed "the life-world" of the patient. Clinical interactions in traditional contexts remain dominated by physicians' perspectives (i.e., disease framework) while patients' perspectives (i.e., illness framework) are minimized (Sharf, Harter, Yamasaki, & Haidet, 2011). The lay experience of illness is quickly overtaken by technical expertise and the complex organization of treatment. Patients' experiences are efficiently reduced to diagnostic related groups (DRGs), formalized accounts that set in place what third-party insurers will pay for medical treatments (Geist & Hardesty, 1992). Pain is reinterpreted as symptoms using specialized language that is at once unfamiliar and overwhelming to many patients. In general, Frank (1995) described this process as *narrative surrender* on the part of patients. "The ill person not only agrees to follow physical regimens that are prescribed; she also agrees, tacitly with no less implication, to tell her story in medical terms" (p. 6).

Montgomery (2006) re-envisioned clinical reasoning to include both the patterned regularities advanced by scientific and instrumental logics and the particularities of lived experience embodied in narrative. In similar fashion, I position narrative sensibilities as worthy of consideration alongside other rationalities that give rise to and shape healthcare. Like Charon (2006, 2009), I believe medicine is a more narratively inflected enterprise than it realizes. Providers need not reject scientific logics or privilege personal stories over evidence-based medicine to acknowledge how patients experience illness in unique ways. In the next section I highlight clinical practices that embrace narrative logics as central to the day-to-day accomplishment of healthcare.

EMBRACING NARRATIVE LOGICS

A scientifically competent medicine cannot help a patient grapple with the loss of health or find meaning in suffering. Along with scientific ability, physicians need the ability to listen to the narratives of the patient, grasp and honor their meanings and be moved to act on the patient's behalf. (Charon, 2006, p. 150)

The coupling of narrative logics with scientific reasoning allows providers to think rigorously and empathically. The emergence of the narrative medicine movement signifies growing acknowledgment of the critical role of storytelling in clinical practice. Dr. Rita Charon, Professor of Clinical Medicine at Columbia University, is a widely recognized authority in the practice of narrative medicine (e.g., Charon, 2006, 2009). She is the founding director of the master of science (M.S.) in Narrative Medicine launched by Columbia University, a program targeting administrators of healthcare organizations and care providers interested in incorporating narrative practices in mainstream medical settings (see http://ce.columbia.edu/Narrative-Medicine). The program includes training in the close reading of literature, and reflective and creative writing.

What is narrative medicine, and how is it practiced? At the Vice-Presidential Plenary Lecture of the 2007 National Communication Association Convention, Charon emphasized that all clinical interactions exhibit a narrative structure. The art of adjusting scientific abstractions to particular cases is a narrative act. As I illustrated earlier, Anne's care providers relied on narrative sense-making to diagnosis her T2DM. On countless occasions she narrated symptoms to providers who reshaped story elements into a recognizable illness script, incorporating information gleaned through questions, test results, and physical exams. That said, some clinical moments are more narrative than others. The potential of narrative is more fully realized when a provider reaches beyond a diagnosis and treatment plan to understand, for example, why a patient like Anne may fail to follow dietary recommendations (e.g., lack of financial resources). Serious and life-threatening illness is disruptive, locating individuals in disorienting social and material circumstances. Ruptures in health expose selves to new dimensions and demands. As such, most people seek more from a doctor than a classification of their malady. Narrative sensibilities allow providers to join with others who suffer and be responsive to their plight. The practice of narrative medicine realizes in practice what Bruner (2001) conceptually argued: Stories construct two landscapes—action and consciousness—occurrences coupled with the thoughts and emotions of characters.

The practice of narrative medicine requires an aesthetic spirit. From Charon's (2006) perspective, the imagination is a "muscular mechanism" by which we enter another person's lifeworld. "The boldness of the imagination is the courage to relinquish one's own coherent experience of the world for another's unexplored, unplumbed, potentially volatile viewpoint" (p. 122). Narratives invite us to stretch our imagination to grasp events befalling another individual. To exercise our imagination is to affirm our capacity to move beyond our own bodies and experiences to appreciate others' realities. Narratively competent providers are those who marshal their clinical imaginations in an effort to comprehend changes patients face and losses they endure. Procedures may be routine, but people are not.

While coproducing the documentary *The Art of the Possible*, I witnessed numerous clinical practices that reflect narrative logics. The opening vignette of this chapter highlighted Dr. Pete's practice of inviting patients and families to participate in the narration of medical dictations. He also coauthors one-page summaries of care with patients and family members. Paperwork (e.g., progress notes, lab reports, x-ray reports) can obscure key problems and turning points in treatment. At the same time, such practices generally fail to include the voices of patients and family members (see critiques by Cassell, 2004; Poirier et al., 1992). In contrast, Anderson invites patients to coauthor accounts of their care, often asking them to sit with him at a computer to construct their updated one-page summaries. Each summary includes diagnostic information, a temporal account of the illness including problem areas, and scanned images of test results. This instrumental information is coupled with photographic images and reflective information provided by patients (e.g., Christine's love of horses). These summaries situate illness in biomedical stories as well as the broader contexts of patients' lives. As illustrated in the documentary, patients and families keep copies of summaries on flash drives provided by MD Anderson Cancer Center. Underlying his use of summaries is a metaphor of partnership—working with patients, families, and other providers to understand illness and make good decisions about care (Anderson & Kaye, 2010).

Another innovative practice highlighted in *The Art of the Possible* is the construction and use of shared calendars to chart and manage treatment. Consider the following documentary excerpt of an interview with Wanda, an oncology nurse at MD Anderson:

> *Communication is such a key when taking care of these kids . . . We all work together on these calendars for these patients. It's a great communication tool. It gives us all, including the family who gets a copy every time they come, an idea of what's going on, when his next chemo is scheduled, when he just had chemo. Here you see where his make-a-wish that he just went on was there on the calendar. He [Dr. Pete] puts everything in. You know, if they're going to school and they have a band concert or they have something going on in their life.* (The Art of the Possible, 2010)

Calendars represent jointly constructed visual aids including prompts for the timing of chemotherapy, medication, blood count checks, scans, and other events of importance to patients (see Figure 3.1).

Dr. Pete believes jointly constructed calendars minimize the effects of "the narrative of anxiety that often accompanies a cancer diagnosis and subsequent treatment" (as cited in Harter, 2009, p. 143).

The co-construction of one-page summaries and shared calendars illustrate *narrative competence in action*—that is, a responsiveness to the thoroughly contextual and contingent nature of health and healing (Charon, 2006). In stark contrast to the depersonalized case histories characterizing mainstream medicine, Dr. Pete's practices transform third-person chronicle into narrative and illustrate the power of integrating patient-oriented evidence that matters (POEMS) with disease-oriented evidence (Donnelly, 1988; Shaughnessy, Slawson, & Becker, 1998). These practices strive to create what Sharf and colleagues (2011) described as an *aligning moment*, "an experience of genuine shared understanding" (p. 46).

When aligning moments occur, they provide *narrative jolts*, creating "a pause in the script of the biomedical practice and focusing both the doctor and patient on the fully contextualized health issue" (Sharf et al., 2011, p. 46). Yet, aligning moments are difficult to achieve, enabled and constrained by several forces. Providers must be open to hearing personal accounts that run parallel to and inform their biomedical stories. Providers are tremendously overworked and overburdened, and not all of them are cognitively and emotionally equipped to realize the narrative potential of aligning moments (Thompson, 2009). Norms of "detached concern" are deeply entrenched institutionalized

FIGURE 3.1: EXAMPLE OF A SHARED CALENDAR

Click here to reset form

Date Printed: **06/17/2011**   MRN: **749588**

Pt Name: **Anderson, Pete (Sample)**

Outpatient Pediatric Calendar

DOB: **07/08/1954** Sex: **M**

Attending Physician: Peter M. Anderson, MD 11279

Page 1 of 1

Time Period (dates): July+ Aug 2011

Allergies: none

Sunday	Monday	Tuesday	Wednesday	Thursday	Friday	Saturday
3	4 Holiday	5	6	7	8 Birthday!	9
10	11	12 scans CT PET-CT	13 clinic appointment	14 IFOS/Mesna	15 IFOS/Mesna	16 IFOS/Mesna
17 IFOS/Mesna	18 IFOS/Mesna	19 IFOS/Mesna	20 IFOS/Mesna	21 IFOS/Mesna bag change	22 IFOS/Mesna	23 IFOS/Mesna
24 IFOS/Mesna	25 IFOS/Mesna	26 IFOS/Mesna	27 IFOS/Mesna	28 disconnect Neulasta	29	30
31	1 count check clinc	2	3	4 count check clinic	5	6

Additional Comments:

hr 175; wt 75 1.9m2 CI IFOS- outpatient x 2 week (monthly)

Ifos 1 gm/m2=1.9gm + Mesna 1gm/m2=1.9 gm daily x 14 days.
7 day bag contains 13.3 gm ifos+13.3 gm Mesna in 665mL ; infuse at 4cc/hr using Gemstar pump
-for nausea: Kytril patch- change weekly
ref: Meazza et al Prolonged 14-Day Continuous infusion of High dose Ifosfamide.. Peds Blood and Cancer
2010; 55: 617-620 ; Anderson P. Continuously Improving Ifosfamide/mesna: A Winning combination. Ped
Blood and Cancer 2010:55:599-600

Pediatric Plan of Care
File under: Allied Health/Pathways
Copyright 2008 The University of Texas M.D. Anderson Cancer Center

Page 1 of 1

PED 00080 V6 03/20/2008

scripts about how healthcare should be performed (Fox, 1980), anesthetizing providers from head to toe. Positioned as a science, medicine easily appropriates a detachment that defends against emotion and vulnerability and promotes distancing between providers and patients.

Detached concern may enable some physicians to work amidst wounded and distorted bodies, nauseating smells, patients' misery and pain, and in the face of inescapable uncertainty (see Morgan & Krone, 2001). Even so, most providers and patients bring their emotional memories into medical encounters and are influenced by emotions they experience in interactions with each other and in anticipation of the future (Roter & Hall, 2011). When it is not balanced by providers' authentic engagement with patients, medicine's practice of detached concern, in the words of Montgomery (2006), is "a frail defense against uncertainty, death, and human emotion" (p. 173). Narrative medicine—the practice of joining in authentic contact with the suffering of another—is *vulnerable medicine* that requires mindfulness, courage, and vigilance (Bochner, 2009). Connection with others makes us vulnerable to grief and loss even as it offers an intimacy that heals and sustains. The challenge remains—to be attentive to another human being without becoming overwhelmed or incapable of exercising clinical judgment.

Narrative medicine is a relational accomplishment. Patients also must be willing and empowered to narrate their experiences. If patients haven't been encouraged to think of their lives in a narrative way, it can be difficult for providers to help them grapple with turning points and ruptures in their life's story (Bochner, 2009; Hauerwas, 1990). Meanwhile, Americans are socialized to be "good patients" who do not openly question and instead defer to the expertise and decision-making power of providers (Suchman, 2011). To often, patients censor their lived truths, tucking them quietly away and choosing the social convention of silence. Unfortunately, voices, when muted, become withered like unused muscles.

Elizabeth Cohen (2010), senior medical correspondent for CNN, encouraged individuals to be "bad patients," especially when providers are dismissive of patients' observations of their own health. "It's your body. It's your health. Doctors and nurses have saved my life and the lives of my daughters and I'll be forever grateful to them," stressed Cohen, "but sometimes *you* will be the one to save your own life, or the life of someone you love" (p. 174; emphasis in original).

Dr. Sherrie Kaplan, Associate Dean of the School of Medicine at University of California Irvine, advocates a standpoint she describes as *planned patienthood* (Cohen, 2010). In lieu of a passive role, Kaplan encourages individuals to consider what they need to get out of appointments, identify questions they need answered, remember what issues are important to them even when providers interrupt, and narrate what they think providers need to know about their life circumstances. Consider the dialogue between Logan and Michelle Boyd, characters in the documentary *The Art of the Possible*:

> *Michelle: First, I'm going to ask him about the Chicago Conference, because that was supposed to be the latest, greatest stuff, to see if there's anything new. I'm gonna ask him, did the x-ray show anything? And he may or may not know. He may not want to do anything yet. Typically when you do radiation for bone cancer you have to do chemo before you do the radiation. So I'm gonna ask him if we have to go ahead and do that, could we throw in the radiation to the back? And then I want to ask him if it's okay to give you Tylenol and ibuprofen.*
>
> *Logan: She googles stuff, and then she writes it all down on her notepad. And then she asks Dr. Anderson questions about it. Can we do this? Can we do this? And he either knows*

about it or he goes and he looks it up. And most of the time we can't do it, but sometimes she finds some good stuff. It's pretty annoying. [Laughter]

Michelle: That was Dr. Pete's idea online. He mentioned that, you know, when you get in there you're intimidated. So you should write down your questions so that when you get in there, because doctors have a limited amount of time, and I understand that. But if I've been waiting all month to ask these questions, if I don't get those questions out, I'm not gonna be happy. So, I just keep my notebook, and as these question pop into my head I write them down for the next time that we're gonna see the doctor.

Dr. Pete: You don't get smart talking to yourself. I'm very impressed how patients now bring me information. I've learned many new things when patients will email me articles or bring them in. My attitude is, I'll try to learn everything I can from each family . . . put yourself in their shoes, from the family-centered perspective, what is needed to complete an episode of care so it's good for everybody? (The Art of the Possible, 2010)

What sorts of actions does this storyline suggest? What identities are called into being in this action sequence? In cancer care, the stakes are high, the science shifting, the providers skilled but imperfect and regularly wrong in the process of being right. Much to her son's feigned dismay, Michelle engages in *planned patienthood*, a performative strategy with emancipatory potential for patients and providers alike. Through their diligent and earnest efforts, Michele and Dr. Pete disrupt the ambient, opaque silence that often surrounds the experience of vulnerability in traditional healthcare contexts.

– CONCLUSION –

Organizations cannot exist apart from the symbolic management of meaning. Individuals' communication practices contribute to the ongoing process of organizing and constituting social reality. Narrative sensibilities provide a robust lens for exploring how healthcare organizations take shape in and through symbolic interactions. Clinical practice is composed of narrative accounts of action and motives of providers and patients who are frustrated and puzzled by circumstance, plagued by uncertainty, rewarded for efforts, and called to account for mistakes.

Providers conduct physical exams, draw blood, use position emission tomography (PET) scans and other tools to detect problems, and achieve therapeutic goals. The value of these activities, though, is quite limited without the social interactions that situate them in a meaningful context for involved parties. Medicine's primary symbolic currency is narrative. Providers encourage patients to narrate chief complaints, use stories as a way to fashion a differential diagnosis and treatment plan, and offer stories back to patients explaining circumstances and charting trajectories of care. Most individuals do not know, for example, that a PET scan, commonly used to detect cancer, simply measures the areas in the body that consume the most glucose (Servan-Schreiber, 2009), nor are they familiar with multimodality treatments for cancer. Clinical success depends in part on the providers' ability to interpret a "shadow" on a scan, convey its causes and consequences, and envision future action as an unfolding story.

In this chapter, I illustrated the narrative nature of healthcare. I highlighted clinical practices that encourage providers to imagine themselves into the role of the other. One-page summaries and shared calendars situate illness in the broader contexts of a patient's life, responding to the particular and contingent nature of suffering. Meanwhile, inviting patients and families to participate in dictating medical records shifts traditional protocols concerning who can talk about what, where, and when. Narrative practices, including who is entitled to tell what story, reinforce and/or resist organizational power structures (Mumby, 1987a, 1987b). Power is distributed more equitably when patients sit beside care providers and participate in the medical dictation process, coauthoring textual representations of their experience and care.

— REFERENCES —

Allen, B.J. (2005). Social constructionism. In S. May & D.K. Mumby (Eds.), *Engaging organizational communication theory and research: Multiple perspectives* (pp. 35–54). Thousand Oaks, CA: Sage.

Anderson, P.M., & Kaye, L. (2010). The therapeutic alliance: Adapting to the unthinkable with better information. *Health Communication, 24,* 775–778.

American Diabetes Association. (2012). http://www.diabetes.org.

Apker, J. (2011). *Communication in health organizations.* Malden, MA: Polity Press.

Barbour, J. (2010). On the institutional moorings of talk in healthcare organizations. *Management Communication Quarterly, 24,* 449–456.

Bochner, A.P. (2009). Vulnerable medicine. *Journal of Applied Communication Research, 37,* 159–166.

Boje, D.M. (2001). *Narrative methods for organizational and communication research.* Thousand Oaks, CA: Sage.

Bruner, J. (2001). Self-making and world-making. In J. Brockmeier & D. Carbaugh (Eds.), *Narrative and identity: Studies in autobiography, self and culture* (pp. 25–38). Philadelphia: John Benjamins.

Cassell, E. (2004). *The nature of suffering and the goals of medicine.* Oxford, UK: Oxford University Press.

Charon, R. (2006). *Narrative medicine: Honoring the stories of illness.* Oxford, UK: Oxford University Press.

Charon, R. (2009). Narrative medicine as witness for the self-telling body. *Journal of Applied Communication Research, 37,* 118–131.

Cohen, E. (2010). *The empowered patient.* New York: Ballantine Books.

Cooren, F., Taylor, J.R., & Van Every, E.J. (2006). *Communication as organizing.* Mahwah, NJ: Lawrence Erlbaum.

Dewey, J. (1980/1934). *Art as experience.* New York: Capricorn Books.

Donnelly, W. (1988). Righting the medical record: Transforming chronicle into story. *Journal of the American Medical Association, 260,* 823–825.

duGay, P. (2000). *In praise of bureaucracy: Weber, organization, and ethics.* Thousand Oaks, CA: Sage.

Eco, U. (1994). *Six walks in a fictional words.* Cambridge, MA: Harvard University Press.

Eggly, S. (2002). Physician-patient co-construction of illness narratives in the medical interview. *Health Communication, 14,* 330–360.

Ellingson, L.L. (2005). *Communicating in the clinic: Negotiating frontstage and backstage teamwork.* Cresskill: Hampton Press.

Ellingson, L.L. (2009). *Engaging crystallization in qualitative research: An introduction.* Thousand Oaks, CA: Sage.

Fairhurst, G.T., & Putnam, L.L. (2004). Organizations as discursive constructions. *Communication Theory, 14,* 5–26.

Fox, R. (1980). The evolution of medical certainty. *Health and Society, 58,* 1–49.

Frank, A.W. (1995). *The wounded storyteller: Body, illness, and ethics.* Chicago: University of Chicago.

Frank, A.W. (2004). *The renewal of generosity: Illness, medicine, and how to live.* Chicago: University of Chicago Press.

Garro, L.C., & Mattingly, C. (2000). Narrative as construct and construction. In C. Mattingly & L.C. Garro (Eds.), *Narrative and the cultural construction of illness and healing* (pp. 1–49). Berkeley: University of California Press.

Geist, P., & Hardesty, M. (1992). *Negotiating the crisis: DRGs and the transformation of hospitals.* Hillsdale, NJ: Lawrence Erlbaum.

Geist-Martin, P., Berlin-Ray, E., & Sharf, B. (2011). *Communicating health: Personal, cultural and political perspectives.* Long Grove, IL: Waveland Press.

Giddens, A. (1984). *Modernity and self-identity: Self and society in the late modern age.* Stanford, CA: Stanford University Press.

Goffman, E. (1959). *The presentation of self in everyday life.* New York: Doubleday.

Greenhalgh, T., & Hurwitz, B. (1999). Narrative based medicine: Why study narrative? *British Medical Journal, 318,* 48–50.

Haidet, P. (2007). Jazz and the "art" of medicine: Improvisation in the medical encounter. *Annals of Family Medicine, 5,* 164–169.

Harter, L.M. (2009). Narratives as dialogic, contested, and aesthetic accomplishments. *Journal of Applied Communication Research, 37,* 140–150.

Harter, L.M., & Hayward, C. (Producers). (2010). *The art of the possible.* Athens: Ohio University.

Harter, L.M., & Japp, P.M. (2001). Technology as representative anecdote in popular discourses of health and medicine. *Health Communication, 13,* 409–425.

Harter, L.M., Japp, P.M., & Beck, C.S. (2005). *Vital problematics about narrative theorizing about health and healing.* In L.M. Harter, P.M. Japp, & C.S. Beck (pp. 7–30). Mahwah, NJ: Lawrence Erlbaum.

Harter, L.M., Patterson, S., & Gerbensky-Kerber, A. (2010). Narrating "new normals" in health care contexts. *Management Communication Quarterly, 24,* 465–473.

Harter, L.M., Scott, J., Novak, D., Leeman, M., & Morris, J. (2006). Freedom through flight: Performing a counter-narrative of disability. *Journal of Applied Communication Research, 34,* 3–29.

Hauerwas, S. (1990). *Naming the silences: God, medicine, and the problem of suffering.* Grand Rapids, MI: Eerdmans.

Hunter, K.M. (1991). *Doctors' stories: The narrative structure of medical knowledge.* Princeton, NJ: Princeton University Press.

Hurwitz, B., Greenhalgh, T., & Skultans, V. (Eds.). (2004). *Narrative research in health and illness.* Oxford, UK: Blackwell Publishing.

Kleinman, A. (1988). *The illness narratives: Suffering, healing, and the human condition.* New York: Basic Books.

Manoogian, M., Harter, L.M., & Denham, S. (2010). The storied nature of health legacies in the familial experience of type 2 diabetes. *Journal of Family Communication, 10,* 40–56.

Mattingly, C. (1994). The concept of therapeutic 'emplotment.' *Social Science & Medicine, 38*, 811–822.

Mattingly, C., & Garro, L.C. (Eds.). (2000). *Narrative and the cultural construction of illness and healing*. Berkeley: University of California Press.

Misher, E.G. (1984). *The discourse of medicine: Dialectics of medical interviews*. Norwood, NJ: Ablex.

Montello, M. (1997). Narrative competence. In H.L. Nelson (Ed.), *Stories and their limits: Narrative approaches to bioethics* (pp. 185–197). New York: Routledge.

Montgomery, K.M. (2006). *How doctors think: Clinical judgment and the practice of medicine*. Oxford, UK: Oxford University Press.

Morgan, J., & Krone, K. (2001). Bending the rules of "professional" display: Emotional improvisation in caregiver performances. *Journal of Applied Communication Research, 29*, 317–340.

Morgan-Witte, J. (2005). Narrative knowledge development among caregivers: Stories from the nurses' station. In L.M. Harter, P.M. Japp, & C.S. Beck (Eds.), *Narratives, health, and healing* (pp. 217–236). Mahwah, NJ: Erlbaum.

Mumby, D.K. (1987a). *Narrative and social control: Critical perspectives*. Newbury Park, CA: Sage.

Mumby, D.K. (1987b). The political function of narrative in organizations. *Communication Monographs, 54*, 113–127.

Pink, D. (2005). *A whole new mind: Moving from the information age to the conceptual age*. New York: Riverhead Books.

Poirier, S., Rosenblum, L., Ayres, L., Brauner, D.J., Sharf, B.F., & Stanford, A.F. (1992). Charting the chart—an exercise in interpretation(s). *Literature and Medicine, 11*, 1–22.

Rawlins, W.K. (2005). Our family physician. In L.M. Harter, P.M. Japp, & C.S. Beck (Eds.), *Narratives, health, and healing* (pp. 197–216). Mahwah, NJ: Erlbaum.

Rawlins, W.K. (2009). Narrative medicine and the stories of friends. *Journal of Applied Communication Research, 37*, 167–173.

Riessman, C.K. (2008). *Narrative methods for the human sciences*. Los Angeles: Sage.

Roter, D.L., & Hall, J.A. (2011). How medical interaction shapes and reflects the physician-patient relationship. In T.L. Thompson, R. Parrott, & J.F. Nussbaum (Eds.), *The Routledge handbook of health communication* (2nd ed., pp. 55–68). New York: Routledge.

Sanders, L. (2009). *Every patient tells a story: Medical mysteries and the art of diagnosis*. New York: Broadway Books.

Servan-Schreiber, D. (2009). *Anti-cancer: A new way of life*. New York: Viking.

Sharf, B.F. (1990). Physician-patient communication as interpersonal rhetoric: A narrative approach. *Health Communication, 2*, 217–231.

Sharf, B.F. (2009). Observations from the outside in: Narratives of illness, healing, and mortality in everyday life. *Journal of Applied Communication Research, 37*, 132–139.

Sharf, B., Harter, L.M., Yamasaki, J., & Haidet, P. (2011). Narrative turns epics: Continuing developments in health narrative scholarship. In T. Thompson, R. Parrott, & J. Nussbaum (Eds.), *Handbook of Health Communication* (2nd ed., pp. 36–51). Mahwah, NJ: Routledge.

Shaughnessy, A.F., Slawson, D.C., & Becker, L. (1998). Clinical jazz: Harmonizing clinical experience and evidence-based medicine. *Journal of Family Practice, 47*, 425–428.

Steinbrook, R. (2008). Personally controlled online health data—the next big thing in medical care? *New England Journal of Communication, 358*, 1653–1656.

Suchman, A.L. (2011). Relationship-centered care and administration. In A.L. Suchman, D.J. Sluyter, & P.R. Williamson (Eds.), *Leading change in healthcare* (pp. 35–42). New York: Radcliffe Publishing.

Sultz, H.A., & Young, K.M. (2009). *Health care USA: Understanding its organization and delivery* (6th ed.). Sudbury, MA: Jones and Bartlett Publishers.

Thompson, T. (2009). The applicability of narrative ethics. *Journal of Applied Communication Research, 37,* 188–195.

Zaner, R.M. (2009). Narrative and decision. *Journal of Applied Communication Research, 37,* 174–187.

– ENDNOTES –

[1]   This vignette is a version of a storyline from *The Art of the Possible* reduced here for the purposes of this chapter.

CHAPTER 4

PREPARING FUTURE PHYSICIANS FOR THE NARRATIVE NATURE OF CLINICAL WORK THROUGH STANDARDIZED PATIENT PROGRAMS

– SPENCER D. PATTERSON AND LYNN M. HARTER –

Medical education historically has emphasized cutting-edge molecular and chemistry-oriented sciences coupled with technical proficiency. Even so, the practice of medicine also involves interpretive sense-making (see Chapter 2). A disjunction too often exists between the vision of medicine as a generalizable science and the practice of medicine as a narrative-based craft that is exercised in the midst of particular and

ambiguous circumstances (Montgomery, 2006). In an effort to better prepare students for a diverse array of responsibilities, medical schools have enlarged the dominant model of education to include experiential pedagogies such as standardized patient labs. Medical schools use standardized patients (SPs)—individuals hired to simulate symptoms—to help students develop their diagnostic and communication skills in safe environments (Feeley, Anker, Soriano, & Friedman, 2010).

Lynn became involved with SP labs in 1995 while teaching at Truman State University (TSU) in Kirksville, Missouri. Adjacent to the TSU campus is the Kirksville College of Osteopathic Medicine (KCOM), one of the first medical schools in the United States to integrate SP labs as part of the formal assessment of students' learning in primary care coursework. Over a period of several years, she explored the professional socialization of future physicians through SP pedagogy and helped to refine assessment protocols (see Harter & Kirby, 2004; Harter & Krone, 2001; Heun, Harter, & Schambach, 1997; Kirby & Harter, 2001). Spencer became involved with the SP program at the Ohio University Heritage College of Osteopathic Medicine (OUHCOM) during the first year of his doctoral coursework in the School of Communication Studies at Ohio University. He witnessed firsthand how students learned to exercise and communicate clinical judgment through SP interactions. Informed by multiple years of fieldwork, Spencer's dissertation offered an ethnographic glimpse of the communication processes composing this pedagogy (Patterson, 2012).

In this chapter, we illustrate the narrative dimensions of SP interactions in three ways. First, we trace the historical development of SP pedagogies and position them as storytelling occasions. Second, we detail how the SP labs at OUHCOM are spatially and temporally organized to simulate realistic clinical experiences. Third, we offer a composite narrative of the SP lab experience inspired by Spencer's dissertation fieldwork (see Patterson, 2012, for an extended discussion of the research design). By framing the narrative as a "typical day in the SP lab," we demonstrate a broad range of processes that accompany an SP experience. As articulated by Ellingson (2005), constructing a composite narrative involves "the partial decontextualization of the interactions and recontextualization of them into different times and in differing juxtapositions" (p. 156). Following Ellingson's lead, we openly acknowledge that this story does not reflect a *real* day in the SP lab—rather, the story offers a *realistic* portrayal of a *realistic* day in the SP lab. We sought to offer enough character development and enough detail to enable readers to develop a sense of the typical scenes that unfold in an SP lab setting.

— STANDARDIZED PATIENT LABS AS NARRATIVE PEDAGOGY —

How can we improve medical education? Can we produce competent and compassionate physicians more efficiently and effectively? How can we reorganize medical education to produce physicians who are able to achieve better health care outcomes for the American people? (Cooke, Irby, & O'Brien, 2010, p. 2)

Medical students are learning a profession wherein they will be expected to alleviate the suffering of individuals facing life disruptions, some of which are significant in scope and consequence. Care providers must enter life stories of patients, ascertain symptoms of problems and potential causes, connect personal stories to biomedical illness scripts, and when necessary chart treatment paths (see Chapter 2). Written exams measure students' acquired knowledge but often fail to assess their abilities to effectively communicate with patients and family members living amidst vulnerability (Weathermon, Erbele, & Mattson, 2000). Dr. Howard Barrows pioneered the use of SPs in the 1960s as a method of evaluating students' skills in facilitating clinical interactions (Barrows, 1993). Guided by scripts that include case histories, SPs are trained to simulate symptoms, abnormal findings, and diverse personalities. Students interact with SPs as though they are interviewing, probing, examining, delivering bad news, and counseling real patients in settings that resemble outpatient exam rooms.

Like other pedagogies, SP labs offer opportunities for faculty to assess students' learning. Specifically, faculty members evaluate how well students exercise clinical judgment in realistic patient encounters. Meanwhile, SPs also appraise students by evaluating information obtained, examination maneuvers performed, and communication skills displayed. Finally, SP interactions typically are audio and video recorded so that stimulated recall techniques can be used with students to enhance the learning experience. By 2000, most allopathic and osteopathic medical schools in the United States had integrated SP programs in preclinical years of education, and the Liaison Committee on Medical Education (the major accrediting body for medical schools) now requires clinical skills training with SPs (Barzansky & Etzel, 2004).

SP interactions reveal the centrality of narrative reasoning to the provision of healthcare (even if unacknowledged as narrative reasoning; see Patterson, 2012). As such, SP pedagogies "integrate new models of rationality" in medical education (Islam & Zyphur, 2007, p. 770), what Mattingly (1994) referred to as *therapeutic emplotment*. "Narrative plays a central role in clinical work not only as a retrospective account of past events," argued Mattingly, "but as a form healers and patients actively seek to impose upon clinical time" (p. 811). In SP interactions, students are urged by the impulse to emplot events befalling patients, search for causality, and develop actionable protocols and interventions.

In summary, SP labs function as spaces in which students try out—that is, *rehearse*—being a doctor and practicing medicine. At OUHCOM, medical students interact with SPs in the newly remodeled Heritage Clinical Training and Assessment Center (CTAC), made possible in part by a $2.3 million gift from Osteopathic Heritage Foundations. In the next section, we describe how the CTAC facilities are spatially and temporally organized to facilitate realistic clinical encounters.

– ORGANIZING SPACE AND TIME FOR LOCALIZED PERFORMANCES –

With its concern for settings of scenes, narrative theory turns scholars' attention toward the *locatedness* of action. Burke, for example, argued "terrains determine tactics" (p. 12), emphasizing *where* action unfolds (see also Chapter 5). OUHCOM spent substantial resources creating high-fidelity (i.e., realistic) learning spaces for the SP experiences. The exam rooms simulate typical settings composing professional clinics in traditional primary care contexts. In this section we explore the strategic creation and use of space in preparing future physicians. Students step into the setting of an SP lab, recreate the scene and the mood it represents, and presumably retain the experience. In this way, architects of the SP program are creating what Croft (1999) and Fiske (1993) would describe as *localized performances*—temporary sites of action in which storytelling unfolds.

A quick tour of an SP lab reveals a familiar setting for anyone who has recently visited a clinic for wide-ranging ailments including sore throats, sprained ankles, or even septic shock. SP labs look like clinical exam rooms at most ambulatory care organizations (e.g., outpatient clinics, retail clinics, doctors' offices). Upon entrance, one's eye is immediately drawn to the brightly colored bags inside sanitary garbage cans marked "hazardous materials." The wall is lined with paper boxes bulging with different-size exam gloves. Mounted between the garbage can and the glove boxes is a container for throwing away sharp objects. The spaces also include container-lined sinks coupled with cabinets and drawers for storing medical equipment (see accompanying photo). Each room includes state-of-the-art software and computers for electronic medical records, and telephones—presumably for managing care among interdisciplinary care professionals, requesting lab results or other information, or even coordinating with third-party payers.

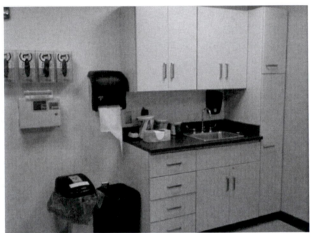

Supplies and storage

Exam beds are prominently centered in the labs, surrounded by wheeled tables, chairs, and stools. Above the beds are storage mechanisms to hold and provide power to the otoscopes, medical devices allowing care providers to see both the outer and middle ear (see accompanying photo). The exam beds are always covered in long sheets of semitranslucent, white parchment paper and they feature foldout stirrups for gynecological exams. Those stirrups, quietly folded away under the tables, are objects made of synthetic plastic and metal. The space they consume is much larger than their mathematical dimensions. The stirrups function as artifacts of uncertainty, anxiety, and exploration for students and SPs alike.

Instruments and supplies rarely used by students fill the drawers (e.g., vision charts, reflex hammers, and various instruments sealed in sterile plastic pouches)(see accompanying photo). These objects—both seen and unseen, used and unused—function as props that frame a setting in ways that shape expected performances (Goffman, 1959). Visual imagery, blood pressure cuffs, and glucometers define settings, providing material parameters for symbolic interactions. In other words, the material dimensions of the settings are inseparable from the improvisational nature of role performances. In many ways, the use of props is similar to the practices associated with method acting.

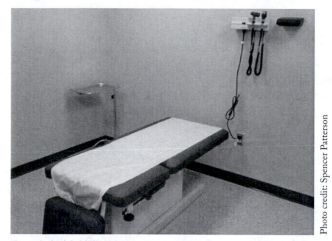

Photo credit: Spencer Patterson

Exam bed with folding stirrups

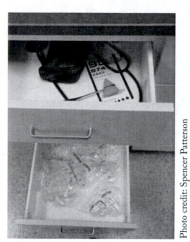

Photo credit: Spencer Patterson

Rarely used drawers

In method acting, characters draw on real, but sometimes unseen, aspects of a scene to experience genuine emotions.

Finally, perhaps the most influential object in the SP setting is the small black object looking down from its perch near the ceiling—the camera (see accompanying photo). As students interact with patients, every word and action is recorded for live and future viewing. The camera serves multiple functions. In the medical school setting, cameras produce trace artifacts that allow students to revisit their interactions. At any time after the initial interactions, students and faculty review the footage for instructional and assessment purposes.

In summary, the space of the SP labs is organized to facilitate localized performances among medical students and patients. The artifacts strewn throughout the space are more than mere decorations or embellishments. Aesthetically, artifacts offer frameworks for action, structuring sensory

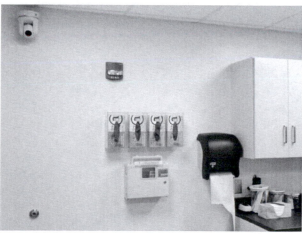

Photo credit: Spencer Patterson

Pivoting video camera

experience and enlarging or constricting the range of possible actions (see Harter, Leeman, Norander, Young, & Rawlins, 2008). In the words of Pam, the lab coordinator, "Exam rooms are outfitted with medical equipment exactly like that found in the doctor's office or clinic . . . [allowing students] opportunity to use their communication and practical skills to develop their confidence and increase their knowledge" (personal communication, March 15, 2012). Technology, sanitation, seating, and tools of the medical trade are some of the obvious artifacts that fill these interactive spaces. But the space is also filled with seemingly inconsequential and sometimes invisible objects and processes that shape how the interactions unfold.

The lab facilitators also temporally organize SP labs to simulate realistic scenes students will encounter in clinical settings. Across industries and occupations, temporal matters remain central concerns. The progressive intensification and commodification of the labor process has positioned time as inevitably scarce in commerce and finance, education, and social services (du Gay, 2009). As a commodity of the industrial process, the value of time rests with its centrality in organizational goals of accumulation and acceleration (Hassard, 1996). As the scarcity of time increases, so does its value. Medical students learn about and confront the temporal demands of their future professions through SP labs.

To begin, a feature of every clinical exam room in the SP lab is a clock (see accompanying photo). The prominence of a clock in each setting is perhaps not surprising given that, in health contexts, time is often highlighted (by patients, providers, and third-party payers) for its positive or negative effects on the process and outcomes of care. As students stumble through the diagnostic process and physical exams in the simulated settings of a lab, they develop what numerous students describe as "rhythm" and "pace." The repetitive experience of working with patients in simulated "real time" provides students with opportunities to develop a temporal flow or a sense of pace. The capacity to develop a rhythmic flow in clinical interactions is certainly one benefit of the SP process that students reap as they prepare to enter professional clinical care settings.

Relatedly, students must hone their abilities to budget time for various tasks. For example, during the summer months, second-year students completed their final labs before leaving for rotations and in preparation for their COMLEX2PE exam. The COMLEX2PE exam is the licensing exam that

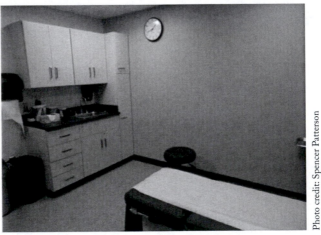

Photo credit: Spencer Patterson

Clock on the wall

includes interaction with standardized patients (National Board of Osteopathic Medical Examiners [NBOME], 2011b). The COMLEX2PE has specific requirements regarding the amount of time students are allotted for each SP interaction as well as the amount of time they have to write their postencounter notes (which have a very particular format). The official orientation guide published by NBOME (2011a, p. 4) outlines the time requirements for the 6-hour examination period:

- Students rotate through a serious of 12 SP interactions.
- In each encounter, students have 14 minutes to evaluate and treat the patient including the interview and history-taking, performing indicated physical examination maneuvers, communicating with and counseling the patient, and performing osteopathic manipulative treatment as indicated.
- After each encounter students have 9 minutes to complete a written SOAP (Subjective, Objective, Assessment, and Plan) note, charting their clinical findings and assessment of the case.

These time requirements function as basic parameters students must observe to pass the exam.

As part of the board preparation process, these guidelines are incorporated into SP settings during medical school. For example, all of the labs are timed and they start and stop with universal sounds and announcements through a PA system heard through all the halls and exam rooms. During the SP labs at OUHCOM, students have more time to complete their labs than they do during the COMLEX2PE, but the pre- and postinteraction instructions as well as the continual chatter in the halls are filled with reminders to adhere to the time requirements.

In summary, CTAC facilities are spatially and temporally organized to facilitate realistic clinical encounters. Next, we offer a composite narrative of the SP setting and typical scenes as a complementary representation of the narrative nature of SP pedagogies. The juxtaposition of our ethnographic description of the labs with a composite narrative is inspired by Ellingson's (2009) vision of crystallization. "Crystallized texts include more than one genre of writing or representation," argued Ellingson (2011). "Crystallization depends on segmenting, weaving, blending, or otherwise drawing upon two or more genres, media, or ways of experiencing findings" (p. 605). There are multiple ways to frame experience. We now invite readers to experience the SP labs from the standpoint of Jane, a first-year medical student.

— A TYPICAL DAY IN THE SP LAB —

During a warm spring day in the third quarter of her first year of medical school, Jane logged into her Blackboard account to check her class schedule. Upon opening her academic calendar through OU's portal for students, she saw that situated alongside many lectures and meetings, she was scheduled for a clinical exam SP lab in 2 weeks. The announcement did not include many details about the lab. Among other calendar announcements, she read:

The following week there will be a standardized patient encounter with a SOAP note. Check your calendar and be sure you attend the correct session. An email with your assignment will NOT be sent out prior to this lab. This will take place in the NEW CTAC in Grosvenor Hall.

Jane did not feel nervous about the fact that her assignment was not available until the day of the lab, as this is a common practice. Even so, she did feel pressure, the sort of anxiety that results in sweaty palms and an increased heart rate. Pressure is not all bad, though, she reminded herself. Those sweaty palms are a reminder to study hard and learn the lecture information. STUDY, STUDY, STUDY . . . that's the best way to do well in the labs and on exams. With upcoming sections on respiratory and circulatory systems as well as a unit on diabetic hypertension and care, Jane had a good idea what to expect in terms of clinical cases. So, along with approximately 120 classmates, she continued to diligently work through the curriculum that led up to the lab.

On lab day, Jane entered the building through the student entrance. Pam, the lab coordinator, always gives clear and firm instructions that students are to enter through one side of the building and the SPs another. She doesn't want providers and patients to see each other or have any other contact prior to the clinical exams. Upon entering, Jane quickly walked into the waiting room, a classroom where she and about 30 of her colleagues awaited instructions regarding the lab and their group assignments. With about 120 students per class, simultaneously accommodating everyone in the SP lab would be nearly impossible. So, the students are generally divided into groups of 20–30 for each lab and then they take turns rotating in and out of the rooms. As one can imagine, the logistical challenge of arranging all the labs is no simple task for Pam.

In the waiting room some of the students sat quietly in their white coats and used the time to squeeze in some more studying for their upcoming exams. Others viewed the time as a break from the normal routine and sat in circles laughing and telling stories as their white coats sat on the desks in front of them. Several students nervously bounced around the room asking questions and seeking reassurance that they were prepared for the lab. Jane noticed that one of them was actually in tears from the anticipated stress of the lab combined with the plethora of other stressors accompanying medical school.

After greeting a few friends Jane sat down and Dr. Smalley, the lead professor, walked in with a few other physician-instructors. She greeted everyone, passed out some handouts, and explained the rotation schedule that included the logistical information of who had to be in which room and when. During the next 2 hours, Jane would see three different patients, write SOAP notes after each visit, and receive individual feedback from each patient as well as her preceptor. She started to sweat as she slipped on her white coat. She felt a bit like an imposter, play acting the part of doctor—a role she was not quite ready for but would someday assume along with responsibility for the healthcare of others.

"After your labs, you should come back here for a debriefing discussion," Dr. Smalley stressed. "Any questions?"

Nobody replied.

She continued, "Okay, then we will go back to the control room and make sure the cameras are working. The first group can come into the hallway and stand in front of your door. Do not knock until Pam gives you permission. Good luck!"

Jane and her classmates nervously and silently filed out to the hallway, each student wearing a white coat and draped with a stethoscope. As they entered the hallway, Pam quickly but quietly relayed a message to everyone, "Stand in front of the door, but don't touch the chart on the wall until I tell you."

Jane felt a lump in her throat. The situation reminded her of kneeling in the starting blocks before a 100-meter dash.

"Alright," Pam said. "You can knock on the door in 3–2–1 go."

Jane knocked on the door and entered the exam room—as physicians do. "Hi, I am Student Doctor Bingham."

"I'm Larry." Sitting on the exam table was a 52-year-old man hunched over a bit and holding his abdomen.

"Tell me why you are here today," Jane encouraged, as she pulled her clipboard and pen out.

Following the script of "gastritis," Larry pointed to the top part of his abdomen and said, "I have a really sore pain in my stomach."

"Hmmm, what does the pain feel like? Is this pain new? Have you taken over-the-counter pain medicine?" asked Jane, and then silently chided herself for asking too many questions at once without allowing the patient to answer.

"Well, I'll start with your first question, it feels really sore, like its kinda burning."

"Larry, have you experienced any other symptoms?"

"Well, I have been sick to my stomach."

"Any vomiting?"

"Nope, just sick to my stomach. But my grandson, Ben, was there with a bag in case I did throw up!"

"That's great. Okay, has there been a change in your appetite, Larry? Any changes in your bowel movements?"

"No changes in my bathroom habits—my bowel movements. But my wife has noticed I'm not as hungry."

"Okay, when did the pain start?"

"Oh, I'd say about 4 or 5 days ago."

As the conversation continued, Jane moved into more specific questions about Larry's past medical history. She learned he has a history of high blood pressure, for which he takes daily medication, and arthritis that acts up when he engages in heavy work around the house and yard.

"Can I listen to your heart?" asked Jane, as Larry concluded his family's medical history.

He complied and she began moving the chest piece of her stethoscope around different parts of his upper body, on top of his shirt, as he breathed in and out. She could feel her own hands shake a bit even as she sensed his breathing patterns and heartbeat. Knowing that she was being evaluated on camera as well as by Larry, Jane took a deep breath and mentally reviewed the step-by-step checklist of procedures she had memorized from previous evaluation forms.

"Oh no!" Jane thought to herself. "I forgot to wash my hands. And I should be listening to his heart under his shirt against his skin." So she excused herself, washed her hands, and restarted the physical exam. Larry just smiled a bit.

As she took a few more vitals, measuring his blood pressure and inducing pupil dilation with a small bright light, Jane mentally reviewed in her mind "OLDCHARTS," a popular mnemonic in medical education that she learned in a lecture for Onset, Location, Duration, CHaracter, Alleviating or Aggravating, Radiation, Temporal, and Symptoms. As she proceeded through the differential diagnostic process, her questions became more specific as she prepared to make a diagnosis.

Jane was startled as she heard Pam's voice echo over the PA system, "You have 2 minutes, 2 minutes." She glanced quickly at the clock displayed prominently on the wall.

"I think you have irritable bowel syndrome," Jane said in a frenzied tone. "And I want you to meet with a gastroenterologist."

Larry looked at her like she just missed the million-dollar question on a game show. So she tried again, "Or, actually, I think you have gastritis."

Larry smiled and they concluded their conversation.

Jane stepped out into the hall and used her full allotment of 10 minutes to write her SOAP note. After summarizing Larry's chief complaint, the history of the present illness, its duration, and symptoms, she articulated her diagnosis and treatment plan.

Jane reentered the room for a second time. However, this entry was much different than the first, because she was there to receive feedback from the patient. So, she sat down as Larry pulled out his checklist and reviewed the details. He was kind, and joked about the fact that he helped her a bit at the end with the diagnosis.

Larry praised Jane for maintaining eye contact with him and other nonverbal gestures. "I really appreciate that you showed interest in me through your eye contact and body language. That is a sign of respect for me, the patient."

Larry had a few recommendations. "Make sure you ask more open-ended questions. And most importantly, listen. Just listen to me talk about my symptoms." Listening is a recommendation Larry makes regularly when providing feedback to students.

Ultimately, when time expired Jane was happy to leave the room knowing that she made a correct diagnosis and the patient perceived her as respectful. One down, two more to go.

After following the same routine with two more patients, Jane returned to the classroom for the debriefing session. The professors also came in and stood in the back of the room while Dr. Smalley led a question-and-answer session from the front. Most of the questions were technical scientific questions about immunology, gastroenterology, and medical classifications. Jane sat quietly and took notes while her peers posed questions, some of which were already on her mind. "What is the differential diagnosis for acute onset gastritis?" and "What diagnostic tests would you have ordered?" were particularly insightful.

Dr. Smalley took a moment to tell a story about a time when she made a mistake in her private practice. She failed to palpate the lymph nodes of a young boy who was visiting for a wellness preventive checkup. Though he felt healthy, the little boy was walking around with a raging infection that manifest itself more strongly a few days later when he was admitted to the hospital.

"So be sure to always follow the entire protocol," she concluded. "That is why we have all these mnemonics and checklists."

At the end of that discussion, the other professors walked through the room and handed out completed evaluations for the students they observed from the control room. Jane was happy to learn that she passed. In fact, she received "satisfactory" marks in all but 1 of the 15 categories. Her preceptors even commended her on the quality of her SOAP notes. Typically, the SP labs are graded as pass or fail requirements rather than the traditional 100-percentage point system for grades. Had she not passed, she would have scheduled a date to redo the lab and make a time commitment that she really could not afford.

— BEHIND THE SCENES —

During the 2 weeks that led up to Jane's lab, a set of complex conditions came together for the lab to be successful. First, Jane was educated on the biomedical information relevant to the lab. Second, the SPs became familiar with the lab through their roles and scripts; and third, the professor at the head of the lab, Dr. Smalley, collaborated with Pam and other faculty to ensure that all the logistics, including patient feedback, forms, and schedules, were in place. This is typical behind-the-scenes work for all SP labs at OUHCOM. Next, we draw on several examples to illustrate activities (including props) that set the scenes that unfold in SP labs.

Typically the unit instructors for the labs also act as teachers in general lectures. This allows the instructors to provide information and handouts pertinent to the labs during the related lectures. For example, in preparation for an oncology lab where students told the SPs that they had terminal cancer, the lecturer, Dr. Marx, shared handouts relevant to the specific creative SP narrative that would be used in the lab. One handout included a creative scenario where the students were presented with a specific role and task. Obviously SPs are hired and compensated to act out the roles; but this was an explicit example of when students were also trained to follow certain roles. Their script revealed that they were to act as primary care physicians who referred their patients, with specific symptoms, to the oncologist. The students also received specific instructions on how to communicate "bad news" to their patients. Finally, the students were presented with a creatively constructed letter from the oncologist who had diagnosed the patient (but had not yet disclosed the information to the patient). The letter included jargon about the cancer type as well as the diagnostic tests that were conducted for the diagnosis.

Lead instructors each conduct their lab differently. In the example with Jane, she did not know her task until she arrived at the scene—a striking contrast in comparison to Dr. Marx's lab in which she informs students weeks in advance. Of course, this realistically portrays how clinical practice unfolds for doctors in diverse practices. Sometimes they walk into the exam room with information from other sources; at other times, they walk in with no history.

Other examples of preparatory information shared with students include straightforward scripts that offer great detail to the students. For example, during one lab, the instructor passed out instructions explaining that the patient suffers from migraine headaches and that the student's job is to diagnose the headache and discuss lifestyle modifications with the patient. In another case, the students were not required to identify any malady, but "to demonstrate communication skills using empathy, support, active listening and appropriate nonverbal behaviors."

In addition to preparing students, the SPs also receive necessary direction. The logistics of getting them to the right rooms with the right scripts on the right days is a big task for Pam, the lab coordinator. She holds regular orientation meetings with the SPs so they know where to park, where to enter, and even how to sit on the tables. As each lab approaches, the SPs are guided on their two roles—acting patients and evaluators. They do not take any drama or acting classes, and they receive their scripts and checklists via email 2–3 weeks before the labs begin. Sometimes the SPs come prepared to perform multiple roles. The scripts do not include word-for-word directions. Instead, they offer narrative details for the patient character they enact (e.g., "you feel worse when you are laying down outside" and "you have only lived in this area of the country since last October"). SPs are also trained to evaluate student performance. They do this via face-to-face feedback, as demonstrated in the composite narrative, and written feedback.

While students interact with the SPs, faculty members sit in a "control room" and watch the interactions unfold live (see accompanying photo). Since the student-to-faculty ratio is greater than one, each faculty member observes multiple interactions simultaneously. As they tune in and out of different interactions, they also complete evaluation forms by checking boxes that rate the students' performances. There are 15 criteria, such as "the student stated the chief complaint clearly" and "the student auscultated the heart." There are also three columns where evaluators can check the quality of the performance as satisfactory, marginal, or unsatisfactory. Due to the pace of the interactions and the increased stress from conducting simultaneous evaluations, the faculty members do not leave many written comments as they observe. However, all the interactions are recorded and stored for future review when necessary.

Photo credit: Spencer Patterson

Control Room

– CONCLUSION –

We juxtaposed our ethnographic description of the CTAC facilities with a composite narrative to illustrate the narrative nature of SP pedagogies. The CTAC facility is home to the SP labs, settings in which typical scenes of healthcare unfold. In the SP lab, students like Jane don their white coats and stethoscopes and interact with patients hired to simulate health problems (i.e, they act out scripts). Student doctors and patients engage in clinical interactions characterized by instrumental, narrative, and scientific rationalities—and vulnerability, fear, trepidation, and excitement. All the while, lab coordinators and faculty members vicariously experience the encounters from an evaluative standpoint.

We developed the creative vignette to embody the narrative features of clinical interactions rehearsed in SP labs—temporality, the ordering impulses of emplotment, and cause and effect. In their finest moments, SP interactions prepare students for the narrative nature of clinical work. Notably, most students and instructors do not intentionally use narrative language in framing the purpose or outcomes of SP experiences. Even so, all that unfolds in the settings of SP labs simulate the narrative sense-making and practices students will engage and experience during professional clinical work. This is accomplished through a complex interplay of institutional strategies (e.g., timed interactions) and environmental elements (e.g., medical instruments). Just as clinical professionals work amidst narrative elements of space, time, acts, characters, and plots, SP experiences, too, are characterized by those same narrative elements. The narrative practices that occur naturally in lived clinical interactions are intentionally planned in SP labs.

For example, OUHCOM created representative clinical spaces for students to *practice* diagnostic reasoning and exercise clinical judgment, both of which rely on narrative sense-making and practices (see Montgomery, 2006). Organizing the clinical spaces with patient chart holders on the outside walls beside the doors entering into the exam rooms is but one example. Inside the exam rooms, the realistic, sterile environment highlighted with latex gloves and red biohazardous bins also indicates that the space is intentionally prepared to simulate professional spaces. Students interact in those spaces performing roles of doctors. Similarly, the clock on wall and the regimented timing of the labs are reminders and reflectors of the realities of time and rhythm that occur in professional clinics. Certainly, students can and will learn much more about their own rhythms and paces as they enter professional settings beyond medical school. But the narrative experiences in SP labs allow them, for example, to reflect on institutional temporal expectations. They learn what it feels like to hold conversations for 5, 10, or 15 minutes about a variety of topics. In other words, the students get *head starts* before they step into the swift currents of professional life.

SP labs represent a rich context for communication scholars to explore how students learn to interact with patients. Like other educational socializing experiences (e.g., internships), SPs offer a realistic job preview of what things will "really be like" as a practicing doctor. In Lynn's research (e.g., Harter & Kirby, 2004) and in Spencer's dissertation (Patterson, 2012), they both explored value sets that are maintained or contested through SP pedagogies from the standpoint of students, faculty members, and administrators. We hope our work inspires other narrative scholars to explore the SP experience from the standpoint of the hired patient. How do SPs understand their role in the professional socialization of medical students? What challenges do they experience when enacting illness scripts? How does the SP experience differ based on the patient's personal history with a particular malady? These questions merit attention.

SP programs, coupled with other innovative medical school experiences, are repositioning medicine as a science—using interpretive and interpersonal practice (see also Dolev, Friedlaender, & Braverman, 2009; Saunders, 2009). As cadavers and chemistry continue to be coupled with practices that dramatize and teach humanizing practices, communication scholars and practitioners are well positioned to contribute to the process through which medical students develop a workable narrative of themselves for use in their future profession.

– REFERENCES –

Barrows, H.S. (1993). Overview of the uses of standardized patients for teaching and evaluating clinical skills. *Academic Medicine, 68*(6), 443–444.

Barzansky, B., & Etzel, S.I. (2004). Educational programs in U.S. medical schools, 2003-2004. *Journal of the American Medical Association, 292*(9), 1025–1031.

Burke, K. (1969). *A grammar of motives*. Berkeley: University of California Press.

Cooke, M., Irby, D.M., & O'Brien, B.C. (2010). *Educating physicians: A call for reform of medical school and residency*. San Francisco: Jossey-Bass.

Croft, S.E. (1999). Creating locales through storytelling: An ethnography of a group home for men with mental retardation. *Western Journal of Communication, 63*(3), 329–374.

Dolev, J.C., Friedlaender, L.K., & Braverman, I.M. (2009). Use of fine art to enhance visual diagnostic skills. *Journal of the American Medical Association, 286*, 1020–1021.

du Gay, P. (2009). *The values of bureaucracy*. Oxford, UK: Oxford University Press.

Ellingson, L.L. (2005). *Communicating in the clinic: Negotiating frontstage and backstage teamwork*. Cresskill, NJ: Hampton Press.

Ellingson, L.L. (2009). *Engaging crystalization in qualitative work: An introduction*. Thousand Oaks, CA: Sage.

Ellingson, L.L. (2011). Analysis and representation across the continuum. In N.K. Denzin & Y.S. Lincoln (Eds.), *The SAGE handbook of qualitative research* (4th ed., pp. 595–625). Thousand Oaks, CA: Sage.

Feeley, T.H., Anker, A.E., Soriano, R., & Friedman, E. (2010). Using standardized patients to educate medical students about organ donation. *Communication Education, 59*(3), 249–262. doi: 10.1080/03634521003628289

Fiske, J. (1993). *Power plays, power works*. London: Verso.

Goffman, E. (1959). *The presentation of self in everyday life*. Garden City, NY: Doubleday.

Harter, L.M., & Kirby, E. (2004). Socializing medical students in an era of managed care: The ideological significance of standardized and virtual patients. *Communication Studies, 55*(1), 48–68.

Harter, L.M., & Krone, K. (2001). Exploring the emergent identities of future physicians: Toward an understanding of the ideological socialization of osteopathic medical students. *Southern Communication Journal, 67*, 67–84.

Harter, L.M., Leeman, M., Norander, S., Young, S., & Rawlins, W.K. (2008). The intermingling of aesthetic and instrumental rationalities in a collaborative art studio for individuals with developmental disabilities. *Management Communication Quarterly, 21*, 423–453.

Hassard, J. (1996). Images of time in work and organization. In S.R. Clegg, C. Hardy, & W.R. Nord (Eds.), *Handbook of organization studies* (pp. 581–598). Thousand Oaks, CA: Sage.

Heun, L., Harter, L.M., & Schambach, C. (1997). Gender and age in relation to perceptions of diverse patient populations: Implications for standardized patient programs. *Academic Medicine, 72*(6), 559.

Islam, G., & Zyphur, M. (2007). Ways of interacting: The standardization of communication in medical training. *Human Relations, 60*(5), 769–792. doi: 10.1177/0018726707079201

Kirby, E.L., & Harter, L.M. (2001). Using standardized and computer-simulated patients as instructional tools for health care interviewing. *Communication Teacher, 16*, 1–4.

Mattingly, C. (1994). The concept of therapeutic emplotment. *Social Science & Medicine, 38*, 811–822.

Montgomery, K. (2006). *How doctors think: Clinical judgement and the practice of medicine*. New York: Oxford University Press.

National Board of Osteopathic Medical Examiners. (2011a). 2011-2012 Orientation guide COMLEX-USA level 2-PE. Retrieved March 2012 from http://www.nbome.org/docs/PEOrientationGuide.pdf

National Board of Osteopathic Medical Examiners. (2011b). COMLEX performance evaluation (PE). Retrieved June 2011 from http://www.nbome.org/comlex-pe.asp?m=can

Patterson, S. (2012). Putting on white coats: Professional socialization of medical students through narrative pedagogy in standardized patient labs. (Doctoral dissertation). Athens: Ohio University.

Sanders, L. (2009). *Every patient tells a story: Medical mysteries and the art of diagnosis.* New York: Broadway Books.

Weathermon, R.A., Erbele, S., & Mattson, M. (2000). Use of standardized patients as an assessment tool at the end of an ambulatory care rotation. *American Journal of Pharmaceutical Education, 61,* 109–113.

CHAPTER 5

DISRUPTING THE META-NARRATIVE OF "ASSEMBLY LINE MEDICINE": CREATING NEW NORMALS FOR UNDER-SERVED POPULATIONS THROUGH MOBILE CLINICS

— KAREN L. DEARDORFF AND LYNN M. HARTER —

Memories are often triggered in the least expected moments from seemingly unre-lated circumstances. Such was the case when I found myself in a meeting between the Community Health Program's (CHP) perinatal coordinator, Molly, and the office and nursing staff at a local doctor's office. During her presentation, Molly outlined how the perinatal program worked, who qualified for referral, and how staff should handle the referrals. "Many of the women who talk to me in the doctor's office probably wouldn't participate if I tried to approach them at home," she emphasized, "for fear of having their children taken away or because they are ashamed of their living conditions." One of the nurses couldn't grasp why women would be concerned about the cleanliness of their homes when a visit from social services or the CHP could provide assistance for the care of their children. Another nurse, Kathleen, suggested, "I think some of them are embarrassed by the way they live, by the condition of their houses. Some of them are ashamed at the way they have to live." Molly nodded her head in agreement, and stressed, "Embarrassment and shame play a major role in women rejecting help via the home visit approach."

I, too, shook my head as I remembered how ashamed I was about the condition of my house growing up. The conversation took me back to seventh grade, a defining moment that lingers with me. The school bus broke down in front of my house. Since it was winter and freezing cold, the bus driver asked my mom if the riders could come into our house to stay warm while they waited on another bus. The situation put me into a state of dual panic. Would I be embarrassed because my mom, who was an extremely closed and private person, refused to take the children inside? Or, would I be horrified to have them see the conditions in which I lived? Or both? Somewhat to my surprise, mom agreed to let the children into our house to await the new bus. As we all huddled in the living room around the lone pot-bellied coal stove that heated our entire house, I remained anxious for the bus to come and rescue those children. My biggest fear was the inevitable need of someone having to use the bathroom because we did not have indoor plumbing—we only had an outhouse (later in life I learned that we were rich by comparison as we had a two-seater outhouse). Luckily my angst was for nothing as no one asked to go to the bathroom that morning. Later on that week one of the riders, Judy Howland, told me that she was surprised how clean my house was on the inside considering how horrible it looked on the outside. When I looked at my house, I didn't see a clean inside. I was focused on what others who were passing by saw—a shack with ripped, and often missing, black tar paper that partially covered the exposed wooden frame. (Karen, fieldnotes)

Individuals living in poverty face countless daily challenges including substandard housing. Living amidst material scarcity and inhospitable environments impacts one's well-being. Health difficulties arise from inadequate or unsafe housing, lack of nutritional food, dangerous work and domestic situations, low paying jobs, and extremely long work hours (Burns, Lovich, Maxwell, & Shapiro, 1997; Zoller, 2005). Mobile health clinics have emerged in the United States over the past 20 years to address unmet needs of underresourced populations (see Carmack, 2010; Liebman, Lamberti, & Altice, 2002; Newman et al., 2004). In this chapter, we present a case study of a mobile health clinic—the Community Health Program (CHP)—that provides free or low-cost services to qualified residents of 21 counties in southeastern Ohio (11 of which are part of the Appalachia region). The CHP is affiliated with the Ohio University Heritage College of Osteopathic Medicine and travels over 14,000 miles per year to provide an array of services including primary care; child and adult immunizations; glucose, blood pressure, and cholesterol screenings; and breast and cervical (B & C) cancer screenings.

Appalachia stereotypically is envisioned as a physically isolated setting populated by backward people and uneducated hillbillies. The region is actually quite diverse in terms of geography, culture, and economic status. Appalachia is best characterized by an "uneven development of its human capital and economic resources" (Latimer & Oberhauser, 2005, p. 269). There are some regions that surpass the national average in per capita income, median-household income, and median-family income. Even so, the region surrounding Ohio University—our employer—is characterized by some of the deepest and most persistent poverty in the United States (Thorne, Tickamyer, & Thorne, 2005). The Ohio Health Issues Poll (2007) found that the percentage of Ohioans living below the 100% federal poverty guidelines (FPG) had increased since 2005, as had the percentage living at 100–200% FPG. The faces of the working poor in southeastern Ohio are primarily women, many of whom are divorced or unmarried with children, and/or who are frequently burdened with low incomes due to labor market inequities (Gilliom, 2001; Ruspini 2001; Shipler, 2004; Towson, 2000).

Poverty presents financial constraints for many individuals who, as a result, lack the resources necessary to seek medical treatment. Issues of geographic remoteness and limited transportation further compound barriers to obtaining healthcare (see Denham, Meyer, & Toborg, 2004; Pistella, Bonati, & Mihalic, 1999). Other barriers to care include an uneven distribution of physicians among geographic areas (McKinley, 2005) and fewer community services (Katz, Wewers, Single, & Paskett, 2007). The social and cultural environment (norms, cohesion, values, and networks) also come into play as "strong values for place, connection to family, and importance of religion are important themes related to health and illness needs of many residents in this region" (Denham et al., 2004, p. 171). Even when healthcare services are available, the shame and stigma accompanying free or low-cost medical care prevents many women from seeking healthcare. In short, discursive, geographic, and economic forces work to separate those living in poverty in Appalachia from mainstream medicine.

By the nature of how it provides services (i.e., mobile, curbside, and community-based care), the CHP disrupts social and material barriers to healthcare. We became involved with the CHP when Lynn met the director, Kathy, in 2005. At that time, the CHP was in need of stories about its efforts to be used in grant applications and for accountability purposes. Lynn formed a research team consisting of herself, Karen, and three other graduate students.[1] Over a period of 12 months, members of the research team traveled over 900 miles, conducted interviews with staff, and spent more than 200 hours observing the interactions between and among CSP staff and clients at various clinics, health fairs, and staff meetings.[2] They composed several short stories used by the CHP in grant applications and for promotional purposes (e.g., http://www.oucom.ohiou.edu/csp/ChangingLanes2008.htm) and authored a chapter for an edited volume on health communication (Harter, Deardorff, Kenniston, Carmack, & Rattine-Flaherty, 2008).

During the fall of 2007, Karen successfully defended her comprehensive exams and turned her attention toward a dissertation project. With Lynn's guidance, she chose to continue fieldwork with the CHP, enlarging the focus of inquiry and discourse collection procedures to more fully include patients' voices. Having experienced intergenerational poverty in Appalachia firsthand, Karen was interested in the development of symbolic and material resources—like the services offered through CHP—that allow individuals to be resilient in the midst of inhospitable circumstances. For her dissertation fieldwork, Karen spent an additional 224 hours traveling with CHP staff and, in addition to shadowing them while they interacted with patients, she assisted with setup and patient intake as needed. She conducted informal and in-depth interviews with patients, staff, and administrators (see Deardorff, 2009 for an extended discussion of her research methods). While completing her dissertation, she wrote three mini stories about the services offered by the CHP now posted on its website (e.g., http://www.oucom.ohiou.edu/csp/PerinatalServicesProgram2008.htm), used in preparing grant applications, and for internal and external reporting. She also worked with the CHP perinatal coordinator and the partnering OB/GYN practice to write a mini story for physicians' use in patient education and for educating the medical community at large.

In this chapter, we explore how the CHP reimagines healthcare in light of shifting scenes and the material and social exigencies of patients' lives. The narrative nature of curbside care offered by the CHP is both different from and similar to the routines and rituals composing traditional health contexts (see Chapter 2). As in traditional contexts, the provision of care through mobile clinics would be impossible if not for humans' capacity for storytelling. For example, patients served by the CHP temporally organize and account for symptoms just as care providers rely on narrative sense-making to diagnose problems, plan treatment protocols, and educate patients. However, unlike the majority of mainstream providers of care, the CHP staff members explicitly acknowledge the narrative nature of their work and foster storytelling in healing relationships (see critiques of mainstream medicine by Charon, 2006; Montgomery, 2006). Meanwhile, in mobile clinics, the *scenes* of care literally shift to homes, community centers, churches, and parking lots. Contextual constraints challenge providers to maintain often taken-for-granted scripts of healthcare. A case in point: It is difficult, and sometimes impossible, to maintain provider–patient confidentiality when medicine is practiced in grocery aisles or parking lots (see Carmack, 2010; Harter et al., 2008). The coordination of privacy scripts becomes more complicated and contested when the settings of care are mobile. The CHP offers a unique opportunity to explore narrative sense-making in a context quite different from the fixed settings composing mainstream medicine.

Health communication scholarship has been critiqued for its implicit assumptions about contexts of healthcare (i.e., primary care physicians' offices, hospitals). "It is insufficient and perhaps misleading to examine clinical communication as if all doctors, patients, and settings are essentially comparable," stressed Sharf (1993). "Taking account of contextual variability will sharpen the utility of our work and clarify which findings transcend these distinctions" (p. 37). Fifteen years later, similar calls continue to be heard as Harter and colleagues (2008) argued, "Communication scholars have remained notably silent about the organizing of health care in non-traditional settings" (p. 314). Narrative theory's attention to the importance of context provides a robust lens through which to expand our discipline's traditional understandings of healthcare settings. The CHP offers a unique opportunity to empirically enrich literature by exploring the storied nature of health and healthcare amidst ever-shifting scenes of activity. To begin, we outline the scope of the CHP and illustrate its significance by situating it within the broader landscape of rural southeastern Ohio. We then move between stories performed and stories told by participants to offer a portrait of healthcare in settings too often unacknowledged by health communication scholars. In doing so, we extend the communication discipline's theoretical and practical reach to include alternative forms of organizing healthcare resources.

– CURBSIDE CARE IN RURAL SOUTHEASTERN OHIO –

The primary mission of the CHP is to provide healthcare to traditionally underserved populations—particularly Appalachian women—who either cannot afford medical care or who have difficulties physically accessing care for themselves and their children. The majority of women living in poverty in southeastern Ohio have little access to healthcare or little disposable income to spend on such care (Reid & Tom, 2006). Those who do work are seldom offered affordable health insurance, and even when access to insurance is available, many cannot meet co-pays and deductibles or pay for prescribed medications. Preventative or routine medicine such as mammograms and cervical cancer screenings are luxuries. As Burd-Sharps, Lewis, and Martins (2008) emphasized, "The agonizing choices women often face are between paying for health care or for other basic needs, such as food, heat, and even housing" (p. 79).

The free or reduced services provided by CHP include breast and cervical cancer screenings, medical clinic services, healthy adult screenings (glucose, blood pressure, and cholesterol), and an adult and child immunization program. Although the CHP offers some services and screenings at a fixed location on a limited basis, most of its clinics are conducted in one of two 40-foot mobile units set up at various outreach sites throughout its service area. To be eligible for these grant-funded services, patients must be 18–64 years old, uninsured, and live at or below 150% poverty level for the free clinics and at 200% of the poverty level for the Ohio breast and cervical (B & C) clinic program.

The outreach sites used by the mobile units vary by location and include parking lots of local hospitals, community or senior citizens' centers, local elementary schools, local grocery stores, or even gas stations. When serving especially rural or Amish communities, it would not be unusual to find a mobile unit parked in a field or in a farmer's driveway. Often, the mobile staff will supplement the limited space inside the unit by using space inside a community health department or another nearby facility such as an elementary school.

The primary CHP staff consists of one director, one administrative assistant, one full-time and two part-time van drivers, one nurse practitioner, one certified medical assistant, six registered nurses, and one or two occasional rotating physicians (primarily at the monthly free clinic). Osteopathic medical students regularly observe and assist the nurse practitioner during mobile clinics. The CHP program also administers a perinatal education program and their perinatal educator works onsite at a local OB/GYN practice with patients who are at high risk for preterm labor. Additional medical services offered by the mobile clinic include bus driver and athletic physicals, a well-child and well-family program for pregnant women and children, and a referral system for other needed services such as mammograms.

As communication scholars, we are interested in how providers and patients narrate their experiences with CHP. First, we draw on participants' narratives to illustrate their perceptions of barriers to quality care.[3] We then move between women's stories of care and the dominant meta-narrative of healthcare in the United States for underresourced populations—*assembly line medicine*. Finally, we illustrate how the CHP advances a new normal of care in southeastern Ohio through its reorganization of space and its temporal rhythms—both of which foster storytelling among providers and patients.

— "FALLING THROUGH THE CRACKS": BARRIERS TO CARE IN SOUTHEASTERN OHIO —

Accessing healthcare while living in poverty is hard for many people to imagine. Individuals who have never gone hungry for days on end have a difficult time grasping the bleak terrain and struggles faced by those just trying to survive. For example, Gina, an AmeriCorps employee who works with the CHP, recalled her first brush with poverty in Athens and nearby counties. "When I moved here and started driving around and exploring, it was like finding the skeletons in the *poverty closet of the United States*," Gina stressed. "I had no idea this type of poverty existed. I figured it did somewhere, but I had never seen it face to face and I was horrified and depressed by it and I was really angry about it." Gina's account illustrates one of the difficulties that people living in poverty face—that of being *invisible* to mainstream society. The evening news is saturated with reports of how governmental cuts in subsidies and programming are eroding an already shaky foundation for "them." Most of us, however, are shielded from many day-to-day realities of those residing in what Gina hauntingly termed "the poverty closet of the United States." Poverty, and its correlates of homelessness, violence, and extreme health inequities, does not happen in "our backyards" (see critiques by Harter, Berquist, Titsworth, Novak, & Brokaw, 2005; Tompkins, 2009).

The majority of patients served by the CHP are women, and most of them shared compelling stories accounting for "why" they needed free or reduced medical care. We share their stories (1) to illustrate participants' precarious financial position and how it impacts their acquisition of, and access to, medical care; and (2) to personalize an otherwise distant public problem. The time and space paths of women living in poverty in southeastern Appalachian Ohio differ from those of the middle class of middle America. We offer their stories as their truths—a form of lived knowledge. We take seriously and value their perceptions, meanings, and experiences. At the same time, we acknowledge our power as coauthors of knowledge claims insofar as we sort, organize, frame, and present women's experiences in public scholarship. In this analysis, we privilege the voices of participants but recognize our position and power in representing and interpreting participants' experiences.

In the words of one patient, Diane, many individuals find themselves and their family members "falling through the cracks" as they struggle to pull themselves out of the poverty cycle. Although gainfully employed, many cannot afford health insurance; they cannot afford standard fees for medical care; and they cannot afford prescribed medications. Holly, a patient who was seen in a free care clinic, did not grow up in poverty but was plunged there when she lost her job and her husband became ill with hepatitis C. "My husband has hepatitis C, and I was tested for exposure to the disease. However, without insurance the doctors won't do further tests to see if I am positive or to see how my husband is doing—no insurance equals no tests," stressed Holly. She described how both she and her husband are falling through the cracks and struggling with their health issues without the benefit of insurance and a steady income. "My husband was on medication for the disease when I had insurance, but he's not on anything now because we can't afford the drugs."

Some patients' take-home pay qualifies them to receive reduced healthcare yet they make just a little too much to qualify for free medical care. Some patients are widowed and have no health benefits through their spouse's pension; others are widowed but not old enough to draw pensions or get Medicaid; and still others have spouses who lost health insurance coverage for the family upon retirement. For example, Katherine, who has had no insurance coverage since her husband died, does not go to the doctor unless she is extremely sick. She realizes that, without preventative care, women are placing themselves in jeopardy for more serious medical problems. But, as she explained, "I realize that women should go more often for health reasons and so they can catch stuff early and get treated. But most can't afford the doctor and they certainly can't afford any treatment needed anyway."

In some situations, patients reported that they opt to either pretend they are not sick or hope that, if they ignore the symptoms and the pain long enough, the problem will disappear. If they cannot afford to pay for an office visit and the tests to see if they are sick, they certainly cannot afford necessary surgeries, medical treatment, or medication. Carol, a CHP nurse practitioner, shared this consistent message she hears from the women she treats:

> What I see mainly is that these women don't have any insurance. Their whole way of dealing with things, I think, is: "Well I don't have any medicine; I'm just going to keep on going and doing the best I can unless there's a super emergency, unless I absolutely have to go." If they have a pain in their stomach, they'll just keep going until they can't move and then maybe they'll go to the ER. Some women who've had breast lumps think, "What's the point? I won't be able to afford the surgery to have it removed anyway so what's the point in going?" It's almost like a hopeless feeling that you hear over and over again—"I can't afford it; I can't afford it."

In other cases, patients have gotten so far into debt after experiencing a comprehensive illness that they had to forego follow-up care and medication. Peggy, for example, suffered a heart attack. "I ran up a $98,000 hospital bill which I can't pay. I was supposed to go back to the specialist for a checkup but could not afford the $150 upfront fee just to see the doctor—so, I just didn't go back," stressed Peggy. "Since I can't afford to go back to the specialist and I can't afford to pay for my heart medicine, I'm not taking any medication for my heart. I haven't seen any doctor since my heart attack for any medical issues until today."

Another barrier that keeps patients from using free medical services is their lack of knowledge about what resources are available to them and where resources are located. Many patients assume that if they are working or receiving some type of pension or aid, they do not qualify for free medical care. One patient, Betty, had a difficult time enrolling in the free clinic once she became aware of it. "I called the medical college to try and find free medical care and got passed around until I finally got someone who knew about the clinics," Betty stressed. "Had I not been scared and desperate, I would have probably given up long before I found someone to help me." Another patient, Jane, suggested that many people fall through the cracks of care because the poverty guidelines, like the minimum wage guidelines, do not adequately depict the cost of living.

Once patients know where and when free or reduced-fee clinics operate, the next obstacle some face is how to get to the clinic locations. Many patients who use the CHP clinics do not have their own mode of transportation and must depend on the kindness of relatives or neighbors. This means, to use the free services, they must first find out where the clinics are located and then see if the date and time works into the schedule of the person who will be bringing them. They are then at the mercy of others, and if something happens and their ride falls through, they miss out on their appointments. This is especially critical when they are being referred for other services that require them to stick to an appointment schedule. Sally, a nurse coordinator, refers her patients to a number of different agencies for assistance. She constantly receives calls from the referring agencies telling her that a certain patient cannot be referred again because he/she missed past appointments. Sally lamented, "A lot of people can't get to referral services. Those are the ones I think about—they couldn't go because they didn't have a car and the agency said you're out because you've missed three appointments."

Fear also prevents many individuals from seeking care. For example, Denice believes that women do not come in for treatment because "they are afraid there is something wrong and their problems would escalate in the aftermath if they couldn't get further financial assistance." Yet, for other women, fear comes in the form of denial—cancer will never happen to me so I do not need to get checked or to do self-exams. We should note that in a couple of cases, the fear of having or getting a life-threatening disease actually brought women in for screenings. Amanda, a 30-year-old woman who was being screened for breast and cervical cancer, was able to convince her mother to come with her. As Amanda explained, "My mom is in her 50s and I brought her with me today for a screening. My bout with cancer scared her and made her realize the importance of screenings. She has never been screened before today." That said, when participants discussed fear it was generally to account for why they chose not to seek care.

Stigma and pride also prevent individuals from seeking care. One of the patients, Judy, made sure that Karen knew she worked on a farm for room and board—that she was not unemployed. During Karen's interview with her, Judy emphasized several times that she is a hard worker, she is not lazy, and farm work is difficult labor. She expressed her fear that medical staff would think, "Here comes a lazy-assed woman who won't get a job." Karen reassured Judy that many of the women served by the CHP were in similar circumstances and that she had yet to meet a "lazy-assed woman" in any of the clinics. Judy, and countless other participants, overtly stressed to us that they did not "choose" their life circumstances, nor were their life circumstances the result of an *immoral character* (see Goffman, 1963). Julie, a nurse coordinator, explained:

> And there's stigma. I've seen this in different places, you know. It's like I'm not going to have my pap test done in a free clinic. We had a patient yesterday that was really uncomfortable and was embarrassed to come because she hated to say that she needed these types of services. It was a pride thing and I try to get that dismissed as soon as I can. I try to make people feel it's okay to come and use these services and to not feel bad because they need them.

In listening to Judy, Julie, and countless other participants, we were reminded of the socially constructed nature of stigma (Goffman, 1963). Stigmatization is usefully understood as a process, the structuring of social relations that produce definitions of outsider and other (see Harter et al., 2005). Such processes reproduce the differential acceptability of various groups, (de)valuations often internalized by marginalized others. The spoiled or tainted identities of those marked as other are difficult to repair (Lindemann-Nelson, 2001), and in fact public health officials position stigma processes as leading barriers to health promotion and treatment for those facing health challenges (Smith, 2011).

The experience of stigma is interlaced with pride. When Karen asked Jane, a B & C screening patient, why she thought more women did not take advantage of free clinics, she reiterated Julie's sentiments about Appalachian pride. "It's humbling accepting free medical services. I think that might be the reason people don't go to get the services because it wounds their pride in some way to accept a handout," reflected Jane. "I think that's characteristic of this whole area. People have their pride in taking care of themselves and in taking care of their own."

As our conversations with patients and staff indicate, providing medical services for an Appalachian population is not just as easy as "if you build it, they will come." Perhaps what is most troubling is the meta-narrative of healthcare for underresourced individuals, described by one participant as "assembly line medicine." In the next section, we explore mainstream care as perceived by participants. We consciously move between women's stories, as shared by them during the course of our fieldwork, and the dominant meta-narrative of healthcare that is both fodder for and outcome of their personal stories.

— THE META-NARRATIVE OF "ASSEMBLY LINE MEDICINE" —

Dorothy, a B & C cancer screening patient, described healthcare in the United States as "assembly line medicine." She extended the metaphor by describing a former male physician's technique of doing pap tests as "like changing auto parts on a car"—he was rough and did not waste time in making small talk or in trying to help patients relax. Dorothy's experience is, unfortunately, one many Americans have experienced (see Beck, 2001). Care providers face competing demands to treat patients as people while at the same time practice cost-effective and efficient medicine. That said, what is different about the stories shared by Dorothy and other women interviewed is that they believe they are subjected to routinized and subpar care because of their socioeconomic status. They feel that many physicians do not want to expend much time or energy on patients whose income stream limits the amount of reimbursement they will receive for services rendered. As Kathleen explained, "Doctors never have time; they rush you and don't listen. Doctors also want money upfront. If you don't have $40, you don't go to the doctor."

Women recalled countless experiences they had with doctors who tuned them out, shut them down, or came across as smug or superior. For example, Jeanette shared that her mother's doctor did not give them the time of day as he was always rushed and they did not feel comfortable asking him questions. She believes that too often doctors treat poor patients, especially women, in a condescending manner. Some care providers appear to adopt what Danielle, a nurse coordinator, called the "treat and street" method of care. For a population that already feels marginalized and stigmatized, the mentality of getting folks in and out as quickly as possible does little to make patients feel appreciated or well cared for. The "treat and street" method of care serves as an anchor in the broader narrative of "assembly line medicine," giving rise to subject positions assumed by both providers and patients.

More than one patient talked about having seen a doctor who limited them to one complaint per visit no matter what health issues they were experiencing. Before joining the CHP, Danielle had worked at a traditional doctor's office and witnessed firsthand a dismissive attitude toward patients. She shared the following example about two physicians she had worked with who operated under the street and treat mentality.

> There are two physicians that I can think of that are here to treat whatever the patient came in for and don't look at anything else. Their attitude is to let somebody else take care of that when we refer them elsewhere. They're "I'm here to take care of their blood pressure today—let's get them in and get them out." They have the mentality of treat and street them.

Carol, a nurse practitioner, has worked in medical offices where patients were not always subjected to kind and considerate treatment. "I've been in places where people are sarcastic and they roll their eyes," reflected Carol. "They're just very impatient and not very understanding of the patients' needs and situations."

Patients also recognize the importance of having their physician conduct a thorough assessment of their overall health. Betty would love to see more physicians treat the whole person and not just the symptoms or the worst medical issue at that appointment. She believes that doctors need to learn about what is going on in the patient's life that may be impacting his or her health because, in her words, "you can't make accurate determinations without knowing the root cause." Importantly, in medical practice, some conditions evoke disgust and distance more than others (see Smith, 2011). For example, the smell accompanying some diseases (e.g., fungating wounds) often leads providers to remain physically and socially distant from poor patients (Lund-Nielsen, Muller, & Adamsen, 2005). It is not surprising, then, that participants in our study generally do not perceive that they receive holistic care.

Assembly line medicine, as narrated by participants, is characterized by *subpar care* for people living in poverty and in some cases is relegated to *subpar settings*. Carol, a nurse practitioner, and Karen were having lunch before an afternoon B & C exam clinic started. Karen was scheduled to have her annual exam the next day and Carol asked her who her OB/GYN was. When Karen told her the physician's name, Carol laughed and told her that she had plenty of experience with him when she worked at the city's health department. In fact, many of her clients used this doctor for their pregnancies and deliveries. She did not have a very high opinion of him because he would make his uninsured or Medicaid patients go to another location for exams and to deliver and would not let them visit him at his nice office. "The poor people get the basement exam rooms with linoleum and cheap furniture. People who are insured, like you and me, get nice furniture and carpeted rooms."

Tina has also experienced subpar care, she believes, largely based on her ability to pay. She currently sees a group of doctors at a practice in her community for heart-related problems. Because this is a group practice, she rarely sees the same doctor at each appointment so whomever she sees never knows her medical history. Once after a 2-hour wait to see a doctor, he told her the computer was down and he could not treat her because he could not access her medical history. "They know we're poor and we're getting our appointments paid for by Medicaid or some other service," stressed Tina. "We're not wealthy and they're not going to make a lot of money from us. Therefore, they can schedule five appointments at 11:00 because our time is not valuable—we're just garbage so it doesn't matter how they treat us." Charon (2006) echoed Tina's concern with her acknowledgment that "the skirmish about waiting room time might be taken seriously—we doctors are never on time, and our assumptions that patients do not mind being kept waiting is a pervasive and powerful message about differential worth" (p. 44).

One of the patients, Stephanie, shared a particularly disturbing experience in discussing the subpar care she received when a male physician lost a tissue sample during a pap smear procedure. "He couldn't find the tissue sample. He had a student there with him and he said, 'Well, I'm going to have to do this again.'" As Stephanie narrated this moment, she recalled "shaking and doing some deep breathing" and he responded by telling her not to worry, "it would just be a little pinch." Unlike many people living in poverty, Stephanie confronted the doctor: "Excuse me, but if I said to you I'm just going to take a little teeny piece off the end of your penis, it really won't hurt very much, what would you think? How would you feel?" recounted Stephanie. "And then, and then, they found the specimen after they did the second biopsy. He found the first one. It was on his glove!" Previous research indicates that lower income patients are perceived as less rational or intelligent than are higher income patients (van Ryn & Burke, 2000). Participants' stories echo existing literature. Stephanie challenged her care provider; many of those living in poverty do not (see Ford & Yep, 2003).

Whether being subjected to the basement exam room, unnecessary procedures due to carelessness, or having their valuable time and health concerns disregarded, many patients definitely have felt the sting of receiving subpar medical care through assembly line medicine. Certainly, not all care providers in mainstream healthcare contexts practice assembly line medicine. And, it is important to acknowledge the broader environment in which providers operate—a culture characterized by soaring costs of medical care and ongoing healthcare reform seeking to contain costs and lower per patient expenses (Harter & Zoller, 2010). That said, class-power dynamics are evident in macro-societal health structures as individuals engage in everyday micro-practices (Allen, 2004). We live in a class-segregated society in which the poor not only live in separate geographic areas but also experience disproportionate health inequities and lower quality of care (if they even have access to care) (see also Ford & Yep, 2003; Ndiaye, Krieger, Warren, & Hecht, 2011). The CHP offers a vision of how to redress health inequities and improve access to quality care for underserved and under-resourced populations.

— ADVANCING A NEW NORMAL OF CARE IN SOUTHEASTERN OHIO —

By design, the CHP breaks down the barriers encountered by the patient base they serve and disrupts the meta-narrative of assembly line medicine. To begin, the CHP reorganizes space to foster a sense of community and invite storytelling among providers and patients. Second, the timing of its services is designed to counteract the temporal rhythms of mainstream medicine and better accommodate patients' lifeworlds.

REORGANIZING SPACE TO INVITE STORYTELLING

The limited and mobile nature of CHP's clinical spaces creates its share of challenges in comparison to fixed clinical contexts (see Deardorff, 2009, for an extended discussion). Even so, the spatial domains of the CHP create opportunities for patients and staff to closely interact. We focus on those opportunities in this chapter. By creating an atmosphere that fosters rapport and trust among providers and patients, the CHP and its staff actively work to disrupt the meta-narrative of "assembly line care." As Sally, a nurse coordinator, explained, "Patients usually tell me a whole lot of things they don't usually tell. I think for some people, this is the only chance they ever get to tell their story and to have someone really listen who is not there to judge what they've done or to judge their personal situation."

Denice was surprised by the quality of medical care she received on the mobile van. She had not been sure what to expect when she climbed up the steps and entered the van's waiting area. She was scared, embarrassed to be the recipient of free medical care, and uncertain whether, as an African American, she would even be welcome. "The environment was so much better than I expected and much different from a doctor's office (in a good way)," stressed Denice when describing her impression of the van. "No one sat behind a glass window and people didn't try to avoid eye contact or talking to each other. No one made me feel ashamed for being there, for being down on my luck." Importantly, for Denice, she felt she was "treated with dignity. They asked questions and then they listened—they really cared about me and they let me talk. The doctor [nurse practitioner] asked about the scar on my breast and I told her it was from an infection I got after a beating from my ex-husband. I don't usually tell people that stuff, but I felt good with her."

The accompanying photographs offer a look at how the clinic's allotted spaces are configured in the primary-use vehicle. Although the CHP has two mobile vans, one is most frequently used for the B & C program and the free medical clinics because the layout of the vehicle is more patient and staff friendly. The space configuration of this most frequently used mobile van somewhat resembles a traditional doctor's office with a waiting area, an intake room, and an examination room. However, a major design factor that separates the mobile clinic from a traditional doctor's office is that patients and staff are not separated from one another by sliding glass partitions, by private lounge areas, or even by private consultation areas. In the mobile van, the waiting area also doubles as office space for the nurse coordinator or whomever is doing the intake and often serves as a consultation area for the nurse practitioner and other CHP staff.

The CHP mobile van

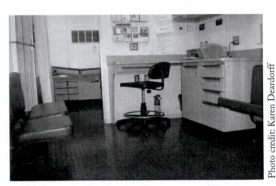

Waiting area in the mobile van

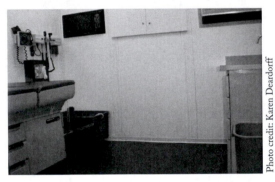

Patient intake room in the mobile van

Exam room in the mobile van

Clinics held in makeshift public venues, such as senior centers, churches, and schools, are also confined to very limited space. These venues are principally used for healthy adult screenings because patients do not need a space to undress for examination, and private consultation between the staff is minimal. During a typical clinic, staff set up three cafeteria-style tables in their allotted space down a hallway, in the corner of a sanctuary, or in a lobby. One table is used for patient registration and intake, one is used for patient assessment (e.g., taking blood pressures), and one holds equipment (e.g., diabetes screening monitors). As on the mobile van, patients and staff have little room for separation or privacy (see Deardorff, 2009; Harter et al., 2008 for an extended discussion). However, these small spaces also afford opportunities for staff and patients to interact on a more personal level. In this way, the reorganization of space in mobile clinics takes on material and symbolic significance.

CHAPTER 5 • Disrupting the Meta-Narrative of "Assembly Line Medicine"

Certainly the limited physical space literally necessitates that patients sit in close proximity to one another and to the CHP staff. However, even when the clinic space is filled with patients who do not know one another, the CHP staff strives to create a social space for patients to comfortably share their lived experiences. One vivid example of this occurred at a breast and cervical cancer screening.

> *Jeanette and Loretta boarded the van together. They have been coming to the B & C clinic together for at least 3 years because only Jeanette can drive and because both are uninsured. The clinic was especially busy and the van had only two seats left which Jeanette and Loretta filled. Loretta started talking about how much she hated to have her yearly exam done and the other two patients, Dorothy and Carolyn, added their thoughts about the procedure as well. Jeanette then began talking openly about being diagnosed with vaginal dermatitis and how she had been doctoring for 2 years and had used every kind of antibiotic and cream the doctors could think of. Carolyn inquired about which doctors she had seen and what kind of medicine she had used. Carol asked if she had brought the medicine with her and Jeanette fished around in her purse and pulled out the tube and handed it to Carol. She also made sure to let us all know that the dermatitis wasn't caused by something she had done sexually; it was just one of those "female" things.* (Karen's fieldnotes)

Sometimes the clinics serve as a reconnecting point for community members or friends. Carol, a nurse practitioner, shared the following story about a group of old classmates who unexpectedly met up on the same mobile clinic.

> *Yesterday, there were some ladies who were classmates and they hadn't seen each other in 5 years since their last class reunion. So, they started talking about their grandchildren and about so and so who was in the hospital. Julie told one of the patients she could go into the exam room now, and I said, "I know you're ready to start the intake, but she's got to catch up with her friend here." Then somebody said, "Why don't you give her your phone number and she can call and you guys can go out for breakfast." Somebody else said, "Yeah, that's a good idea—Mary give me your phone number." They were yelling through the exam room door— it was kind of cute. A lot of women come in and just by accident see people they know or that they used to work with or that were old classmates. We see a lot of people reconnect.*

To disrupt the barriers of mobility and flexibility in receiving healthcare, the mobile clinics often set up in small towns throughout their service area. In its finest moments, this practice helps break down the barriers of stigma and pride by sending a message that people living in these areas are important enough to make an effort to bring care to their doorstep. For example, the mobile clinic has held several free medical and cancer screening clinics in a small, rural, economically depressed community. The van opens up shop in front of the local senior center, which is housed in one of the nicest run-down buildings in town. Marie, a CHP nurse, told Karen that trust was hard to establish in this town, and as a result, the first few clinics had very few patients. However, as part of her church's outreach program, she started coming to the senior center once a week to take blood pressures. Through this interaction, she was able to establish trust and to eventually convince people to give the mobile clinic a try. The day Karen observed there, the clinic was heavily scheduled with patients all day. The last patient of the morning invited everyone to come to the senior center with her for lunch. After lunch, the staff agreed they had made the right decision by sharing lunch with them—through breaking bread they had joined medicine with the spirit of the community.

Metaphorically, patients are given the space they need during the intake and examination to talk about not only their health issues but also underlying factors that might be contributing to their health challenges and/or to the challenges of family and friends. Judy, a patient in a B & C clinic, found that the CHP staff provided a comfortable, caring, and competent atmosphere in which to tell her story: "They not only took good care of me, they allowed me space to talk about personal issues. I told Carol about a medical problem my sister was having and Carol gave me information on the free clinics and encouraged me to get my sister an appointment."

In other instances, the clinics serve as a venue for social networking while also providing an educational component. During a healthy adult program (scheduled to coincide with a food pantry distribution) in the lobby of a small community church, three sisters came over to the screening area to have their glucose, blood pressure, and cholesterol tested. While the three were taking turns getting screened and learning what their numbers meant, three or four other friends who had received their food allotments came over to see what was going on.

> As I watched the patients and their friends exchanging personal medical information, I could not help but think that HIPPA would have a field day here with the lack of patient privacy. Everyone was asking everyone else what their numbers were and leaning over the screening tables to observe the testing process. Gina, who was doing patient intake, remarked to me that you just didn't see this kind of community in larger cities—this was Appalachia at its finest. She also thought this reaction was in part due to the small, comfortable setting. (Karen's fieldnotes)

The healthcare promoted by CHP fosters what Burke (1969) might have described as *consubstantiality*, or common ground. By creating a physical and social space that allows patients to engage in storytelling about their lives, a bond is forged in a common space that promotes communication between self and other.

Carole, a nurse practitioner who did not grow up in Appalachia, was surprised at the sense of community the staff engender with patients. She shared the following encounter she and her husband had with a former clinic patient.

> In the first 2 weeks of working this job, my husband and I were in the Pomeroy area and we stopped at McDonalds. The lady behind the counter said, "You're that lady from the van, aren't you?" I recognized her then. My husband thought that was pretty funny, that you're far away from home, far away from Athens, and someone recognizes you and treats you like an old friend. That's a good feeling to know that you're touching people's lives in these communities.

Many CHP staff noted that their connections with patients deepened when they also shared personal stories about their families, hobbies and interests, and personal experiences with health-related issues (e.g., surviving breast cancer, efforts to quit smoking). For example, Danielle's willingness to talk about her faith and church attendance led a patient to seek additionally needed medical care.

I wouldn't have found that out [cancerous lesion between breasts] had I not talked to this patient about church and had we not gotten real comfortable with one another. She was there for blood pressure only and had I not been able to establish a rapport with her and share some of my experiences with her, the cancer might not have been found before it was too late for any treatment. She wasn't going to show the doctor—she was there for her blood pressure and nothing else. When she opened her blouse and showed me her breasts, I was stunned that she had been living with this sore and had not told anyone. She's had surgery and is taking chemo and radiation now. I call her every couple weeks to see how she's doing—we still don't know if we caught the cancer in time but it's important to me to let her know I'm still here and I still care about her.

Sally, another staff member, was quick to stress the importance of establishing common ground with her patients:

Sometimes I think if they've never talked about things before, they think that they are the only people this has ever happened to or that are feeling that way. It helps if I can say not only has it happened to you, it's happened to me and it's happened to a whole bunch of people out there. It's not just a common bond, it's helping the patient understand that they're not crazy or weird or alone.

Throughout its various clinics, CHP staff regularly used stories to create a common bond with patients, ease the sting of stigma, honor tradition and culture, preserve a sense of dignity and pride, and create what Hyde (2004) might term a *dwelling space*. For Hyde, dwelling spaces represent the life-giving gift of acknowledgment—acknowledgment of difference, being, hardship, and suffering. "Acknowledgment provides an opening out of such a distressful situation," he argued, "for the act of acknowledging is a communicative behavior that grants attention to others and thereby makes room for them in our lives" (p. 63). We witnessed time and again how storytelling at CHP clinics opens up a dialogic thread, discourse that instrumentally helps medical personnel dig deeper into the root causes of illness or health issues.

In many ways the narrative practices of the CHP reflect Tannen's (1990) concepts of rapport-talk (i.e., sharing personal information) and report-talk (i.e., discussing medical issues and treatment). Julie, a nurse with the B & C cancer program, shared a vivid example. She occasionally shares with her patients that she is a breast cancer survivor. When Karen asked Julie why she chose to share such intimate details with strangers she replied:

Sometimes I do share my personal story of breast cancer, it depends on the case. If I see someone hesitant about getting their mammogram I do, and I've swayed them to get their mammograms before. Because I've been through it I can say here's a perfect example because I had no family history of breast cancer, and I had been getting routine mammograms, and I had no breast lump, and wham, one year they found it on a mammogram, and I was 48. I'm the perfect example. I tell that to women who are hesitant about getting their mammograms, and I can usually sway them. I think it helps if patients know you've gone through a similar situation because they tend to trust what you're telling them. I think it also helps staff connect with that person on the other side of the exam table. Patients feel more comfortable when they realize that their doctor or nurse is human too and that they are speaking from personal experience.

Sally, a nurse coordinator, is quick to let her patients know that she has walked in their shoes. She believes such disclosures foster more open and honest communication, build trust, and alleviate the stigma and shame many experience from being referred to her for medical evaluation and intervention. As she explained:

> I've shared very personal trials in my life, or I say, "I understand that" or "that's my history, too," so that patients know it's not so shameful. It helps that I can talk about what I went through and how it took time and hard work to get things turned around. They need to know that I didn't feel so damaged that I didn't do some healing from getting help. In order to help with the medical and behavioral issues, I've got to get them to tell me what's really going on. Once they feel comfortable enough to give me the whole picture I can start talking with them about treatment and intervention options. I think what makes me pretty good at my job is that I can talk to people coming from the same place I've come from and they don't have to protect themselves any more. They can let some of that guard down and we can talk honestly about things that maybe they've never talked about before.

One patient, Judy, suggested that a nurse practitioner's use of personal stories helped her to understand the treatment or medical issues more clearly. "She never gave the names of anyone, but she'd say I've been through this with my family and this is what they went through and then I would better understand what she was talking about." Another patient, Wendy, also remembered how Carol's stories brought a different perspective to the medical care she received.

"When we were in there and we were talking about arthritis and things, she was talking about her family and how it affected her dad and she got more on a personal level," shared Wendy. "That made me realize that she wasn't talking about something just as a doctor, she was talking about something she had experienced firsthand—something she personally knew about."

Through the blurring of personal (rapport-talk) and professional (report-talk), staff members share their personal and family stories of health and healing with patients in the waiting areas and during medical examinations. We witnessed firsthand how this storytelling put patients at ease, established common bonds, fostered a sense of community, and helped build connections and trust that often extended outside the physical clinic walls. By creating a dwelling space where patients feel comfortable sharing their lived experiences, CHP staff members disrupt the meta-narrative of assembly line care.

TRANSFORMING TEMPORAL RHYTHMS

The CHP also transforms the traditional temporal rhythms of mainstream care. The time care providers spend with patients is critical for constructing what Montgomery (2006) described as "a recognizable clinical account of the patient's illness," enabling providers to "transform details of the patient's illness narrative into clues that will match one disease plot better than others and clinch the diagnosis" (p. 61). Numerous national reports issued by the Institute of Medicine (IOM, 2001) and by the American College of Physicians' Charter on Medical Professionalism (ABIM Foundation, ACP-ASIM Foundation, & European Federation of Internal Medicine, 2002) have positioned patient-centered care as central to safe and quality care. In this context, patient-centeredness is shorthand for the full inclusion of patients' perspectives in medical interactions (Roter & Hall, 2011). In assembly line medicine, though, patients routinely spend considerable time sitting in a room waiting for their turn to see a physician. The patient is rewarded for this wait by getting to spend approximately 10–15 minutes (if the patient load is light) with their physician. And, more often than not, the physician will only treat one chief complaint per visit. Certainly, we do not conflate quantity of time with quality; however, a "treat and street" mentality allows little time for patients to share much more than the location of a pain or the most pervasive symptoms they have been experiencing. Underscoring this problem is the fact that underserved patients typically present with multiple interrelated problems and challenges that providers must triage in order to treat.

The CHP staff realizes that "between the activity of narrating a story and the temporal character of human experience there exists a correlation that is not merely accidental but that represents a transcultural form of necessity" (Ricoeur, 1984, p. 52). Blood tests, x-rays, medications, and other tools are limited if providers cannot meaningfully situate them in the patient's broader lifeworld. To counteract the temporal rhythms of assembly line medicine, the CHP clinics are scheduled to provide shorter waiting times and allow for longer patient–provider interaction in a slower paced, more relaxed environment. Granted, the CHP staff does not generally have patient quotas to fill or a specific number of billing hours needed to produce an income stream most practices depend on to stay in business. Although the staff is aware of the tenuous position the clinic is in because of shifting and eroding funding (see Deardorff, 2009), this lack of constant financial dependency allows staff to practice a more patient-centered medicine by spending the time needed to elicit the myriad factors that contribute to patients' health challenges.

Charon (2006) argued that clinical care is transformed when it is practiced with a respect for time and timeliness. Time is central in diagnosis, in prevention, in palliation, or in treatment. Taking the time to listen, the time to care, and the time to recognize each individual patient's story of illness is an irreplaceable ingredient in the healing relationship. Danielle, a CHP nurse, believes mobile clinics like the CHP provide a unique sense of space and an allotment of time for each patient that is not typically found in mainstream medical environments. Before accepting a position with the CHP, Danielle worked for several years as a nurse for a group of doctors in a primary care facility. She bases the following viewpoint on the differences she witnessed between her former position and her current position working on the mobile vans.

> *Sometimes we're the only place patients get to tell what they want to tell someone who will listen to them. I think it's important to their care. They are getting the best nursing care and the best physician or nurse practitioner care because they have our undivided attention. We don't have phones ringing; we don't have patients walking in and out wanting certain things; and we don't have a lot of staff needing things. I feel like we have a lot of time to do one-on-one. I think they get better care than you and I get when we go to our physician's office and our insurance pays.*

Dr. Roberts spoke about the importance of combining the psychological and social aspects of healthcare along with the biological or scientific model. Believing that there is a difference between "taking a patient's history" and "hearing the patient's story" (Frank, 1995), Dr. Roberts spends as much time talking with patients as is needed to obtain a comprehensive overview of their medical and personal stories. CHP nurse Danielle believes that Dr. Roberts embodies a narrative mindset when talking with patients. When Karen asked Danielle to explain why she felt Dr. Roberts provided a different type of care to patients, she responded:

Dr. Roberts never gets in a hurry when he's with a patient. He may disappear with a patient for an hour if that patient wants to talk to him. He asks them questions about everything and has a conversation with them. You just never know what you're going to hear that's going to help you understand patients better and enable you to treat them. The mobile clinic is the ideal setting for Dr. Roberts because we have the time for him to spend with each patient. Dr. Roberts' people and interpersonal skills are amazing—he makes time to listen. He understands that making time to listen leads to making better decisions in regard to diagnosis, treatment, care, and the subsequent healing of our patients.

The patients we met were quite vocal in their appreciation for environments that foster more face-to-face contact with medical personnel. For example, Judy had not sought medical treatment for some time because of her financial situation and because the environment always seemed cold and rushed. She appreciated that the staff took their time with her and did not try to hurry her out the door: "That means a lot, especially when you are hesitant to seek treatment in the first place. It is a good feeling to know that they (medical staff) are not looking at you as just a body but as a human being."

– CONCLUSION –

At the end of the first decade of the 21st century the Healthy People 2010 goals for reducing health disparities remained unmet. In a country where health-related expenditures exceed 16% of the gross domestic product, it is ironic at best that 43.6 million people under the age of 65 remain uninsured (see http://www.cdc.gov/nchs/fastats/hinsure.htm). For those Americans who qualify for free or reduced care, many experience what one participant in our study described as "assembly line care." The CHP offers a hopeful vision of curbside and community-based care for individuals who face persistent barriers to quality healthcare, including the stigma and shame of poverty. It disrupts geographic barriers by shifting the settings in which services unfold. Staff members provide patients with the physical and emotional space as well as time to narrate their lives, positioning illness in broader social circumstances. In doing so, the CHP creates a new normal for its constituents and serves as a model for how to organize healthcare resources for underresourced and underserved populations.

The very process of operating a mobile clinic lends itself to efficiently serving its patients. For example, mobile clinics have the ability to set up shop quickly and in virtually any location, function with minimal staffing and overhead, and administer a variety of healthcare services and screenings quickly so patient wait time is minimal. By bringing healthcare to the doorsteps of its patients, the mobile clinic reduces barriers exacerbated by the lack of available and affordable transportation and lessens the need for patients to take large chunks of time off from work in order to receive care.

Storytelling is central to the activities of the CHP. As argued in Chapter 1, the lived experiences of health, healing, illness, and chaos represent calls for stories (see also Brody, 1987; Frank, 1993, 1995; Lupton, 2003; Sontag, 1978). The telling of stories can be empowering insofar as it "allows individuals to construct meaning from otherwise devastating life events, repair the disruption caused by illness to their healthy life narrative, and reclaim power from other narratives of the experience, including the medical narrative" (Das Gupta & Hurst, 2007, p. 1). It is important to note, though, that not all patients may want to engage in extended narration about their lives. The CHP staff allows patients to maintain their dignity and control over what aspects of their story they choose to share (if anything).

Although the CHP staff is changing the experience of healthcare for this underserved population, there are times when it is not easy or possible to challenge "assembly line care." Rules and regulations get in the way, socioeconomic situations pull at already overburdened budgets, and some patients still do not trust care providers or feel empowered. In fact, for some patients, the lack of privacy during CHP clinics functions as a deterrence rather than incentive for seeking care. Meanwhile, challenges arise from the very essence of being mobile—mechanical problems with the van or generator, medical equipment malfunctions, inclement weather (either for traveling or for patients who might have to wait in line outside the van), a limited number of staff to care for patients, and limited space onboard to accommodate those patients. Clinics in rural areas often lack cell phone service, making it difficult for staff and patients to schedule follow-up screenings for mammograms or other diagnostic services (see Carmack, 2010, and Deardorff, 2009, for an extended discussion of the challenges associated with mobile clinics).

Our analysis offers one reading of the CHP's efforts; we recognize other possibilities exist. We close by noting our discomfort in celebrating the efforts of an organization that exists because segments of society lack access to quality healthcare. Discourse, scholarly or otherwise, risks naturalizing health inequities as normal. We hope that neither our narrative about the CHP nor the development of mobile clinics more generally romanticizes the grueling conditions of poverty and individuals' abilities to confront it. The strategies exhibited by the CHP, powerful as they are, cannot counteract the many forces that affront those living in poverty in southeastern Ohio. Those of us who enjoy relative privilege must take responsibility for acknowledging and responding to differences that matter—including social class. Scholars and practitioners alike must shift attention to the broader social domain where healthcare is provided and rendered meaningful. Clearly, the healthcare concerns and needs of those living in poverty are positioned differently than those with more resources.

Our lives have been enriched in the process of learning with CHP staff and stakeholders. We hope our representation of our encounters inspires additional inquiry and interpretations about the possibilities and limits of mobile health clinics and community-based care.

− REFERENCES −

ABIM Foundation, ACP-ASIM Foundation, & European Federation of Internal Medicine. (2002). Charter on medical professionalism. *Annals of Internal Medicine, 136*, 243–246.

Allen, B.J. (2004). *Difference matters: Communicating social identity.* Long Grove, IL: Waveland Press.

Beck, C.S. (2001). *Communicating for better health: A guide through the medical mazes.* Boston: Allyn and Bacon.

Brody, H. (1987). *Stories of sickness.* New Haven, CT: Yale University Press.

Burd-Sharps, S., Lewis, K., & Martins, E.B. (2008). *The measure of America: American human development report 2008-2009.* New York: Columbia University Press.

Burke, K. (1969). *A rhetoric of motives.* Berkeley: University of California Press.

Burns, A.A., Lovich, R., Maxwell, J., & Shapiro, K. (1997). *Where women have no doctor: A health guide for women*. Berkeley, CA: The Hesperian Foundation.

Carmack, H.J. (2010). "What happens on the van, stays on the van": The (re)structuring of privacy and disclosure scripts on an Appalachian mobile health clinic. *Qualitative Health Research, 20*, 1393–1405.

Charon, R. (2006). *Narrative medicine: Honoring the stories of illness*. New York: Oxford University Press.

Das Gupta, S., & Hurst, M. (Eds.). (2007). *Stories of illness and healing: Women write their bodies*. Kent, OH: The Kent State University Press.

Deardorff, K.L. (2009). Catalytic innovations in Appalachia Ohio health care: The storying of health care in a mobile clinic. (Unpublished dissertation). Athens: Ohio University.

Denham, S.A., Meyer, M.G., & Toborg, M.A. (2004). Tobacco cessation in adolescent females in Appalachian communities. *Family & Community Health, 27*, 170–181.

Ford, A.L., & Yep, G.A. (2003). Working along the margins: Developing community-based strategies for communicating about health with marginalized populations. In T. Thompson, A.M. Dorsey, K.I. Miller, & R. Parrott (Eds.), *Handbook of health communication* (pp. 241–262). Mahwah, NJ: Erlbaum.

Frank, A.W. (1993). The rhetoric of self-change: Illness experience as narrative. *The Sociological Quarterly, 34*(1), 39–52.

Frank, A.W. (1995). *The wounded storyteller: Body, illness, and ethics*. Chicago: University of Chicago Press.

Gilliom, J. (2001). *Overseers of the poor: Surveillance, resistance, and the limits of privacy*. Chicago and London: The University of Chicago Press.

Goffman, E. (1963). *Stigma: Notes on the management of spoiled identity*. Englewood Cliffs, NJ: Prentice-Hall.

Harter, L.M., & Zoller, H.M. (2010). Organizing healing and health care resources. *Management Communication Quarterly, 24*, 446–448.

Harter, L.M., Berquist, C., Titsworth, B.S., Novak, D., & Brokaw, T. (2005). The structuring of invisibility among the hidden homeless: The politics of space, stigma, and identity construction. *Journal of Applied Communication Research, 33*, 305–327.

Harter, L.M., Deardorff, K.L., Kenniston, P., Carmack, H., & Rattine-Flaherty, E. (2008). Changing lanes and changing lives: The *shifting* scenes and *continuity* of care of a mobile health clinic. In H. Zoller & M. Dutta-Bergman (Eds.), *Emerging issues and perspectives in health communication: Interpretive, critical, and cultural approaches to engaged research*. Mahwah, NJ: Lawrence Erlbaum Associates.

Hyde, M.J. (2004). The ontological workings of dialogue and acknowledgement. In R. Anderson, L.A. Baxter, & K.N. Cissna (Eds.), *Dialogue: Theorizing difference in communication studies* (pp. 57–76). Thousand Oaks, CA: Sage.

Institute of Medicine. (2001). *Crossing the quality chasm: A new health system*. Washington, DC: National Academy Press.

Katz, M.L., Wewers, M.E., Single, N., & Paskett, E.D. (2007). Key informants' perspectives prior to beginning a cervical cancer study in Ohio Appalachia. *Qualitative Health Research, 17*(1), 131–141.

Latimer, M., & Oberhauser, A.M. (2005). Exploring gender and economic development in Appalachia. *Journal of Appalachian Studies, 10*(3), 269–291.

Liebman, J., Lamberti, M.P., & Altice, F. (2002). Effectiveness of a mobile medical van in providing screening services for STDs and HIV. *Public Health Nursing, 19*(5), 345–353.

Lindemann-Nelson, H. (2001). *Damaged identities, narrative repair.* Ithaca, NY: Cornell University Press.

Lund-Nielsen, B., Muller, K., & Adamsen, L. (2005). Malignant wounds in women and with breast cancer: Feminine and sexual perspectives. *Journal of Clinical Nursing, 14,* 56–64.

Lupton, D. (2003). *Medicine as culture: Illness, disease and the body in Western societies* (2nd ed.). London: Sage.

McKinley, A. (2005). Promoting access and care in rural and underserved areas. *Healthcare Financial Management, 59,* 16–17.

Montgomery, K. (2006). *How doctors think: Clinical judgment and the practice of medicine.* Oxford, UK and New York: Oxford University Press.

Ndiaye, K., Krieger, J.L., Warren, J.R., & Hecht, M.L. (2011). Communication and health disparities. In T.L. Thompson, R. Parrott, & J.F. Nussbaum (Eds.), *The Routledge handbook of health communication* (2nd ed., pp. 469–481). New York: Routledge.

Newman, E.D., Olenginski, T.P., Perruquet, J.L., Hummel, J., Indeck, C., & Wood, G.C. (2004). Using mobile DXA to improve access to osteoporosis care. *Journal of Clinical Densitometry, 7,* 71–75.

Ohio Health Issues Poll. (2007, October). Ohioans' experiences with poverty: A demographic profile of poverty in Ohio 2005-2007. From The Health Foundation of Greater Cincinnati. Retrieved October 7, 2008 from http://www.healthfoundation.org/publications/documents

Pistella, C.L.Y., Bonati, F.A., & Mihalic, S. (1999). Social work practice in a rural community collaborative to improve perinatal care. *Social Work in Health Care, 30*(1), 1–14.

Reid, C., & Tom, A. (2006). Poor women's discourses of legitimacy, poverty, and health. *Gender & Society, 20*(3), 402–421.

Ricoeur, P. (Translated by Kathleen McLaughlin and David Pellauer). (1984). *Time and narrative.* Chicago: University of Chicago Press.

Roter, D.L., & Hall, J.A. (2011). How medical interaction shapes and reflects the physician-patient relationship. In T.L. Thompson, R. Parrott, & J.F. Nussbaum (Eds.), *The Routledge handbook of health communication* (2nd ed., pp. 55–68). New York: Routledge.

Ruspini, E. (2001). The study of women's deprivation: How to reveal the gender dimension of poverty. *International Journal of Social Research Methodology, 4*(2), 101–118.

Sharf, B.F. (1993). Reading the vital signs: Research in health care communication. *Communication Monographs, 60*(1), 35–41.

Shipler, D.K. (2004). *The working poor: Invisible in America.* New York: Alfred A. Knopf.

Smith, R.A. (2011). Stigma, communication, and health. In T.L. Thompson, R. Parrott, & J.F. Nussbaum (Eds.), *The Routledge handbook of health communication* (2nd ed., pp. 455–468). New York: Routledge.

Sontag, S. (1978). *Illness as a metaphor.* New York: Vintage.

Tannen, D. (1990). *You just don't understand: Women and men in conversation.* New York: William Morrow and Company, Inc.

Thorne, D., Tickamyer, A., & Thorne, M. (2005). Poverty and income in Appalachia. *Journal of Appalachian Studies, 10*(3), 341–357.

Tompkins, P.K. (2009). *Who is my neighbor? Communicating and organizing to end homelessness.* Boulder: Paradigm Publishers.

Towson, M. (2000). *A report card on women and poverty.* Ottawa, ON: Canadian Centre for Policy Alternatives.

van Ryn, M., & Burke, J. (2000). The effect of patient race and socio-economic status on physicians' perceptions of patients. *Social Science and Medicine, 50,* 813–828.

Zoller, H.M. (2005). Women caught in the multi-causal web: A gendered analysis of *Healthy People 2010. Communication Studies, 56*(2), 175–192.

– ENDNOTES –

[1]   The other members of the research team included Heather Carmack, Elizabeth Rattine-Flaherty, and Pamela Kenniston.

[2]   See Harter, Deardorff, Kenniston, Carmack, & Rattine-Flaherty, 2008 for an extended discussion of the research design.

[3]   Pseudonyms are used instead of participants' actual names when integrating testimony.

CHAPTER 6

THE POETIC POSSIBILITIES OF LONG-TERM CARE

– JILL YAMASAKI –

It's four o'clock in the morning, and 91-year-old Margaret Carlson is baking cook-ies. This is her third early morning in a row with one more to go until the annual quilt show and bake sale cosponsored by the Happy Sew & Tell Quilting Group and Prairie Meadows Senior Living, but Margaret doesn't mind. "My best baking mood comes early in the morning," she always tells baffled people with a smile. She sifts flour in the "one-at-a-time kitchenette" of the apartment she shares with her roommate, Ada,

and measures sugar from the 25-pound bag they bought together in anticipation of the sale. By sunrise, the aroma of freshly baked cookies fills her apartment and wafts down the hall in a warm greeting for the housekeepers arriving to work and the residents starting to stir. Ada wakes to join her for their usual breakfast of a homemade bun and cup of coffee; then, Margaret frosts with white fluffy frosting the chocolate cake she made for the weekly resident-staff social gathering that afternoon. She promises to vacate the kitchen to let Ada make her famous fudge, but the two will reunite there later that evening when Margaret makes her peanut brittle. Since Margaret is diabetic, Ada will taste each batch for consistency; since Margaret has trouble seeing, Ada will read the thermometer. "We get along just fine," says Margaret, "because we like a lot of the same things."

Margaret, who moved to Prairie Meadows after her husband of 71 years passed away 2 years ago, seems to "get along just fine" with just about everyone. Residents and staff members sing her praise and flock to her treats. "She bakes like you would not believe, and I think she'll make a baker out of me yet," says Bonnie, the head housekeeper. "I called her when we went to Washington. I wanted to make her frosting but couldn't remember the ingredients. You know, my frosting always gets a crust on it. Well, hers never does. And she got the biggest kick out of that." They affectionately call her the "Cookie Grandma," and they encourage her to submit her baked goods for judging at the county fair. When she wins four blue ribbons—for chocolate chip cookies, oatmeal peanut crisp cookies, pumpkin pecan cookies, and peanut brittle—they use her likeness to advertise the facility's quilt show and bake sale in her small town's weekly newspaper. By the time we finally meet—in her apartment over a scrumptious piece of white cake with homemade lemon filling and the white fluffy frosting that never crusts—I have read about her in the newspaper, sampled her cookies at a facility social, and learned of her from staff members, other residents, and various adults living in town. "Have you met Margaret yet?" they ask me. "You need to talk to Margaret."

Margaret lives in an assisted living community. It's located in the same small Minnesota town where she raised her four children, where she realized her declining health meant she could no longer live safely on her own, and where, not so long ago, her only option for long-term care was the county nursing home. Nationwide, assisted living has emerged as a popular residential alternative for physically or cognitively frail older adults like Margaret who can no longer function independently but do not need the 24-hour care provided in traditional nursing homes. Although assisted living environments vary greatly in size and service, they share a general person-centered approach to care that emphasizes resident autonomy, choice, privacy, and engagement in a homelike setting with community connections and family involvement. With these philosophical tenets in mind, Margaret's story seems to exemplify assisted living at its best. She participates in reciprocal relationships with individuals within and outside of the Prairie Meadows community; spends her time pursuing meaningful activities; and receives the assistance she needs to function independently despite frail bones, declining eyesight, and chronic diabetes.

Of course, no one wants to think they'll end up in an assisted living community, much less a nursing home, and not all long-term care is this positive. As elderly adults live longer and with more chronic health conditions, residents in assisted living communities have become increasingly older, sicker, and more like those commonly found in nursing homes (Hawes, Phillips, Rose, Holan, & Sherman, 2003). Many of these residents exhibit mild-to-moderate confusion, memory loss, or impaired judgment (Carder, 2002); and an estimated one fourth need help with three or more activities of daily living (Hawes, Rose, & Phillips, 2000). Some assisted living administrators even suggest the changing realities of old age present real-world constraints to the future of assisted living's philosophical goals, particularly when health or cognition needs challenge resident autonomy (Eckert, Carder, Morgan, Frankowski, & Roth, 2009). Still, as long-term care strives to move from the nursing home's institution-centered medical model of health care toward assisted living's person-centered social model of care, more practitioners across the spectrum are embracing a new culture of aging in contexts that are life-affirming, humanizing, satisfying, and meaningful for staff, residents, and their families (Calkins & Keane, 2008).

Imagining new normals in long-term care requires that we reexamine what it means to be old in our society. "The biology of aging and of age-related illness coexists with cultural images that help shape how we view the elderly and how the elderly view themselves," argued Morris (1998). "The fate of the elderly depends to a large degree on what dominant narratives a culture constructs about the last years of life" (p. 236). Residence in any senior-segregated setting calls forth a number of unsettling labels and despondent images that often serve to further isolate older adults and increase fears or apathy toward our own aging. When old age is medicalized as an illness or disability, "it is a tragedy of accumulating deficits, diminishing reserves, and deteriorating attractiveness and strength: nothing more than denouement" (Randall & McKim, 2008, p. 4). From this decidedly thin view of aging, it's easy to see residents as nothing more than bodies in a perpetual state of decline. A biographical view of aging, on the other hand, privileges individual experiences over biological evidence by focusing on the *inside* of aging (Ruth & Kenyon, 1996). From this perspective, older adults are positioned as unique individuals with rich histories, storied possibilities, and continued potential who actively *grow* rather than passively *get* old (Randall & McKim, 2008). Their lives as stories (Kenyon, Clark, & de Vries, 2001) are far from finished.

The most hopeful health intervention within these care communities, then, may also be the greatest challenge: provide for continuity of life experience and personal identity within the normal daily elements of social and supportive living (Kane, 2001). Just as Dr. Pete demonstrates at MD Anderson Cancer Center (Harter & Hayward, 2010), a growing number of medical providers are recognizing "the capacity of narrative sensibilities to disrupt the narrowing gaze of the biomedical model" (Harter, Patterson, & Gerbensky-Kerber, 2010, p. 466) and, in so doing, are honoring the lived experiences of individuals receiving care (see Charon, 2006). With that in mind, narrative care—what Kenyon, Randall, and Bohlmeijer (2011) define as "acknowledging and respecting a person's lifestory" (p. xv)—should be just as important as bodily care in long-term care settings.

Narrative care as core care "suddenly makes us see that we don't have to try and *add something to* the way we care for frail older adults," argued Ubels (2011). "All we need to do is *change the way we look at* what we do when we operate in care organizations" (p. 321, emphasis in original). Indeed, *imagining new normals* in long-term care means viewing residential settings not as institutions but rather as narrative communities in which care providers (a) recognize, respect, and sustain the personal identity of older residents through biographical attentiveness; and (b) draw from their own biographical energy in reciprocal relationships with residents. This dialogic approach dissolves barriers between "professional" and "patient" by focusing instead on the relational and enacted nature of narrative construction. Stories told by residents embody their fundamental individuality, including essential information about their values, beliefs, and accrued knowledge over a lifetime of experiences. When care providers connect with residents and are responsive to and appreciative of these lived stories, they can better identify inherent strengths, talents, and resources that residents can draw from and care providers can utilize to individualize care and, most importantly, improve quality of life.

Driven by the philosophy of person-centered care and the life-as-story metaphor, scholars and practitioners have implemented a variety of narrative interventions to promote psychological well-being and quality of life in long-term care. As in other clinical settings (see Chapters 3, 5, and 7 in this book), these programs enable disenfranchised individuals to forge meaningful understandings and build genuine community through creative expression. For instance, Basting (2009) highlights a number of innovative programs that use the arts as a conduit to inspire hope, stimulate self-expression, and facilitate emotional connection between individuals with dementia and willing partners or receptive audiences. Performance programs like To Whom I May Concern, TimeSlips, and Songwriting Works help residents imaginatively and eloquently capture the inside of aging through words, while art-making programs such as Memories in the Making, Arts for the Aging, and Art-Care enable them to aesthetically communicate personal perspectives beyond words (see Chapter 2). Combined with other day-to-day activities, including quilting, scrapbooking, and reminiscence or guided autobiography, these narrative approaches offer the meaning-making, growth, connectedness, and empowerment needed to effect deep transformations in how we treat aging individuals, in general, and residents in long-term care settings, especially (Noonan, 2001).

In the remainder of this chapter, I demonstrate the possibilities that can arise when narrative care, in the form of creative engagement and humanizing communication practices, is woven naturally into the fabric of daily life in long-term care settings. For more than a decade now, I've been fortunate to work as a volunteer, employee, and/or scholar in a variety of excellent assisted living communities. The four communities[1] profiled in this chapter differ in size, location, level of care, affiliation, profit status, and resident characteristics, yet they all strive to create moments of meaningful engagement that honor the residents' rich histories and biographical selves. In so doing, they challenge assumptions about aging, embrace person-centered care, and, most importantly, honor the humanity, dignity, and uniqueness of the older adults residing within (Kenyon et al., 2011, p. xiii).

Photo credit: Jill Yamasaki

Flower Garden #1 – A Life Lived in Bloom

– A FAMILIAR SPACE –

At Christmastime at home, I really decorated. I'd get a piece of plywood, and I'd put cotton on there for it to look like snow, and I'd put some blue paper under some glass for it to look like a pond, and I'd put a gazebo in it, and I'd put some people ice-skating on that glass, and then I had a town that I put around that. This was out in the middle of the town. I had the big Christmas tree at one end, and I had a town. I had an opera house. I had a drugstore. I had a church. I had a fire station. Just a regular town. And then this park was out in the middle. And then I had a train that went around the whole thing. So I wanted to set that up. The girls up in the office liked that idea and told me to put it down in the front where, you know, people come in and see it. If I'm still around, I'll put it out next year, too, because it really made me feel good. It made me finally feel like this is home. (Walt, resident)

Most of us have a deep understanding of and attachment to our homes. There, we establish social patterns, nurture intimate relationships, and express ourselves through the accumulation of artifacts and mementos. Not surprisingly, our ability "to sustain a sense of physical, social, and auto-biographical insideness, and to organize the space within our home in a manner consistent with our needs and personality, may, as we grow older, become increasingly significant in preserving a sense of identity and continuity amidst a changing world" (Rowles, 1993, p. 67). Owing to the importance of place in a person's historical continuity, as well as a longstanding societal desire to grow old in a familiar environment, assisted living's social model of person-centered care calls for homelike settings that more closely resemble conventional households than caregiving institutions. In the best of these communities, hallmarks of the traditional nursing home—fluorescent lights, nursing stations, multipurpose day rooms, pungent odors—have given way to accessible outdoor environments, richly textured interiors, intimate spaces, and even inviting aromas of fresh food or flowers. The four communities profiled in this chapter are pleasingly decorated with plants, comfortable furniture, a variety of colors, and art. All of the residents in these communities enjoy private rooms or small apartments, each furnished with personal possessions that reflect their interests, histories, and sense of self. At Arbor Terrace, accumulated treasures from Walt and other residents fill the public spaces, as well.

Arbor Terrace is located in College Station, Texas, home to Texas A&M University. A nonprofit community operated by a Protestant-affiliated company, it sits on a main thoroughfare directly across from the area's major medical center and shares the same neatly manicured grounds and beige brick construction as the hospital it faces. Its resident population is comprised primarily of Protestant, Caucasian, widowed females from smaller towns across Texas.

Admittedly, Arbor Terrace, which was built as a nursing home in 1964, feels more like the traditional institution it once was than the contemporary assisted living residence it aspires to be. The activities area is located with the physical therapy room off the lobby, and residents live and eat in wings radiating from a central nurses' station. Colored stripes on the linoleum hallway floors differentiate the level of independence or care needed in each wing and, since each hall looks alike, also serve to guide residents to and from their rooms. Still, like many assisted living communities, Arbor Terrace strives to incorporate philosophical ideals of resident independence and interdependence in its daily practice. Residents have a private room with full bath and eat their meals in a community dining room. They also have access to transportation and beauty services, as well as a program of planned activities, weekly shopping trips, and nondenominational religious services.

My wife and I shared a big queen-sized bed. At the convalescence ward, I had a single bed. I couldn't dare turn over because if I turned over one way I'd fall to the concrete floor with that real thin indoor-outdoor carpet on the concrete, so I'd have a concussion. If I turned over the other way, I'd run my head through the sheetrock. My wife, by the way, she has Alzheimer's, and she's in a nursing home. So when I came here, the first thing I asked for was our queen-sized bed. I really enjoy my big bed. It's my favorite thing here. And now I have the bed all by myself. I have big pillows, so I just curl up with a pillow—her pillow—and make believe it's her. (Ernest, resident)

Within Arbor Terrace's decidedly institutional shell, the residents' accumulated personal possessions—what Hepworth (2000) deems biographical objects—spark conversations and invite stories. Many of the residents, like Ernest, sleep on the beds they shared with spouses under quilts pieced together from fabrics collected over a lifetime of memories. Pictures of children, grandchildren, and friends adorn their walls, as do diplomas, crosses, mirrors, and clocks—all treasured items that have survived various household moves or been gifted from previous generations. Dorothy's room contains a large collection of the professional journals she once contributed to and consulted as a public health professional, while Walt's room displays dozens of the Kachina dolls he painstakingly carved and dressed over the years. Outside of their rooms, Hazel's grand piano graces the great room, Lily's antique writing desk (with her grandson's initials scratched in the corner) sits in the reading room, and Edith's watercolors line the corridors. As external expressions of inner selves (Hepworth, 2000), these biographical objects offer a sense of the familiar to their owners and an intimate inside view of the residents to others.

Photo credit: Jill Yamasaki

Baking with Betty

Arbor Terrace also places special emphasis on the kitchen, considered the heart of the home for many of us. Although the staff must contend with a variety of dietary restrictions when preparing food, they strive to incorporate in their daily menus dishes and ingredients popular to areas in Texas where most of the residents have spent much of their lives. They also use recipes supplied by the residents themselves, believing that familiar foods prepared in familiar ways will intrinsically link residents to memories of home (see Eckert et al., 2009, p. 155). Finally, while all residents eat their meals in the congregate dining room, each wing is equipped with a small kitchen and eating area where residents can help themselves and often gather for snacks or coffee. "Sometimes, with a little help, I like to bake cookies or a pan of brownies," said Betty. "It's always nice to have a little something special when the girls get together." *The girls*—a group of four to six residents who live on the same hallway—gather together a couple evenings a week to chat over tea. Residents also frequent these small kitchens throughout the morning for coffee and into late night for bedtime snacks from the stocked cabinets or refrigerators.

The home is perhaps the strongest formative—and certainly most emotive—influence of place on self (Hepworth, 2000). Ultimately, the collective efforts at Arbor Terrace to nurture a familiar space help ensure that the residents' separation from the various places in their lives before assisted living does not ensure a separation from self within the new realities of long-term care. Indeed, as argued by Rowles (1993), a focus on "facilitating the transfer of artifacts, photographs, and other memorabilia that are the cues to an individual's vicarious immersion in the places of their lives" (p. 69) could allow older people to retain biographical continuity and at least a partial sense of aging at home, even when physical relocation is unavoidable.

– HUMANIZING CARE –

I've learned a lot for myself about aging, and my parents are aging—my dad now has dementia—and it's easier for me to accept him for who he is now. I think that's the biggest thing. If families can just accept them for who they are now—not for who they were because they will never be that person again—that's the difficult thing for families. And I tell them, "You know, they're really great now, too. Just be comfortable with it." That's what I've learned, to be comfortable with who they are now. One day, one of our residents was sitting there and he's kind of looking sad, and I came in and I said, "So, Richard, do you have any words of wisdom for me?" And he thinks a minute and he said (mimicking), "Yep. Get up early, stay up late, and work hard in between." And I said, "Remind me never to ask you again!" (laughs) And he chuckled. And, you know, if you can get them to laugh, that's a big thing for a whole day. Makes your day, makes their day, and makes everybody else's sitting around the table. Because he was laughing—I don't know if they recognized what his response was—but because there was joy there, they picked up on it and they were all smiling and kind of chuckling. That's so important. Everyday should have smiles and laughs, I think. (Ruth, caregiver)

Few illnesses incite more fear, invite more stereotypes, or invoke more stigma than Alzheimer's disease and related dementias. Certainly, the realities of dementia, including lost memory, declining abilities, and changing personal characteristics, prove frightening experiences for diagnosed individuals and their loved ones. But a life lived with dementia can also be much more. "Core fears—of being a burden, of being out of control, of being violated or robbed, and of a meaningless existence—can be eased by changes in attitude, awareness, and care practices and policies," argued Basting (2009). "I don't pretend that we can eliminate the fear of dementia. We can, though, learn to feel *more* than fear. We can learn to feel and act with respect and compassion and to believe in purpose for those with dementia and those who love and care for them" (p. 11).

Cypress Court is located on a tree-lined street in suburban Houston, nestled between a luxury apartment complex on one side and an established neighborhood of single-family homes on the other. A secured wrought iron fence circles the building and its attractive yards with covered patio, playground, vegetable garden, and paved walkways. Inside, four "neighborhoods" based on resident care needs radiate from the common areas. The residents sleep in private or semiprivate rooms and spend their time with other residents in the common areas or in their neighborhood's kitchen or TV lounge. Sunlight streams through the many large windows, an aviary with chirping birds lines one wall of the activities room, and the community's three large adopted dogs wander freely throughout the building.

Cypress Court is one of approximately 20 assisted living communities nationwide that operate as part of a for-profit eponymous organization dedicated exclusively to the life-affirming care of individuals with Alzheimer's disease and related dementias. Its resident population includes individuals in the early, middle, and late stages of dementia. Until recently, the standard model of care for individuals with dementia included physical and pharmacological restraints aimed to manage disruptive behaviors, such as wandering, screaming, or crying. At Cypress Court, the standard model of care is *normal life*, a philosophy that both honors the biological continuity of residents and prioritizes their quality of life.

Using narrative sensibilities, staff and family members continually strive to engage residents at Cypress Court through multisensorial experiences that nurture the body and celebrate the person. Connecting with residents in various stages of dementia requires creativity. On any given day, for example, staff members will gather a small group of residents in a neighborhood kitchen to bake bread. The residents don aprons. They measure flour, stir, and roll the dough, either independently or hand-over-hand with the staff, while the warm aroma of baking bread from two bread machines on the counter fills the air. Staff members dab warmed butter on the lips of those who are too frail to participate and smile as the residents thoughtfully lick or pleasingly smack their lips. The physical motions and the sights, smells, tastes, and sounds of food preparation prompt conversations and stories for some; for others, a simple smile, deep inhalation, or sustained attention signifies a meaningful connection.

Normal life at Cypress Court also means properly bathing, dressing, and grooming each resident every morning. The men have clean-shaven faces, and the women wear makeup. Hair is styled; clothes are clean. Attending to the residents' appearance preserves their dignity as well as their biographical continuity, sense of self, and identity. Virginia, for example, was married to an oil executive for more than 50 years and, at the height of his career, lived a lavish life of travel and entertaining. Her sons said they never saw her without coifed hair, full makeup, tailored clothing, and matching jewelry. Now a widow in the later stages of Alzheimer's disease, Virginia can no longer recall her husband's name or much of their life together. Still, engrained personality traits remain. She constantly smoothes her slacks and blouses (polyester and cotton now, instead of linen and silk), and she marvels at the colorful costume jewelry she's never without, as demonstrated in one of our late-morning conversations:

Virginia: I got this thing here to look at. I'm excited. I sure do like it.

Jill: Yes, your necklace is very pretty.

Virginia: Yeah, I just got it a few minutes, a minute ago. And I got real excited about it. I've never seen one like that before.

Jill: They're pretty beads. It's a nice necklace.

Virginia: I just now got it. Somebody gave it to me, and I don't even know who that person was. But it turned out just, just as pretty as it could be.

Jill: They must like you, Virginia!

Virginia: And it, it kind of makes me feel a little bit better.

Jill: Well, sure. It makes you look special.

Virginia: It was just what I wanted.

Memory boxes outside every room at Cypress Court also capture the residents' unique personalities and storied lives. Each resident has a cabinet that contains memorabilia, photos, and treasures from happy moments and special occasions. These cabinets provide opportunities for the Cypress Court community to celebrate the human spirit and to rejoice in the residents' collective accomplishments and successes. Most importantly, according to Cypress Court's website, the memory boxes serve as a reminder that "our residents are dignified, respected, successful individuals with lives, accomplishments, and families…They help us see our residents through the eyes of loving families and friends and help us know them without the debilitating effects of dementia. They help us honor, celebrate, and truly connect with our residents."

Cypress Court staff also strive to engage the residents in supportive communication by validating their feelings, listening with undivided attention, offering empathic responses, and laughing with them when warranted (see Table 6.1, my conversation with Jack, a Cypress Court resident in the middle stages of Alzheimer's disease). In these conversations, veracity and eloquence matter much less than creative expression and emotional connection. Indeed, Basting (2009) advocates that we forget memory and try imagination instead in our efforts to create better lives for people with dementia.

Photo credit: Jill Yamasaki

Memory Box

TABLE 6.1: A HAIRY SITUATION, BY JACK G., AGE 87

I had an interesting story—well, an interesting life—in World War II. I became a B-25 pilot. That's a twin-engine bomber. I flew something like 70 missions and, uh, cracked up a couple of airplanes when I brought them home and didn't know that my tires had been shot out.

Wow.

Yeah, wow. I didn't know that I'd had my tires shot out. So, as I put the weight on the wheels, the whole, the whole mess collapsed to the left. The gas tanks were full of gas, and they spread all over the place. All the airplane practically melted in the flames. I didn't know it, but the two tires on the left side had been shot out and had holes in them. So when we hit the ground, the wheels collapsed, the whole airplane collapsed, and we spun around, and the whole airplane burned.

That sounds scary!

Yeah, it sounds so now. (laughs) I guess we didn't worry about it in those days.

How did you get out?

Well, we managed. We had escape techniques. But, the funny part is, uh, my tail gunner got a little nervous and excited, and he tried to go out over the tail gun, which was sticking up in the air. And everything around him was burning. So, he'd, I'd say, panicked. (laughs) And he forgot to remove his Mae West, and it caught inside the airplane. So there we were. The airplane was burning, so a Jeep came out to pick us up, and I asked them to drive me up right close to the burning airplane, and I got the kid's Mae West off of him.

And what was a Mae West?

It went over your head and zipped up the front, and it had air pressure chambers in it. It was a little bit clumsy, but you could wear it and not really bother you. So if you crashed in water, you just pulled the plug on the Mae West. You pulled the plug on it, and it inflated the whole thing. Well, this guy got nervous 'cause he could see the front end of the airplane burning, and he didn't think he had any way out except over the back. He couldn't see a way out the front, so despite the fact that he had instructions on where to go, he looked down there (laughs) and saw the flames and tried to get out over the rear. But he forgot to take off his Mae West. So he tried to get out the back of the airplane over his, over the gun. There's a gunner out the rear end, and there's guns all over the place in some kind of consideration.

Did he make it out?

Yeah, eventually he got out. The Jeep came to pick us up and everybody in the airbase knew what was happening. And I called the Jeep up to the rear of the airplane. The front end was burning from the engines, of course. And, uh, doggone if he didn't go get himself stuck in—the safety belt caught on, uh, some of the pipes and stuff inside the airplane. (laughs) He forgot to take off his Mae West and, sure enough, that catches on something, and he's stuck. He's stuck in the rear end of the airplane and just his head is visible out the rear end. First instruction that he should've done was get rid of the Mae West. We're already on ground, you know. I could just reach his hands almost, and every time he looked over his shoulder, he saw the red fire burning behind him. So I stood on the front end of the Jeep and managed—the part of his Mae West was holding him back—I managed to get it loose and pull him through.

So you saved him!

Yeah. I stood on the hood of the Jeep and was able to get a hold of him and undid his buckle or something and got him off and pulled him unceremoniously through over the gun. He went out of there with a Mae West on, and, uh, his normal equipment. He had a lot of obstructions going through a narrow space. It wasn't any wider that that cabinet up there. And he had to get through that. Meantime, the front end of the airplane is burning, and he looks over his shoulder, he can see it. (laughs) He can visualize his toast on there burning.

Ha! Was he hurt?

Oh, I don't know. (laughs) He was out. I pulled him through and just dropped him on the ground. (laughs) I think his dignity might have been hurt more than anything else. The whole airplane melted down. The flames just consumed the whole airplane. I went out to look at it, and there was a big puddle of molten metal which was, had been, the airplane.

That sounds so scary.

It was scary for awhile, but the funniest part is one of the gunners in the tail. He got all panicked and forgot to take off his Mae West. (laughs)

— EXPRESSIONS OF SELF —

Dear Mark and Jill,
It was an honor to participate in your wedding. May God bless your love, your marriage, and your future together with a lifetime of joy.

Wishing you the very best,
Rev. Dave

While many older adults view assisted living as a positive alternative to the traditional nursing home, crisis—rather than thoughtful research or careful planning—often precipitates the transition from the family home to a long-term care community. "They either ignore the options in their community or simply don't know what's available until the social worker says Mom can't move back home," bemoaned one administrator I interviewed. "Then they're in crisis mode, the move is negative, and everyone is miserable. I wish people would visit, see how nice the place can be, and then, two years later when they need it, they can say, 'Remember when we toured there, Mom, and you liked it?'" As an even more appealing solution for some, continuing care retirement communities offer a tiered approach to the aging process by accommodating residents' changing needs from independence to potential skilled nursing care in one location for the duration of their lives (www.aarp.org).

Aspen Grove is part of Centennial Homestead, a faith-based 27-acre retirement campus outside of Denver that is owned and operated by one of the nation's largest nonprofit senior housing providers. As a continuing care retirement community, Centennial Homestead offers a variety of residential options and services across the long-term care continuum, including independent living, assisted living, and skilled nursing care. Aspen Grove, its assisted living community, is comprised of approximately 40 studio or one-bedroom apartments with private baths and kitchenettes. Physically located between independent apartments and patio homes on one side and the skilled nursing building on the other, Aspen Grove provides its residents with the services and amenities offered by the other communities in this chapter, as well as access to additional resources from the larger Centennial Homestead campus overall.

Ideally, older adults will relocate to Centennial Homestead when they are active and well, knowing that their residential contract ensures they will be cared for if and when their health needs change. In reality, most of them choose Centennial Homestead for that peace of mind but dread ever having to move next door to Aspen Grove. Consider, for example, what happened with Nelly, a 99-year-old independent resident. As a part-time receptionist at the front desk of the six-story apartment building, I knew Nelly as a quiet woman who had trouble hearing, hunched over her walker, and often communicated by letter with an elderly niece who seemed to be her only family. The well-liked residents who lived below her knew Nelly as a cantankerous pest who left her water running by mistake on two separate occasions, necessitating repairs in both apartments and sparking a giant feud in the building. Many residents demanded Nelly move immediately to Aspen Grove, Nelly steadfastly refused, and administration called for multiple meetings between Nelly, her care providers, the staff, and her niece, who proved to be just as stubborn as her aunt. It took 7 months of legal wrangling and community unrest before Nelly was moved against her will to Aspen Grove, where she lived until her death a few months later.

In this climate, where planned-for transitions may result instead in what Ginny, another resident, deemed a "forced demotion," biographical attention helps narrow the gap between a resident's current mindset and preferred view of self. Specifically, staff at Aspen Grove—and even residents and staff from the larger Centennial Homestead community—solicit and draw from the residents' storied histories for "narrative solutions" (Enron & Lund, 2003), or better understandings of who they are and who they want to be. How do they define themselves? What were their primary roles before Aspen Grove or Centennial Homestead? What attributes or character traits are most important to them? What experiences were most meaningful?

Centennial Homestead offers "a Christian heritage of fellowship and service," and many of its residents across the continuum are retired missionaries or ministers. The chaplain on staff calls on a number of these residents to lead community Bible studies or prayer groups and to counsel fellow residents in need. I first met Reverend Dave when he lived in the independent apartment building with his wife, Marilyn. After they relocated to Aspen Grove almost 2 years later, I asked him to officiate my wedding. Mark and I planned an intimate outdoor wedding attended by our closest friends and families. Neither of us had close connections to a particular church, but we wanted a meaningful service that incorporated our faith. Reverend Dave counseled us in the months leading to the wedding, wrote and presided over the service, and led the prayers immediately following at our reception and then weeks later at an informal party in our honor at Centennial Homestead. Unlike what happened with Nelly, Reverend Dave's biographical continuity—and preferred sense of self—persisted despite moves to Centennial Homestead and then Aspen Grove.

Relatives, staff, and other residents who notice preferred qualities and attributes and then incorporate them into conversations and activities enable Aspen Grove residents to bridge the gap between past, present, and future with hope and possibility (Enron & Lund, 2003). Once a month on Sunday afternoons, for example, staff, residents, and their families gather for a resident show-and-tell of sorts in which two or three featured individuals play music, read poetry they've written, or share photos and tales of interesting travels. The gatherings have become a much-anticipated event for all involved. I watched residents spend weeks preparing for their turn and then, in the weeks following their performance, I heard them fielding compliments and questions. More informally, as demonstrated at Arbor Terrace and Cypress Court, residents at Aspen Grove still enjoy a variety of hobbies, including woodworking, gardening, scrapbooking, needlework, baking, and floral arranging. Their finished products are displayed throughout the building, and staff members strive to recruit residents with certain interests for specific tasks. For example, during my tenure there, Marjorie often arranged flowers for special events, and every month the scrapbooking club helped assemble the community's bulletin boards. They even had some residents help the office staff distribute newsletters or memos, while others liked folding towels for the housekeepers. Combined, these various activities helped the residents at Aspen Grove sustain lifelong interests and valued roles beyond that of long-term care resident.

Our Wedding

Photo credit: Karen Jones

– COMMUNITY CONNECTIONS –

Thank you to all the friends, neighbors, and relatives who attended my 90th birthday party at Prairie Meadows. What a special memory! And thank you to my children, grand-children, and great-grandchildren for putting on my party. God Bless! Ada (published in the Dodge County Independent, Wednesday, 2/13/08)

Prairie Meadows Senior Living, home to Ada and her roommate, Margaret, from the beginning of this chapter, is a pleasant 61-unit assisted living and specialized memory care community located off the main park in Kasson, a small rural town in southeast Minnesota with a population of approximately 5,500 people. Built in 2005 in partnership with the City of Kasson, Prairie Meadows offers residents private apartments and access to a number of common areas, including the community dining room, library, movie room, chapel, lounges, outdoor patios, and a beauty/barber shop. Most of the residents have lived most, if not all, of their lives in Kasson or the surrounding area. Charlotte explains:

> *My son, a couple years ago, insisted that I should sell my house and move in with them in Indiana so they could take care of me, and if I didn't want to move in with them, why, they'd help me buy something and they'd take care of it. They had it all figured out. I told them—I did give it some serious thought, the pros and cons. My daughter doesn't have a big enough house, but my son does. And I finally told him that to me it just isn't a feasible thing to do. The load would be on his wife, and I don't know, there were just lots of reasons why I thought I should stay here. They just didn't want me in a nursing home so far away. I said, "Well, just remember one thing. You're the ones who moved away. It wasn't me." (laughs) Besides, you know, Prairie Meadows is an awfully nice place to live.*

Kasson has seemingly embraced Prairie Meadows as a natural extension of the community. The city council conducts its monthly meetings at the facility; members of the Lions Club, churches, and schools regularly volunteer their services; and the Kasson Public Library delivers books biweekly to residents through its Books on Wheels outreach program. Reciprocally, Prairie Meadows opens its kitchen and dining room to Kasson residents for large fundraising events (e.g., pancake benefits) and Sunday brunch (offered buffet-style at $10 for anyone visiting residents or simply wanting a nice meal after church); hosts holiday parties, weekly card tournaments, and entertainment programs for all generations; provides respite services to family caregivers; and sponsors ongoing health seminars for the Kasson community.

Prairie Meadows also embraces community connectedness, a key tenet of the assisted living philosophy. "A strong sense of community is part of the reason assisted living works so well," claims Prairie Meadows on its website. "Although we recognize the importance of independence when wanted, here at Prairie Meadows we believe that it is interdependence that gives value and dignity to life." To that end, staff members encourage residents to eat their meals in the dining room with revolving tablemates, residents and staff members socialize together at weekly community mixers (called Sweet Treats), and residents elect members to represent them on the Resident Advisory Council, which meets once a month and reports to the administration. Prairie Meadows also en-

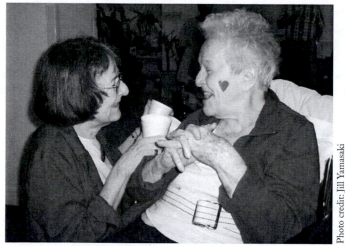

A Mother-Daughter Moment

courages family participation in the daily life of the community, and grown children or younger grandchildren often visit for extended periods of time.

In addition to spending time with family, other residents, and staff, some of the residents create their own opportunities for socialization, meaningful activity, and valued roles, within Prairie Meadows. For example, Gretchen and Hazel decided to lead a prayer group one Sunday afternoon in the chapel. "She's the one that came up with the idea," explains Hazel. "I thought it was a good one because there are some people here that don't get out to their own churches or they're not from Kasson so their home churches aren't close by. If there's enough interest, we'll start doing it regularly, and hopefully we'll get volunteers to read scriptures and say prayers and so on. I hope it's a success." At the inaugural service, with nine residents dressed in their Sunday best, Hazel and Gretchen took turns at the altar and led the group through prayers for Prairie Meadows and the country's servicemen and women, as well as the Lord's Prayer, the Prayer of Saint Francis of Assisi, and a period of silent reflection. Three readings and a number of hymns with Dorthy accompanying on the piano rounded out the half-hour service. "I was so nervous!" exclaimed Gretchen later in her apartment. "I can't hear, so I never know how loudly to speak. And I wasn't sure what would appeal to everyone, so I just picked my favorites." And the good news is these resident-led Sunday afternoon services are still a regular and well-attended event.

Andy and Harold organized another resident-led activity, this time a support group for residents caring for or living apart from spouses with Alzheimer's disease or other dementias. The group, which usually fluctuates between four and six members, meets once a month in the conference room for approximately 2 hours over dessert and coffee. Although they declined the social worker's offer to attend in favor of the privacy afforded by closed-door meetings, they do ask Laura, the activities director, to publicize their meetings on the monthly activities calendar. "We just use the time to share what's going on," says Andy. "Of course, we talk throughout the month, as well, but this is our chance to reach out, to ask questions and to answer questions. I look forward to it."

Because most of the residents at Prairie Meadows are from the Kasson area, Kasson residents continue to embrace them as active members of the outside community and encourage them to participate in community-based events, as well. Former neighbors invite them to block parties, friends include them in weekly card games, and church members offer them rides on Sunday or to various church-related meetings (e.g., Bible study, quilting, Circle) throughout the week. Ongoing family, friend, and community relationships also extend to shared histories between staff members and residents. Consider Bonnie, a part-time housekeeper and long-time Kasson resident, for example. Alice, Hazel, Dorthy, Gladys, and Andy knew her previously from church, and Margaret, Harold, and Gretchen were once her neighbors. Ethel taught her children at the local high school, Hazel's husband sold her first house, and Lucille's children bagged her groceries. These prior relationships and local connections offer a sense of belonging and social affinity beyond the assisted living community that is integral to quality of life but often missing in other long-term care settings.

– CONCLUSION –

Last Thursday, it was my turn to lead worship at Prairie Meadows. As I left the building I talked with the residents sitting outside at the front door. We all agreed that it was a beautiful day. The sun was warm, but not hot, the breeze was blowing, but not strongly, and the scent of freshly mown grass was in that breeze. There was a couple sitting on the bench holding hands. They had been married many years and were remembering numerous other times when they had sat in the early summer sun holding hands. There was a woman patiently waiting for her son to pick her up and then they were off for a marathon of activities: picking up plants, watching grandchildren's ballgames, and eventually planting those flowers at the cemetery to celebrate the lives of loved ones. The other woman sitting there was an old friend and a long-time member of the church. I had just spent some time catching up with her. It was a beautiful day because there was evidence of God everywhere: in the delightful aromas, warmth, and wind of that moment and in the relationships that make life worthwhile. (Pastor Marie, St. John's Lutheran Church, Kasson, MN)

Narrative care in long-term care communities, like narrative medicine, is inherently relational (Harter, 2009). While compassionate assistance and competent medicine comprise quality care, meaningful connections and creative engagement ensure quality of life. In their finest moments, the four long-term care communities profiled in this chapter serve as narrative environments that honor relationships and celebrate the unique personhood and biographical continuity of each participant. Even under the institutional constraints of staffing, scheduling, regulatory accountability, and increased care needs, these communities have transformed the one-size-fits-all model commonly imposed on older adults in long-term care settings to reflect resident desires and personalize activities and place (Geboy & Meyer-Arnold, 2011). This inherently dialogic perspective acknowledges the power of stories for making sense of lived disruptions, including the corporeal and social threats of aging in long-term care settings. Most of all, it embraces the storied nature of aging. A biographical approach to long-term care costs little financially but requires much commitment, intentionality, and imagination—with profound results at individual, interpersonal, organizational, cultural, and societal levels. Valuing older adults, in general, and long-term care residents, in particular, as biographical selves with complex histories, meaningful presence, and futures alive with possibility can ultimately shape thicker versions of late life and inspire new normals in long-term care.

– REFERENCES –

Basting, A.D. (2009). *Forget memory: Creating better lives for people with dementia*. Baltimore: The Johns Hopkins University Press.

Calkins, M.P., & Keane, W. (2008). Tomorrow's assisted living and nursing homes: The converging worlds of residential long-term care. In S.M. Golant & J. Hyde (Eds.), *The assisted living residence: A vision for the future* (pp. 86–118). Baltimore: The Johns Hopkins University Press.

Carder, P.C. (2002). The social world of assisted living. *Journal of Aging Studies, 16*, 1–18.

Charon, R. (2006). *Narrative medicine: Honoring the stories of illness*. New York: Oxford University Press.

Eckert, J.K., Carder, P.C., Morgan, L.A., Frankowski, A.C., & Roth, E.G. (2009). *Inside assisted living: The search for home*. Baltimore: The Johns Hopkins University Press.

Enron, J.B., & Lund, T.W. (2003). The narrative solutions approach: Bringing out the best in people as they age. In J.L. Ronch & J.A. Goldfield (Eds.), *Mental wellness in aging: Strengths-based approaches* (pp. 273–298). Baltimore: Health Professions Press.

Geboy, L., & Meyer-Arnold, B. (2011). *Person-centered care in practice: Tools for transformation*. Verona, WI: Attainment Company.

Harter, L.M. (2009). Narratives as dialogic, contested, and aesthetic performances. *Journal of Applied Communication Research, 37*, 140–150.

Harter, L.M., & Hayward, C. (Producers). (2010). *The art of the possible* [Motion picture]. Athens: Ohio University Scripps College of Communication.

Harter, L.M., Patterson, S., & Gerbensky-Kerber, A. (2010). Narrating "new normals" in health care contexts. *Management Communication Quarterly, 24*, 465–473.

Hawes, C., Phillips, C.D., Rose, M., Holan, S., & Sherman, M. (2003). A national survey of assisted living facilities. *The Gerontologist, 43*, 875–888.

Hawes, C., Rose, M., & Phillips, C.D. (2000). *A national study of assisted living for the frail elderly: Results of a national survey of assisted living facilities*. Beachwood, OH: Myers Research Institute, Menorah Park Center for Senior Living.

Hepworth, M. (2000). *Stories of ageing*. Buckingham, UK: Open University Press.

Kane, R.A. (2001). Long-term care and a good quality of life: Bringing them closer together. *The Gerontologist, 41*, 293–304.

Kenyon, G., Clark, P., & de Vries, B. (Eds.). (2001). *Narrative gerontology: Theory, research, and practice*. New York: Springer Publishing Company.

Kenyon, G., Randall, W.L., & Bohlmeijer, E. (2011). Preface. In G. Kenyon, E. Bohlmeijer, & W. L. Randall (Eds.), *Storying later life: Issues, investigations, and interventions in narrative gerontology* (pp. xiii–xviii). New York: Oxford University Press.

Morris, D.B. (1998). *Illness and culture in the postmodern age*. Berkeley: University of California Press.

Noonan, D. (2011). The ripple effect: A story of the transformational nature of narrative care. In G. Kenyon, E. Bohlmeijer, & W. L. Randall (Eds.), *Storying later life: Issues, investigations, and interventions in narrative gerontology* (pp. 354–365). New York: Oxford University Press.

Randall, W.L., & McKim, A.E. (2008). *Reading our lives: The poetics of growing old.* New York: Oxford University Press.

Rowles, G.D. (1993). Evolving images of place in aging and 'aging in place.' *Generations, 17,* 65–70.

Ruth, J-E., & Kenyon, G. (1996). Biography in adult development and aging. In J. Birren, G. Kenyon, J-E. Ruth, J. Schroots, & T. Svensson (Eds.), *Aging and biography: Explorations in adult development* (pp. 1–20). New York: Springer Publishing Company.

Ubels, G.M. (2011). Implementation of narrative care in The Netherlands: Coordinating management, institutional, and personal narratives. In G. Kenyon, E. Bohlmeijer, & W. L. Randall (Eds.), *Storying later life: Issues, investigations, and interventions in narrative gerontology* (pp. 319–337). New York: Oxford University Press.

– ENDNOTES –

1. I conducted ethnographic research (participant-observation, interviews, and focus groups) with IRB approval at three of the four communities. In one of those communities, I worked as a paid part-time employee for almost a year before deciding to formally conduct research. I did so with full support from the administration, residents, and their families, as well as my university's IRB. In the fourth community, I worked as a paid full-time employee for more than 3 years and, for purposes of this chapter, have relied solely on my private journals from that time. All organization, resident, and staff names are pseudonyms except for those associated with the Prairie Meadows and Kasson, Minnesota, communities. Participants from that research project specifically requested I use their real names in all written and oral presentations, and I received IRB permission to do so.

CHAPTER 7

COMMUNICATING HEALING IN A THIRD SPACE: REAL AND IMAGINED FORMS OF INTEGRATIVE MEDICINE

— BARBARA F. SHARF, PATRICIA GEIST-MARTIN, AND JULIA MOORE —

Recently, I did a holistic nursing consultation for an individual. He's 92 years old and he came to me because he didn't have good balance. He was having trouble walking up stairs and he had been to, you know, ears, nose, and throat doctors, primary care doctors. He had been to physical therapy. He was in good shape. I mean he exercised 3 days a week at the gym and he swam 2 days a week . . . . And so one of the things I started doing was, I just started going over, you know, his health conditions in his past

and he had had a CVA, a cerebrovascular accident. He had some mild carotid artery stenosis. He had a left hip replacement.

And, man, I just started thinking, you know, there was this really interesting research study in the Journal of Clinical Nutrition *not that long ago and what they did was they looked at people's carotid arteries and they took an ultrasound of the carotid artery before and after the intervention, which I'll mention in a minute. But these people did have mild to moderate carotid artery stenosis. So the intervention was 6 ounces of pomegranate juice every day. They had these people for—I don't know if it was 4 months or 6 months or a year, but basically the carotid artery ultrasound before and after was significantly different. It was able to regress the stenosis of the carotid, with pomegranate juice. I mean they used Pom Wonderful from the grocery store.*

So I was like, okay, you need to be drinking pomegranate juice, 6 ounces every day and, you know, oh, you're on a statin, you need to take Co-Q10 and, well you know, your cholesterol you might get off that statin if you take a fish oil and, man, it just started coming… Oh, he has insomnia as well and so [takes] melatonin. You know, and it was really interesting just standing there and talking to him about these supplements, which nobody had ever really talked to him before. Of course, at the end of the day I was like, "Well, make sure you talk to your doctors and they don't have any problem with it because I want to keep them happy." But at least I put the bug in his ear. (Filipa Lechtin, 2011)

This description of a patient consultation was presented by Filipa Lechtin (2011) at a conference with her nursing colleagues. Filipa is an experienced holistic nurse and cofounder and former co-owner of Brazos Healing Center located in College Station, Texas. The active, elderly patient she references may be in the forefront of the aging demographic in the United States. At the same time, her overall appraisal of his health conditions and her therapeutic suggestions are unusual. We may wonder if she is merely atypical or in the vanguard of a new direction for American healthcare.

In this chapter we describe how complementary and integrative forms of medicine, healing, and wellness activities in the United States are forming a *new normal*, in part through healthcare organizations that are attempting to meld alternative healing modalities with conventional medical practices. However, melding in this context signifies creating something beyond a combination of the constituent parts. Documenting organizational efforts to generate integrative forms of healthcare is the focus of this chapter. Our first task will be to provide an explanation of what alternative and complementary forms of healing are, and how, in some ways, these practices once considered odd and marginal are becoming more generally accepted and mainstream. To describe how this new normal is evolving, we use the rhetorical concept of *symbolic transcendence* (Burke, 1984) and the metaphorical language of the *"third space"* (Moje et al., 2004; Soja, 1996), a term that's been adopted by scholars in diverse disciplines.

— FROM CAM TO CIM —

Complementary and alternative medicine (CAM) is described by the National Center for Complementary and Alternative Medicine as "diverse medical and health care systems, practices, and products that are not generally considered part of conventional medicine" (NCCAM, 2012). This is an extremely broad, confusing definition (Coulter & Willis, 2004). While alternative modalities denote a departure or separate realm from allopathic or biomedicine, complementary approaches are different from but harmonious with conventional medical practices. That distinction at first seems to make sense, but when operationalized, the difference is less clear. Some products and practices once viewed as alternative have become more widely accepted by Western medical practitioners, especially as research findings support the efficacy of such options. Still, there is not always agreement as to what counts as valid evidence. Even with research support, insurance companies have been reluctant to reimburse nonallopathic treatments and services.

The use of complementary and alternative modalities can be traced back to the 18th century in the United States (Gevitz, 1988). American medicine began with a pluralistic environment, in which alternative and complementary therapies were readily available, and formally trained medical doctors were only accessible to the wealthiest citizens (Kaptchuk & Eisenberg, 2001). The sharp dichotomy between "elite educated physicians" and practitioners of other categories of healers began to erode in the early 1800s; however, alternative medicine continued to have a "pronounced presence in health care throughout U.S. history" (Keptchuk & Eisenberg, 2001, p. 3). Americans have continuously utilized CAM for over 200 years, but statistics on CAM use were not recorded until the second half of the 20th century. The documented use of CAM has been increasing since the 1950s (Kessler et al., 2001). In 2004, over half of the U.S. population reported using CAM (Robinson & McGrail, 2004). In 2007, 1.5% of total healthcare payments were paid out of pocket on CAM products, classes, and visits—a total of $33.9 billion (Nahin, Barnes, Stussman, & Bloom, 2009).

While CAM definitely still has its detractors and draws some sharp criticism, it has a growing presence within conventional medical institutions met with a range of grudging to enthusiastic acceptance (Freedman, 2011). The increase in demand for CAM care has led several U.S. medical [and nursing] schools to offer some form of instruction in selected complementary practices (Massey, 2006), along with the establishment of academic and community-based clinical centers varying in size and mission for what is now referred to as *integrative medicine* (IM) (Barrett, 2003). Such centers incorporate complementary and conventional forms of medicine, drawing from multiple paradigms of healing. With growing awareness and experience in what integrative practice entails, some of the leaders who have helped pioneer this growing movement have begun to refer to complementary/integrative medicine, or CIM, in place of CAM (Cohen, 2011).

However, integrative medicine is more than a mix of modalities; "rather, it is a philosophy of and attitude toward what constitutes health" (Cohen 2011). The Bravewell Collaborative, a philanthropic organization that works to improve health, defines integrative medicine as "an approach to care that puts the patient at the center and addresses the full range of physical, emotional, mental, social, spiritual, and environmental influences that affect a person's health." Horrigan, Lewis, Abrams, and Pechura (2012), reporting on behalf of Bravewell, go on to explain that IM employs personalized strategies that are responsive to "the patient's unique conditions, needs, and circumstances, it uses the most appropriate interventions from an array of scientific disciplines to heal illness and disease and help people regain and maintain optimum health." CIM focuses on the patient rather than the ailment; it cultivates patient–physician relationships (Geist-Martin, Sharf, & Jeha, 2008); and emphasizes preventative medicine and wellness of mind, body, and spirit (Snyderman & Weil, 2002). Academic CIM centers offer a broad variation in clinical care generally for adults, but with some facilities also serving pediatric, adolescent, and geriatric needs. Delivery of care may be in the form of CIM consultations with conventional practitioners, comprehensive care coordinated by integrative physicians (possibly including inpatient hospital services), and primary care across the lifespan. Self-referrals by patients or clients to CIM centers predominate (Horrigan et al., 2012).

In short, with the development of centers of CIM, the divide between conventional and alternative practitioners that once helped to delineate modern medicine in the United States is lessening. Medical education and practice are gradually moving toward a normalized integrative approach, a new normal in conceptualizing healthcare. However, complications and dilemmas exist between the imagined collaboration of biomedical and CIM providers and the actual realities of integrated practice.

Integration is not easily achieved, as illustrated through the research on CIM in medical education and on the operation of CIM centers. Despite a gradual increase in acknowledging CIM within medical school curricula, there remain negative attitudes toward this material among many students and faculty (Abbott et al., 2011; Kreitzer, Mitten, Harris, & Shandeling, 2002). Conversely, three-quarters of students in CAM institutions have a difficult time communicating with conventional practitioners (Frenkel, Ben-Arye, Geva, & Klein, 2007), signaling barriers that exist in both conventional medical and CAM training.

Not surprisingly, research on CIM centers indicates similar difficulties with enacting integration. Clinical centers of integrative medicine must carefully find the right practitioners to foster trust and success (Boon & Kachan, 2008). Promoting collaborative teamwork has proven difficult even when medical physicians and complementary providers express interest in cooperation (Ben-Arye, Frenkel, Klein, & Scharf, 2008). Dual education to overcome divergent paradigms has been shown to foster interprofessional collaboration at these centers (Gadboury, Bujold, Boon, & Moher, 2009); however, studies demonstrate that dominant biomedical patterns of communication still persist, inhibiting full integration (Gadboury et al., 2009; Hollenberg, 2006).

For these clinical centers, it is a tall order to create ways of achieving truly functional integration of philosophies, knowledge bases, and services characterized as interdisciplinary and nonhierarchical with the goal of developing individualized wellness plans (Boon, Verhoef, O'Hara, & Findlay, 2004), based on shared vision and mutual respect. Elsewhere we have characterized such efforts as "trailblazing health care" (Sharf, Geist-Martin, Cosgriff-Hernandez, & Moore, 2012); that is, creating new spaces that transform accustomed meanings of health and wellness, and that transcend familiar patterns of how healthcare is organized and communicated.

TRANSCENDENCE INTO THE THIRD SPACE

As a way of helping to understand the change processes through which forms of CIM are creating a new normal in healthcare, we have borrowed vocabulary and conceptual understandings developed through other fields of study.

Transcendence. How change in human affairs occurs is frequently discussed in the works of Kenneth Burke, an influential American literary and rhetorical theorist and critic whose writings spanned approximately 50 years, from the 1920s through the 1970s. Burke focused on how the use of language and other symbol systems serves to shape and motivate human activity, with examples from politics, literature, religion, among other social systems. For this chapter, we are most interested in Burke's notion of "transcendence," a term that has been interpreted in many ways by a variety of scholars (Jasinski, 2001). Burke (1984) defines transcendence in a deceptively simple, yet puzzling way: "When approached from a certain point of view, A and B are 'opposites.' We mean by 'transcendence' the adoption of another point of view by which they cease to be opposites" (p. 336). So, it seems that some sort of movement—literal or figurative—transforms a conflictual situation to one of coexistence or perhaps even harmony. Rhetorical scholar James P. Zappen (2009) posits that Burke accounts for such transformation through a process of dialectic; that is, "a merger of opposing ideas at higher levels of generalization through a process of linguistic abstraction and transformation that respects a diversity of individual interests, even as it seeks to transcend them in larger unities" (pp. 280–281). It is important to underscore that this dialectical change does not seek to destroy or discredit the original separate components, but recognizes that the individual perspectives are "partial and incomplete without the others" (p. 281). Thus, Zappen explains that social exchanges should " . . . seek to encompass a diversity of individual voices in larger unities that preserve, but transcend, any one of them" (p. 281). In essence, transcendence is not only a change away from conflict but toward a more encompassing, inclusive level of functioning. Zappen concludes that Burke's notion of transcendence

> *...challenges rhetoric as a socially responsive endeavor to view not individual discourses alone but* **individual discourses in relationship to each other**, . . . *[N]ot only to persuade others in their own best interest but also* **to create larger communities of interest that transcend individual and group ideologies and interests**. (p. 281; emphasis added by authors)

Starting with this somewhat abstract concept of transcendence from partisan views to a more unifying perspective as a motive for human behavior, we move on to a related, but more grounded notion of the creation of a "third space" as a metaphoric and material basis for conceptualizing an integrative practice of healthcare.

Third Space Theory. A cursory Internet search using the term "third space" reveals a wide variety of meanings and applications. In the field of community and urban planning, third space refers to social surroundings separate from the two usual social environments of home and workplace; described by urban sociologist Ray Oldenburg (1989), third spaces are places that anchor community life such as coffeehouses, community centers, and hair salons. Geographer and urban planning scholar Edward Soja (1996) discusses the turn to spatial thought as having been limited to either material (e.g., mapping) or mental/symbolic forms. He conceives of an alternative approach that acknowledges both the material and mental dimensions, but also extends beyond these conventional forms to new forms of thinking. Education theorists (Moje et al., 2004) have adapted Soja's conceptualization to study phenomena such as literacy in the context of "intersections and disjunctions between everyday [first space, e.g., home, community, peer network] . . . and school [second space, e.g., formalized settings such as school, work or church] funds of knowledge and discourse," leading to the construction of a third space of learning. These scholars impute a critical perspective in their work, asserting one set of spaces to be privileged or dominant contexts, with the other set as marginalized (which is which depends on the perspective of the participant). For Moje and her co-authors, the third space emerges from a creative process of hybridity, serving as a bridge connecting the first two spaces, a navigational device that permits coexistence within diverse cultural groups, and, perhaps most important, "as a space of cultural, social, and epistemological change in which the competing knowledges and discourses of different spaces are brought into 'conversation'" (Moje et al., p. 44). In their study of schoolchildren, the third space of literacy emerges through the learning environment of popular culture such as rap music and social media.

Outside academic applications of third space theory, there are examples of everyday uses, such as 3RDSPACE, a private club that fosters creativity in San Diego, California (http://3rdspace.co/), on its web page as:

> less by what it is as what it becomes by our growing community of interesting, talented and active members. . . . The flowering of ideas, innovation and inspiration, whether in a society or an individual, happens in more organic, fertile environments of connectivity and activity.

Throughout this varied array of uses for the idea of third space, there is a certain consistency of meaning. In all these contexts, the third space is conceptually related to, yet distinctly different from the first—the most common, dominant, or privileged—and the second, contrasting or alternate, space. In many cases, it combines elements or traces of the other two spaces, but it is *not* the sum total of the other spaces. Rather it is transcendence into a unique, separate entity. Thus, it is our intention to explore how the construction of a third space for integrative medicine is occurring in contemporary healthcare.

Closer to the focus of our study of third space is another virtual address of an organization described as "London's Premier Health and Fitness Club." The web page depicts this club, The Third Space, as enacting four major activities: fitness classes and equipment, pilates, spa services, and medicine. The fourth category, medicine, is what seems the most unusual in this group of health club offerings. Under the heading of medicine, there is a list of over 20 practitioners including medical physicians and surgeons, as well as doctors of homeopathy, chiropractic, podiatry, and Chinese medicine; physiotherapists; sports medicine specialists; nutritionists; and others. Beyond offering access to such a broad range of expertise, the Third Space's description of medical services promises:

> One database for all practitioners to record patient notes and treatments. This improves the communication between practitioners and reduces time spent asking for duplicate information from our patients, and builds a better diagnostic and information profile for each patient.

Further, the description promises "integration with [club services] to aid in rehabilitation, posture assessment, gait analysis, range of movement etc. for training and many other medical issues and treatments" (http://www.thethirdspace.com/home/medicine/practitioners.aspx). In summary, The Third Space health club presents the image of a comprehensive, seamless site for maintaining a healthy lifestyle while also offering integrative services for a wide variety of health problems, a striking departure from most commercial health clubs and medical clinics. Not visible in this public image are the struggles and efforts entailed in creating such a space.

In the remainder of this chapter, we examine two organizations in U.S. communities that are trying to create a new normal for wellness and healthcare. They are, by definition, variants of a third space, transcending the separate, often conflicting, paradigms of biomedicine and complementary approaches to health and healing.

– HOW WE INVESTIGATED –

We've taken a case study approach in which we tell the stories of two CIM centers in order to focus on the discourses, symbols, and processes that characterize how each center imagines its third space and the realities of enacting the imaginary. The centers were intentionally selected because each is relatively local, embedded in a particular community setting (as opposed to academic, research-oriented centers). Each has a multispecialty staff that to some degree integrates conventional medical practices with complementary modalities. Beyond those basic similarities are distinct differences of geography, years in operation, services offered, and leadership styles.

Our descriptions of each center are based on a combination of ethnographic methods, including in-depth interviews with center leaders and other available staff, onsite observations and participation in center activities, and examination of archival materials, such as pamphlets, media reports, websites, and photographs. Given the prestated differences between the centers, our goal is not to provide an explicit comparison, but to offer detailed exemplary portraits of how centers for CIM are developing in the United States, and to articulate the issues and questions that emerge from such depictions.

– TRANSCENDING DIALECTICAL TENSION BETWEEN IMAGINED AND REAL –

The story of The Center for Health and Wellbeing (CHWB) reveals the struggles to move from the imagined "We up in the sky" to the reality of a center that accomplishes integration.

THE IMAGINED

Located in San Diego, CHWB has been in operation for 16 years. Dr. Janette Gray, cofounder and medical director, leads the team of 17 providers who take a "whole-person approach," providing a "healing experience that bridges the gap between conventional allopathic medicine and alternative and complementary therapies" (http://chwbonline.com/). CHWB's website describes its vision as "providing integrative medicine that emphasizes the patient-provider partnership and encourages patients to take an active role in their health care." However, as her educational path reveals, this imagined concept was a long time in coming.

Photo Courtesy of The Center for Health & Wellbeing

THE PATH TOWARD INTEGRATIVE HEALTHCARE

Dr. Gray was trained in internal medicine and focused on primary care because "I always enjoyed just how everything connects." She began in a center for women's medicine where an integrative approach, including acupuncture and massage, was being utilized. She was fascinated with how patients seemed to be driving the move toward integrative medicine: "They realized that the regular medical model wasn't enough, seeking out acupuncturists and others who could provide more." In her view, most doctors are isolated and have "minimal exposure to anything alternative, complementary."

When the women's medical center closed down, Gray had to make the difficult choice of working for an HMO, going into private practice, or something else. Serendipitously, in 1996, the opportunity arose to rent space and begin practice with another physician who valued CIM by including a massage therapist and nutritionist in his practice. Gray indicated that she "didn't see a practice just being me or a group of primary care doctors. It . . . just felt natural to have a team." A year later, when the other physician retired, she had the space to herself with the nurse practitioner, Barbara Whiteside, and made the decision right away to add an acupuncturist and a chiropractor. In her words,

> So basically all at the beginning I started accumulating a team. Again what was I doing? I am sort of envisioning this integrated model. I didn't know what it would look like or where it was going. . . . I was still evolving myself and still am, like you know, what are the pieces?

Dr. Gray found sources of information and insight all around her. A turning point moment was reading the study by Eisenberg and colleagues (1998) that reported on the rising trend of alternative medicine in the United States. As she indicated, "It appealed to me to be able to offer people more levels [of care]."

Another valuable source of knowledge for Dr. Gray was John Weeks's blog, *The Integrator—Integrative Medicine and Complementary and Alternative Medicine News* (http://theintegratorblog.com); Weeks has been writing about integrative medicine since 1983. Calling it her "mini Bible," Dr. Gray told the story of how the knowledge it provided helped her to begin filling out her notion of what a center for integrative medicine should look like. She explains, "I would look at how they'd build [a center] and what the modalities were and how they shared information, you know, things from a common [patient] chart to having four different charts or whatever."

ENVISIONING THE STRUCTURE AND CORE MODALITIES

From the beginning, Dr. Gray wanted to construct a model of patient care that was truly integrative. Rather than just having a building where providers rent out spaces and vie for a place at the front counter to display their business cards, she wanted to create a center where collaboration and integration were central to providing optimal patient care. For Dr. Gray, it was all about shared vision:

> The collaborative, integrative holistic model is . . . you are going to actually create collaboration if there is somebody there that shares your vision . . . not just part in, but that is their

vision. So it is shared *vision as opposed to my vision superimposed upon others. [Emphasis added to reflect her vocal emphasis]*

An important element of the vision for Dr. Gray was deciding what would be the core modalities included in the center. In addition to the acupuncturist and chiropractor already on board, she "started accumulating a team, sort of envisioning this integrative model, still evolving myself." It was important "to find a cover that wasn't too far out there" under which patients who were more familiar with a medical model would be willing to try other therapies. This was the collaboratively constructed imagined vision—the "we" as Dr. Gray explained:

> So the "we" is the big "We up in the sky," right? So we kind of wanted to focus on stuff that wasn't considered too far out there. So we considered okay, primary care medicine was the center and that was because of my training and realizing that you don't want people to not be getting their physical or their pap smear or things that are fundamental medical care— diabetic care, hypertension. And then you want to be able to treat those kinds of conditions and preventions in more alternative, safer, natural ways so they can come in with a condition and maybe we can actually treat it in a safer non–pharmaceutical way. But initially that is also a way of getting someone in.

Once in, patients could then discover and learn about CIM approaches that might benefit their health as a whole person, not just treating a particular disease or illness. This vision is represented well in the reception area of CHWB as revealed in the accompanying photo.

What began as a core of primary care medicine, acupuncture, chiropractic, and massage expanded to include naturopathic. In addition, transformational counseling was added as a "really good match [in that] it is the integrative, collaborative approach to mental health." Dr. Gray believes that once the core is decided upon, other modalities could be "snap-ons" that add to the core. The CHWB web page describes transformational counseling in this way:

"An understanding that our stories, beliefs, relationships, and culture influence our behavior and biology is the foundation for the Family Therapy Program and our collaboration with patients and health care providers at CHWB."

Photo Courtesy of The Center for Health & Wellbeing

One snap-on for this center is a gastroenterologist who comes in one half-day a week. Another snap-on is IV infusion and nutritional therapy which was added as an "expansion of the naturopathic functional medicine piece." Other snap-ons include podiatry, health screenings and lab testing, bio-identical hormone therapy, weight management, and skin rejuvenation. What is core and what are the snap-ons seems to be evolving, indicating that what at first may be a snap-on, eventually could become core, and vice versa.

Today, CHWB emphasizes healthy lifestyle over treating sickness, such as the use of massage therapy, as depicted in the accompanying photo. Dr. John Humiston, who was trained in family medicine, and hired recently as an integrative provider, explains, "The idea is we really want to get you back on your feet and to enjoy the health that we enjoy." Nurse Whiteside promotes "laughing and being happy. . . . and mak[ing] healthy lifestyle choices." However, she also encourages her patients to see the integrative physicians at CHWB because conventional medicine is her area of expertise. Similarly, Dr. Humiston refers his patients to the Chinese medicine practitioner. The idea of internal referrals is critical to the organizational functioning of the center as teamwork, one of the foundational components of CIM centers (Boon et al., 2004). Dr. Gray and the other CHWB practitioners emphasize internal referrals to maximize patient outcomes and expose patients to new modalities with which they may be unfamiliar.

Although internal referrals are paramount to how this organization functions, integration is not achieved solely through referrals. Indeed, integration is a constantly evolving process. Dr. Humiston emphasizes the difficulty of starting an integrative health center, followed by the importance of ongoing organizational evolution: "To get the rocketship to lift off just takes way too much. . . . Here they're almost a little bit too much. . . let's try this, let's try that, but that's refreshing, we've just had to tame it a little bit." However, with a constantly evolving organization in terms of changing practitioners, modalities, and strategies, CHWB continues to face new and recurring obstacles. While this section has characterized the imagined or idealized vision of the center, the following section considers the realities of constructing an integrative health center in a third space and the challenges that restrict collaboration.

Photo Courtesy of The Center for Health & Wellbeing

THE REALITY OF THE IMAGINED

The challenge CHWB faces on a regular basis is collaboration across the different modalities so that the clinical group brings together all perspectives on behalf of the patient. Dr. Gray states, "The integrated work that we have been trying to do here [means that] the client's voice shows up equally to the providers' [voices]." Even with this guiding principle, the center struggles with how to systematize collaboration and integration of the wide array of providers and modalities.

Practitioners of all backgrounds at CHWB acknowledge the obstacles faced, including member resistance, physical space limitations, meeting opportunities, patient record-keeping, and insurance practices. First, the organization faces resistance from staff and practitioners. "There are some staff members who could maybe do a little better," says Nurse Whiteside laughingly. "They're getting there, the staff members are getting on board with what we do." Staff members currently have the opportunity to participate in any of the services offered at CHWB, free of charge, but some have been hesitant to take on the offer. Organizational members reveal that certain co-workers are also hesitant about other modalities. Kathleen Bundy, a registered dietician, describes how practitioners see health and wellness through different lenses that do not always match up, making full collaboration difficult to achieve: "With other practitioners, they have their own thing and it's hard to get them to buy into my thing."

Second, physical space proves to be a hindrance to integration. The building that houses CHWB is two stories tall with offices and treatment rooms located on all floors. Dr. Gray explains, "I thought we would be able to all be on one floor but the timing was such that practitioners were separated with admin on the second floor and practitioners on the first and second floors." However, the center attempts to transcend spatial obstacles by having "all the alternative and medical providers get together once a month." So as a third factor, these meetings are a particularly important time for conventional and complementary practitioners to come together and discuss current cases and troubleshoot problematic cases.

However, efforts to communicate systematically face-to-face with one another have failed. While the idea of meeting a few times a month on a regular basis to collaborate and coordinate patient services is the imagined, the reality is that these meetings are difficult logistically for everyone. Dr. Gray explains:

> We have the provider get-together, and then we have an all-staff. So again, depending upon who's actually available—because you know, people tend to work half days, they tend to work one day, like Dr. Corey never works a Thursday so he can rarely make it all the way down from Encinitas for the Thursday meeting, so there's logistical problems. But still, I mean, I can't tell you how many people [say], "Oh I forgot to clear my schedule." It's like, how many years have you been [here]? I've done the math and well, it must not be a priority. And that's why I am going a little backwards in ... looking at how people can be a little bit more independent, like run their own practice and the thought is that if it's the right person, if it's that type of provider who really does care and wants to be . . . in a healing center and share this integrative model, then they'll make an effort to come to the meetings because they want to come to the meetings, not because they're an employee or something.

Within this reality is the seed of an idea that has recently unfolded and come into being at CHWB, which is to move toward a model of independent providers, not employed by the center, but committed to integration and hopefully working collaboratively in the same space. Interestingly, this is the model of San Diego's 3RDSPACE, mentioned earlier, where independent artists work side by side and discover opportunities for collaboration.

Fourth, the imagined centralized electronic medical record, in which all providers type their notes into one patient record has, in reality, not been operationalized. While all providers do engage in their own note taking, constraints on time keep them from entering their notes in the electronic medical record where all could see. Elaborates Dr. Gray:

> *Right now, it's been more one-on-one cases. We have an electronic medical record which is helpful because I can send individual messages off to providers about individual patients; we might talk about a couple points or aspects. We might see each other in the lunchroom or in the hall and we might have a couple meetings a month where there's an exchange of patients.*

Despite the potential of the computer program, the imagined process of collaborating daily through the electronic medical record does not occur in reality, for a number of reasons, as Dr. Gray further explains:

> *That's another theoretical benefit, and the idea was that everybody would scan in their own notes. So you know, each department would scan their own notes in and then they'd have them for referring and then the other providers could look at those notes. And I even had a series of meetings where one person would bring their notes and pass out a copy and kind of teach them how to read their notes. And so the idea was to make it—you can write your stuff like oriental medicine has all these lines and stuff you can fill out at the bottom, assessment and plan, you know, . . . so where you can kind of distill it a little bit and get an idea of the non-oriental medicine or non-chiropractor. But again there, you have to say that having them scan in their notes was like twisting their arm, no one wanted to do it . . . . Before I know it, I'd find them all dumped on somebody, one of my employees, so she's got a pile in front of her that they dumped on her when no one's looking. . . . And then the second part of it is [laughs] that they're not even reading each other's notes anyway.*

So the realities of the day-to-day do not transcend to the imagined third space, but for Dr. Gray, the creation of an integrated new normal may be envisioned in more than one way and that is exactly what CHWB is in the process of figuring out.

Fifth, insurance systems constrain integration because many plans often pay for conventional or certain complementary treatments, but deny coverage for other therapies that are prescribed as part of a total treatment plan. This issue has been present since the center's inception and healthcare reform leaves the future uncertain. Nurse Whiteside details the complex insurance practices that are curbing transcendence: "We try to use insurance as much as we can to help patients out," she stressed. "We're starting to cut back on it because it is hard to get reimbursed for some things so we had to switch over to more cash pay for some stuff." The realities of reimbursement for some therapies including massage constrain the efforts of CHWB.

Additionally, some patients "come with medical benefits and not necessarily mental health benefits," says Dr. Jan Ewing, a marriage and family therapist at CHWB. This makes access to integrative healthcare a socioeconomic issue. Dr. Ewing has "a heart and concern for the disenfranchised around health" and has started a non-profit that is housed within CHWB, but operated separately to provide free or low-cost mental health services to low-income patients.

The successes and challenges discussed candidly by Dr. Gray and her staff vividly depict the ideals and complexities of organizing CIM successfully as a new normal in healthcare. Challenges to creating an integrative center continue at CHWB where the shared vision they still hope to achieve remains an ideal and not a reality. As a result, Dr. Gray made the decision recently to move to a decentralized center, where providers pay rent and bill their own patients, rather than centralizing billing and payment. Other challenges emphasized by Dr. Gray not only include decisions about what modalities to offer, but also how to select practitioners who are truly collaborative; finding appropriate resources in space, time, and technological support; and coping with reimbursement policies or lack of health insurance that prevents access to services.

— SHIFT HAPPENS: EVOLVING THE BRAZOS HEALING CENTER —

Photo Courtesy of Brazos Healing Center

Our second exemplar has some similar features to CHWB, but is marked by different strategies, challenges, and directions, and perhaps a more optimistic discourse.

THE IMAGINED BECOMES REALITY

> Lisa: *You know, we were a center before we were in my head.*
> Barbara: *In your head?*
> Lisa: *Filly knows I was calling it Brazos Healing Center, so I had the website up and running as of January of 2009, and that was just me. And people were calling about the Center and I would say, "It's just me."*

Lisa Tauferner and Filipa Lechin are two young women who became cofounders/co-owners of the Brazos Healing Center (BHC), located in College Station, Texas, in April 2010. As this later conversation indicates, Lisa had already imagined and created on the Internet what such a center might become, even as a sole individual without a place, staff, or adequate resources to make it an actual reality. Stated Lisa during a radio interview soon after the opening of the BHC:

> *In early 2009, I had the idea of forming a center that would basically meld my passions of yoga, and energy therapies, and other holistic health therapies with expansions in career, and doing something more professional with it, rather than just as a hobby.* (L. Tauferner, 2010)

Lisa earned humanities degrees, a BA in German and an MA in history. She works full time at Texas A & M University as a study abroad advisor. Filipa's educational and vocational background is quite different. She received a BS in nursing, then later an MS in nursing with certification in holistic nursing. She has worked full time as a nurse in several conventional medical settings. The two women met through their common interest and experiences in yoga practice and instruction. Both are credentialed instructors in several forms of yoga. Also, each has obtained advanced training in forms of energy therapies.

Soon after the time of BHC's actual locational opening in 2010, there were three more staff, an additional yoga instructor, a tai chi instructor, and a massage therapist. While all center staff are part-time employees, the initial menu of services and classes offered through the center was surprisingly versatile, as described by Lisa:

> *Basically we offer, just to give you the breadth of what we do, yoga for various styles and levels; energy therapy treatments, healing touch and reiki; . . . various therapies related to mindfulness relaxation, so meditation, guided visualizations, relaxation in general. . . .*
>
> *Filipa also does holistic nursing consultation. The "baby" of the center is the 6-week holistic lifestyle intensive, a great program. What she is doing this year is working with a small group of clients to have weekly meetings, do an initial nursing consultation assessment, and each week have a different topic, for instance, aromatherapy, yoga, energy therapy, things like that. We also include one class per week with the clients, yoga class as well as one 30-minute energy therapy treatment a week. So essentially they get a package [deal] to try. And over the 6-week period, she's having them do homework . . . journaling and helping to encourage each other.* (L. Tauferner, 2010)

To understand how BHC represents a move toward a new normal at the local level, it is necessary to understand something about the indigenous community in which the center exists.

COMMUNITY CONTEXT

The Brazos Valley includes the "twin cities" of College Station and Bryan, constituting a metropolitan area of more than 200,000 people, excluding the temporary population of close to 50,000 students at Texas A & M University, plus several small rural towns in Brazos and contiguous central Texas counties. For a population of this size, there is a considerable infrastructure of "first space" conventional medicine institutions and practitioners. Among the first space players are two multispecialty hospitals with approximately 300 combined inpatient beds and several outpatient satellite clinics throughout the region; a large outpatient clinic operated by a physician-owned HMO organization; a University Health Sciences Center, including residential schools of medicine, nursing, and public health, as well as various research institutes and enterprises; a specialty-oriented, physician-owned outpatient center with a small number of additional inpatient beds; and hundreds of independent and group practices of physicians, dentists, chiropractors,[1] psychologists, physical therapists, and other conventional health practitioners.

There is also a surprisingly robust, though much more clandestine, network of individual practitioners that constitutes the second space of complementary and alternative healthcare in this area. The presence of this network and the constituency that supports it are described as surprising because of the notoriously conservative nature of the larger community, known for its allegiance to Republican politics, the dominance of numerous Christian churches and religious organizations, and reverence for traditions related to the university as well as Texas history and civic values. The range of available CAM services and treatments for adults and children includes, but is not limited to, massage, herbal supplements and medications, acupuncture, essential oils, movement therapies such as yoga and pilates, nutritional counseling, and lesser-known treatments such as cranial-sacral manipulation and Astin patterning. Some variations of these CAM modalities are rooted in specific cultural and religious traditions deriving from India, China, Mexico, and other countries of origin for immigrant populations in the area. Though many of these CAM practitioners are well known to one another and make referrals among themselves, overwhelmingly CAM in this area is conducted by solo practitioners or small group practices, specializing in a particular modality. Within this group, a few individual physicians and nurses can be characterized as integrative insofar as they are combining conventional biomedicine with complementary modalities and practices related to other systems of medicine. Such efforts to integrate the first and second spaces have been limited and difficult for many potential users to locate.

Filipa and her physician husband have spent considerable time and effort at their own expense attending conferences on CAM and visiting some of the major integrative medicine centers throughout the country. It is from this well-educated perspective that they commented on the breach that they perceive between an interested patient population and a resistant medical community in the Brazos Valley.

> When you start seeing patients here, you realize that there is really an interest, but there is not a setting for that to take place. A lot of the people who come to our center though have been doing it. They've always been interested and they always say, "Oh, I've been waiting for something like this to come to town." You know, they take their retreats to Scottsdale and the California coast or whatever and so they know and they've been looking . . .

However, their conversation also acknowledged the gap between what patients want and what practitioners are willing to offer:

> If I were to get chemo and radiation, I would like a place where I can relax, have either relaxation or meditation or healing touch, or something that would put me in relaxation that I'd like to be ready for that kind of harsh therapies. And it's just not happening. I don't see that. The gap is definitely there.
> [Barbara: Maybe it's because it's not covered by insurance?]
> I think that is a multifactorial thing, but there is a barrier that is thick and it is just very—It's not an easy-to-break deal.

Thus, the 2010 opening of the BHC, publicized through various media, self-referred to as a "complementary" approach to healthcare and well-being, represented an ambitious, multifaceted effort to carve out a third space of integrative healthcare in the geographic region.

DEVELOPMENT OF LITERAL AND SYMBOLIC IDENTITY

At the yoga studio in Austin, Texas, where she'd worked as an instructor, Lisa participated in a workshop called Business for Yoga Teachers. As part of that training, she learned about submitting business ideas to logo designers around the world via the Internet. According to Lisa, she didn't have a precise logo idea in mind but when she saw the sun motif (pictured on the center's outdoor sign), she said, "I just knew when I saw it that was it, and I knew everyone [would] see it differently so I love that too."

The name of the center was an important step toward establishing its identity, distinguishing it from other establishments in the vicinity and conveying its intended functions. Initially, the yoga classes seemed to dominate the center's agenda. In Filipa's words, "Yoga gets people in the door." Lisa elaborated:

> I think of us more as [the] therapeutic yoga site studio, if people are looking for yoga, that we offer more therapeutic type of applications. . . . How can we distinguish ourselves from other people in town, but how can we also make sure that we're supporting the mission of what we're trying to do and that's to really help people to feel better where they are at.

In other words, Lisa's intent was to differentiate the BHC yoga classes from others offered through other facilities as primarily physical fitness exercise. Thus, the word "healing" was an intentional choice meant to underscore that therapeutic association: "It means certainly we do want to treat the body, mind and spirit, without trying to focus on alleviating that physical condition." However, that choice was not without controversy. Both Lisa and Filipa admitted that "healing" may have negative connotations for some people. Lisa posited, "Healing can maybe scare people off if they think it could be something religious, you know, from a spiritual context." Filipa added another interpretation: "It's something uneasy. Paranormal or something." Despite those initial reservations, the Brazos Healing Center as a central part of Lisa's imagined conception has stuck.

Another key decision in making the center a reality was finding a strategic, yet affordable location for the startup enterprise. Early on, the cofounders decided that a desirable place for the center would be within College Station's "medical corridor." This area in the southern end of the city and near the north–south interstate includes one of the aforementioned hospitals, several large "professional buildings" including clinics, practitioners' offices, and medically related businesses. An additional hospital, under construction, and a proliferation of recently built residential subdivisions and local businesses are also prominent parts of the surrounding environment. A conscious desire on the part of Filipa and Lisa was that being in the vicinity of the College Station Medical Center would facilitate referrals for their classes and services from physicians. However, real estate rental in this prosperous neighborhood is predictably expensive. Lisa described their discovery of a space for the center at the front of the professional building adjoining the hospital as "synchrony," the intersection of forces and events that complement one another with positive effects:

> Filipa: [The center's location] was just an empty space for 6 or 8 months and...
> Lisa: Nobody pointed it out, so what happened was we were standing in the lobby and we look to the right and it just looked vacant. And I remember asking Filly, "What's this space?" and you said, 'Oh that's a little pharmacy shop that's been vacant for awhile now and then you ended up I think calling, right? And the lady was like 'I've been looking to sublet this thing for . . . "

> *Filipa: ...8 months. Yeah, we sublet from her until October. . . .*
> *So for the first 6 months we were literally paying half of what we would have paid. It allowed us to establish ourselves and then take over once we had, you know, clientele.*

The location obtained through these fortuitous circumstances was a rectangular space with large windows open to the front of the professional building, equipped with blinds for privacy. Moveable chairs, blankets, massage tables, and yoga mats enabled the space to be used for multiple purposes. A sink and shelves were incorporated into the space, while a restroom was available to all first-floor residents of the building.

In fact, the visibility of BHC within the hospital environment resulted in some of the once-imagined physician referrals (less than 20% of the center's clientele). Filipa noted: "We're getting referrals from the local rheumatologist, cardiologist, psychologist, and the chiropractor." Neighboring health professionals have also participated as clients in BHC's classes, while a volunteer from a nearby hospice was sent to receive training in energy therapies. It is also possible that the BHC's medical corridor location had some negative effects with potential clients. For example, Melissa, one of the center staff shared:

> *I have heard people who do a lot of energy moving, say—I don't know this personally, I haven't tested it or done it—that when you're attached to a hospital or a funeral home or something like that, the energy level is not quite as high. . . . I talked to one person in particular and said, "Have you gone to the Healing Center?" and they said, "It's attached to a hospital; I won't go."*

Lisa and Filipa made it clear that their ways of operating are purposely distinct from those of conventional medicine. Staff of BHC do not refer to patrons as patients, but as "clients" because, according to Filipa, "clients just feels better or maybe more equal, working-on-it-together kind of thing." In fact, the notion of doctors' directives has been supplanted by client empowerment, as Filipa described:

> *[B]eing holistic is meaning that we are a partnership. . . . My doctor will tell me what I do and I don't need to understand it and then it will just happen. I mean we're throwing that to the wayside . . . We are collaborating in your health and it's not for me to tell you what to do, but rather it's me to kind of walk with you in that road to something better.*

Still, those boundaries could be uncomfortable with their medical neighbors; Lisa observed, "We're tenants there and there is no other way to say it. . . . It's kind of like we're outsiders looking for a way in."

In addition to naming and location, the center's website has been an important way of communicating information about BHC's objectives, staff, activities, and overall identity. For instance, as shown during yoga instruction at the center, there are a number of elements conveyed, including male clients and relatively uncomplicated positions that won't intimidate newcomers or people who are not in good physical conditions. Lisa explained:

> *We stick to basic positions. We want to emphasize the kind of gentle yoga that we offer. It's also important to me that we show the environment of the center—clean wooden floors and large yoga mats.*

Photo Courtesy of Brazos Healing Center

QUANTUM ENERGY AS A DEFINING METAPHOR AND ACTIVITY

Yoga was the modality that was initially common to both Lisa and Filipa and attracted several initial clients. However, since yoga is recognized and available throughout the community, these classes are not the feature that defines BHC as a third space form of healthcare.

Much less known and accessible in this area prior to the opening of the center is the concept of energy healing. Though both had training and experience with reiki, Lisa is certified as a reiki master, while Filipa has more training in healing touch, another form of energy healing. (For purposes of a brief explanation in this chapter, reiki will be the focus.) Energy therapies are based on an understanding of all phenomena, including the human body, mind, and spirit; other living beings, objects, and processes, as composed of energy. At its most encompassing level, this is called quantum energy which "binds all matter together into a field of oneness" (Tauferner, 2011). Various cultural belief systems and modalities (including yoga) posit how energy is disturbed and can be rechanneled for purposes of clearing energetic debris to facilitate forms of positive change. Reiki is a Japanese system of energetic healing dating from the late 19th century, with a well-established heritage of master teachers; certification is based on training developed through this lineage. The word *reiki* itself translates to "universal life-force." The practice of reiki requires that the practitioner be both intentional and intuitive in order to become a clear channel through which energy can flow. To help another person (or being or situation), the practitioner strives to feel a pattern of auras or chakras though which energy flows. The process of sensing energy flow may occur through touching the body, or feeling the auras surrounding a body, and can even be done at a distance.

As visualized in the photo, depicting reiki is not easy to convey and it may seem exotic or even incredible to those unfamiliar with what it is and how it works. In essence, this is energetic vibration in space that is sensed, felt, but not seen. Within BHC, reiki is offered both as a service (i.e., one may receive energy therapy) and as classes. Clients who take the classes are taught from the beginning level that they are now themselves reiki practitioners and are equipped to direct or channel energy on behalf of others, as well as themselves. In effect, to learn this system of energy healing is a form of self-empowerment. Reiki can be described as "prayer in action," so within this community, Lisa sometimes substitutes "god-force" for "life-force." Beyond reiki as a specific change-enhancing

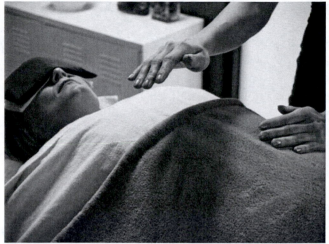

Photo Courtesy of Brazos Healing Center

modality, energetic flow is a way of framing and communicating about everything from worldwide situations (global conflicts, economic recession, climate change) to individual situations (relationships, health status, job security), to plants, animals, even inanimate objects that symbolize living complexities. Recently, quantum biofeedback—the use of computerized interactions to assess and balance energy fields—was added to BHC's repertoire of therapeutic services. Lisa told the following anecdote as an illustration of the versatility of energy therapy:

> *There was a graduate student who's been taking reiki classes with me for a while. She graduated with her doctorate in December, but hadn't been able to find a job, and was getting discouraged and depressed about her situation. A few weeks after taking the Reiki 1 training class, she got the idea to give reiki to her cv. Soon thereafter, she was invited for an interview. We'll never know if that made the difference, but she called me later to say that the interview had gone very well, and she was offered the job.*

Introducing energy therapies as a complementary form of transformation in this conservative community is truly an entrée into a third space on several levels—physical, metaphysical, and metaphorical.

COMMUNITY OUTREACH

In addition to the aforementioned referrals from local physicians and healthcare organizations, BHC maintains keen awareness of the value of being connected to various segments of the community in which it is located. Since the university is a major entity in the area, BHC welcomes and seeks opportunities for partnerships including participation in the current study and Lisa's working with a faculty member to develop a freshman seminar in wellness. Outside the university, BHC strives to initiate ways to interface with the public. These endeavors have included media presentations, participation in health fairs, an open house with demonstration of services at the center, and periodic guided meditation sessions and energy therapy shares during which participants work with one another and pay small donations going to a community agency. An active, up-to-date electronic newsletter alerts recipients to a continuously updated schedule of special workshops and speakers.

THE CENTER'S EVOLUTION CONTINUES

In December 2011, Filipa amicably separated from BHC to pursue other personal priorities. Several more changes within the center soon followed, including the hiring of additional staff and the re-opening of BHC in a new location, a few miles away from the medical corridor in a small strip mall nestled among such everyday enterprises as a coffee shop and a hair salon. Holistic nursing consultations have been supplanted by physician wellness consultations conducted by an integrative physician from a neighboring city. While there are small alterations in the classes and services offered, BHC's initial objectives remain constant:

> The mission of the Brazos Healing Center is to support those in the greater Brazos Valley community seeking a central place to: access complementary medical therapies and holistic health care consulting; learn more about various methods to enhance one's personal development, and meet others to exchange ideas for balancing and strengthening the mind-body-spirit connection. (http://brazoshealingcenter.com)

BHC's slogan, imprinted on the front of t-shirts, is "Shift Happens," a play on the popular saying "shit happens," meaning things, including bad things, occur and we adapt. Shift Happens is amusing shorthand for the notion that change is a regular occurrence. In the context of the Brazos Healing Center, shifts happen at multiple levels. For individuals, a yoga stretch becomes more flexible; consciousness transcends to greater depths of awareness; physical health may be stymied, but spiritual and emotional growth continues. For the organization, people come and go, business challenges emerge and need to be resolved, community alliances arise and are withdrawn. The realization that shifts happen is the platform upon which BHC continues to strive for transcendence into a yet-to-be-discovered third space.

— THE CIM NARRATIVE CONTINUES: TRANSFORMATION OR CO-OPTION? —

Our investigation portrays two community-based, complementary/integrative medicine centers, each striving to create its own version of a third space for healing, evolved from the founders' imagined visions, and shaped by living realities. Not surprisingly, given their very different circumstances, the discourses and directions that emerged in each case were quite distinct. The issues characterizing

CHWB tend to be inwardly focused, with the emphasis on the problematics of achieving a shared model of integrative team collaboration. For BHC as a startup organization, the focus has been more outward, with key decisions that communicate a particular identity and relationship with the surrounding community. It is noteworthy that BHC's leadership tends to frame challenges as opportunities for change.

Shifting our gaze to a broader social level, we wonder how the ongoing story of the ways that complementary/integrative medicine continues to evolve will eventually impact American healthcare. We have argued repeatedly in this chapter that CIM is creating new physical, psychological, spiritual, organizational, and discursive spaces for wellness and healing, in effect establishing expectations for a new normal as to how health practices can and should be enacted—both for health professionals and recipients of care. However, this evolution may play out in alternate ways.

One possibility for this evolution is that integrative medicine won't function well on a grand scale, and that complementary and alternative medicine (CAM) will continue to exist as an option for the public, albeit unreimbursed and regarded as unorthodox. However, given the increasing incorporation of CIM curricula in medical education, the proliferation of clinical CIM centers across the country, and the ongoing research on CAM modalities, it appears that CIM is moving from a position of marginality to one of mainstream acceptance; hopefully, health insurance will follow suit. Still, it is far too early in the (r)evolution to know whether conventional medicine will colonize and co-opt CIM for its own dominant purposes (e.g., using CIM centers primarily as a marketing tool to bring in more paying patients).

From our viewpoint, a more positive perspective, CIM will enable a transformed biomedicine to take a new, improved narrative turn, one that increasingly humanizes the relationship between practitioners and patients/clients; expands treatment options; promotes wellness and disease prevention; and encourages improved collaboration among practitioners and expansion of available modalities. Clearly, as these two case studies reveal—how centers frame this evolution, the language they use to describe the changes, the ways they communicate within the physical spaces and communities they inhabit—could all be opportunities to accomplish the vision they have set out to achieve.

— REFERENCES —

Abbott, R.B., Hui, K.-K., Hays, R.D., Mandel, J., Goldstein, M., Winegarden, B., & Brunton, L. (2011). Medical student attitudes toward complementary, alternative, and integrative medicine. *Evidence-Based Complementary and Alternative Medicine.* Retrieved from http://www.hindawi.com/journals/ecam/2011/985243/

Barrett, B. (2003). Alternative, complementary, and conventional medicine: Is integration upon us? *The Journal of Alternative and Complementary Medicine, 9,* 417–427.

Ben-Arye, E., Frenkel, M., Klein, A., & Scharf, M. (2008). Attitudes toward integration of complementary and alternative medicine in primary care: Perspectives of patients, physicians and complementary practitioners. *Patient Education and Counseling, 70,* 395–402.

Boon, H.S., & Kachan, N. (2008). Integrative medicine: A tale of two clinics. *BMC Complementary and Alternative Medicine, 8,* 1–8.

Boon, H.S., Verhoef, M., O'Hara, D., & Findlay, B. (2004). From parallel practice to integrative health care: A conceptual framework. *BMC Health Services Research, 4,* 1–5.

Burke, K. (1984). *Attitudes toward history.* Berkeley: University of California Press.

Cohen L. (2011, April). Visitor program discussion. Integrative Medicine Program, MD Anderson Cancer Center, Houston, TX.

Coulter, I.D., & Willis, E.M. (2004). The rise and rise of complementary and alternative medicine: A sociological perspective. *The Medical Journal of Australia, 180,* 587–589.

Eisenberg, D.M., Davis, R.B., Ettner, S.L., Appel, S., Wilkey, S., Rompay, M.W., & Kessler, R.C. (1998). Trends in alternative medicine use in the United States, 1990-1997. *The Journal of the American Medical Association, 280,* 1569-1575.

Freedman, D. (2011, July/August). The triumph of new-age medicine. *The Atlantic,* 90–100.

Frenkel, M., Ben-Arye, E., Geva, H., & Klein, A. (2007). Educating CAM practitioners about integrative medicine: An approach to overcoming the communication gap with conventional health care practitioners. *The Journal of Alternative and Complementary Medicine, 13,* 387–391.

Gadboury, I., Bujold, M., Boon, H., & Moher, D. (2009). Interprofessional collaboration within Canadian integrative health care clinics: Key components. *Social Science & Medicine, 69,* 707–715.

Geist-Martin, P., Sharf, B., & Jeha, N. (2008). Communication healing holistically. In H. Zoller & M. Dutta (Eds.), *Emerging perspectives in health communication: Meaning, culture, and power* (pp. 83–112). New York: Routledge.

Gevitz, N. (1988). *Other healers: Unorthodox medicine in America.* Baltimore, MD: The Johns Hopkins University Press.

Hollenberg, D. (2006). Uncharted ground: Patterns of professional interaction among complementary/alternative and biomedical practitioners in integrative health care settings. *Social Science & Medicine, 62,* 731–744.

Horrigan, B., Lewis, S., Abrams, D., & Pechura, C. (2012, February). *Integrative medicine in America: How integrative medicine is being practiced in clinical centers across the United States.* The Bravewell Collaborative: www.bravewell.org.

Jasinski, J. (2001). *Sourcebook on rhetoric: Key concepts in contemporary rhetorical studies* (pp. 588–591). Thousand Oaks, CA: Sage.

Kaptchuk, T.J., & Eisenberg, D.M. (2001). Varieties of healing. 1: Medical pluralism in the United States. *Annals of Internal Medicine, 135,* 189–195.

Kessler, R.C., Davis, R.B., Foster, D.F., Van Rompay, M.I., Walters, E.E., Wilkey, S.A., Kaptchuk, T.J., & Eisenberg, D.M. (2001). Long-term trends in the use of complementary and alternative medical therapies in the United States. *Annals of Internal Medicine, 135,* 262–270.

Kreitzer, M.J., Mitten, D., Harris, I., & Shandeling, J. (2002). Attitudes toward CAM among medical, nursing, and pharmacy faculty and students: A comparative analysis. *Alternative Therapies in Health and Medicine, 8,* 50–53.

Lechtin, F.P. (2011, October 29). *Brazos Healing Center: CAM in the Brazos Valley.* Presentation to the 1st Annual Texas Holistic Nursing CAN Conference, Temple, TX.

Massey, P.B. (2006). Physician training in integrative medicine. In M.P. Mumber (Ed.), *Integrative oncology: Principles and practice.* Boca Raton, FL: Taylor & Francis.

Moje, E.B., Ciechanowski, K.M., Kramer, K., Ellis, M., Carrillo, R., & Collazo, T. (2004). Working toward third space in content area literacy: An examination of everyday funds in knowledge and discourse. *Reading Research Quarterly, 39,* 38–70.

Nahin, R.L., Barnes, P.M., Stussman, B.J., & Bloom, B. (2009). Costs of complementary and alternative medicine (CAM) and frequency of visits to CAM practitioners: United States, 2007. National Health Statistics Reports, U.S. Department of Health and Human Services.

National Center for Complementary and Alternative Medicine [NCCAM]. (April, 2012). What is complementary and alternative medicine? Retrieved from http://nccam.gov/health/whatiscam/

Oldenburg, R. (1989). *The great good place: Cafes, coffee shops, community centers, beauty parlors, general stores, bars, hangouts, and how they get you through the day.* New York: Paragon House. ISBN 978-1557781109. (Hardback)

Robinson, A., & McGrail, M.R. (2004). Disclosure of CAM use to medical practitioners: A review of qualitative and quantitative studies. *Complementary Therapies in Medicine, 12,* 90–98.

Sharf, B.F., Geist-Martin, P., Cosgriff-Hernandez, K-K., & Moore, J. (2012). Trailblazing health care: Institutionalizing and integrating complementary medicine. *Patient Education and Counseling.* doi:10.1016/j.pec.2012.03.006

Snyderman, R., & Weil, A.T. (2002). Integrative medicine: Bringing medicine back to its roots. *Archives of Internal Medicine, 162,* 2381–2383.

Soja, E. (1996). *Thirdspace: Journeys to Los Angeles and other real-and-imagined places.* Hoboken, NJ: Wiley-Blackwell.

Tauferner, L. (2010, September 19). Brazos Healing Center. *Our Voices, Ourselves.* Radio interview with Vandy Ramadurai, KEOS, Bryan, TX. Retrieved from http://ourvoicesourselves.com/2010/10.

Tauferner, L. (2011, February). Reiki 1 class notes. Brazos Healing Center, College Station, TX.

Third Place. http://en.wikipedia.org/wiki/Third_place. Retrieved November 13. 2011.

Zappen, J.P. (2009). Kenneth Burke on dialectical-rhetorical transcendence. *Philosophy and Rhetoric, 32,* 279–301.

– ENDNOTES –

[1]   Chiropractors are categorized by the National Center for Complementary-Alternative Medicine as a form of manipulative and body-based CAM modality. The status of chiropractors is probably one of the most contested as to whether their practice belongs in the first or second space. We have included chiropractors in the first space in this chapter because they serve as primary care practitioners for many people within this community. Simultaneously, it is also important to note that local chiropractors in the Brazos Valley often incorporate massage, acupuncture, and naturopathic regimes within the services offered in their practices.

CHAPTER 8

ORGANIZING FOR SOCIAL CHANGE: PERSONAL STORIES AND PUBLIC HEALTH ACTIVISM

— LYNN M. HARTER, MICHAEL BRODERICK, SAMUEL VENABLE, AND MARGARET M. QUINLAN —

On September 17, 2007, my husband Vince and I had the sitcom life: two beautiful daughters (Mackenna, age 10 and Colleen, age 8), two dogs, and a two-car garage. On September 18, a malignant lesion was discovered on Colleen's right femur, and our lives were profoundly and irreversibly changed forever.

It was unfathomable. I dare say that was the worst day of my life. And it would be followed by a similarly harrowing 8-month journey for Colleen and our family. During that time, we interacted with three primary hospitals and learned firsthand just how inconsistent and inadequate our nation's pediatric oncology wards were at providing the emotional and spiritual support these children so desperately needed. Early on, we received some of the best psychosocial care one could hope for. But later, we were faced with such a dearth of emotional and spiritual support; it made what was already a nearly unbearable situation considerably worse . . .

. . . Colleen died on June 9, 2008. A couple of weeks before she died, the doctor had told us that it was time to tell her that the doctors and nurses couldn't help her anymore. I needed to tell her that we had to cancel her Make-a-Wish trip. I needed to tell her that the only way for her to feel better was to go to Heaven and be healed. Even on this horrible day, we were not provided any support services.

After Colleen died and I began to feel called to address this need, I researched the issue. Eight out of the top 10 hospitals that are excelling in emotional and spiritual support are doing so through donor funding. Regrettably, insurance companies do not easily pay for this type of support. In fact, another local hospital where Colleen had been treated lost some of their grant funding, and their support services suffered as a result. I sadly learned that the problem is widespread.

In my darkest hours, I sometimes cry out, "Why us?" I wish I could answer that. It haunts me. For now, I just know for certain that God is leading me to passionately pursue the improvement of emotional and spiritual support for children with cancer. It is my prayer that Colleen's tragedy will result in an increased awareness of this issue and, as a result, increased support for kids with cancer. (http://www.striving4more.org/page/our-inspiration)

Photo credit: Diane Moore

Colleen and Mackenna

No one leaves this world without wounds—or alive. In the United States, cancer is a leading cause of death for children and adolescents between ages 1 and 14, second only to accidents (Jemal et al., 2009). The American Cancer Society (2012) estimates that over 12,000 children in the United States will be diagnosed with cancer in 2012. In 2007, the Moore family found themselves on the wrong side of the statistics, a grim departure from the usual routine of playdates and ramshackle lemonade stands. Colleen traded in her childhood for doxorubicin, a chemotherapy drug that interferes with how cancer cells multiply even as it unsettles family routines, strains relationships, and shifts one's sense of self. What resources do families need to survive when adversity strikes? When bodies are vulnerable? When reckoning with the causes and consequences of illness? When treatments are opaque to common sense? When a cure remains allusive in spite of medicine's best efforts? These questions motivate Diane Moore's health activism.

Striving for More is a non-profit organization founded by Diane to increase the emotional and spiritual support available to children and families living with cancer and its treatment. Like other founders and directors of non-profit organizations, Diane is a consummate storyteller, rendering narrative central to *knowledge-making* in organizational practice. Through storytelling, narrators identify protagonists and victims, detail dilemmas, interpret cause and suggest redress, approve and discount social orders (see Chapter 1). As visitors enter the virtual reality of Striving for More, they encounter stories—of a child's lost innocence, a family touched by tragedy, a well-intended but limited healthcare system. With the click of a mouse, they also glimpse turning points in dialogue, moments that inspire our collective social imagination and commitment to crafting a different way to be together.

What is the role of storytelling in health activism? How do health advocates circulate narratives? How does storytelling function to invent spaces for resistance? In this chapter, we engage these questions and explore the narrative dimensions of health activism as embodied in the activities of Striving for More. Like Zoller (2005, 2012), we understand health activism as including efforts to question and extend or change the norms, values, social structures, policies, and relational dynamics

Diane in Office

in health arenas. In the United States, health activism includes collective actions related to patient advocacy, disability rights, healthcare reform, disease prevention, environmental justice, and even public safety. Striving for More focuses its efforts on shifting the terrain of pediatric and adolescent cancer care.

Striving for More, hereafter referred to as S4M, is an advocacy organization conceived by a founder who was directly impacted by the problems she seeks to change. S4M serves multiple roles as a non-profit organization. To begin, members engage in *communicative labor* as they articulate social problems and possible solutions. Communicative labor is a form of symbolic power or capital linked to social legitimization and cultural values (Dempsey, 2009). In other words, communicative labor produces information, knowledge, ideas, values, and emotions.

S4M also raises funds and in turn underwrites initiatives related to its mission. Its financial support comes from individual donors, community associations, a handful of local companies, and fundraising events. In-kind donations support fundraising efforts and events. The headquarters of S4M is located in Raleigh-Durham, North Carolina. S4M is a volunteer-based organization that relies on contract labor as needed (e.g., web design).

In this chapter, we move between narrative theory and practice as we profile the communicative efforts of S4M as it seeks to broaden the scope of pediatric cancer care. First, we explore the narrative *inception* of S4M as a health activist organization. Advocacy organizations are imagined and known in stories stakeholders tell about them. In other words, they consist of symbolically constructed and shared meanings, interpretations, rituals, and identities. Stories, in this sense, bind individuals together as they articulate their values and mission. Second, we demonstrate how storytelling guides *initiatives* of S4M and the actions of its associates. "Although narratives are a *mirror* that show the group its defining characteristics," argued Fine (2002), "they can also be a *lamp* that directs group action" (p. 238, emphasis in original). Health activists rely on narrative logics to prioritize interests and fund and implement initiatives. Third, we explore the *narrative capacity* of S4M—its mechanisms and processes for circulating narratives in order to advance its cause. Along the way, we join other scholars and practitioners committed to exploring the communicative labor involved in advocacy-based organizing (e.g., Dempsey, 2009; Zoller, 2005, 2012; Quinlan, 2010).

– ORGANIZATIONAL INCEPTION –

During the latter part of the 20th century, social scientific methods—in their quest for testable and verifiable unbiased observations of behavior—proved limiting in understanding the human condition and created a crisis of representation. In the study of organizational life, the dominance of realist epistemologies privileged, in Boje's (1995) words, an "impersonal, functional, mechanistic social order over the personal" (p. 1004). Organizational communication scholars and practitioners turned to narrative as a framework for studying how meaning is performed and intersubjectively negotiated (e.g., Coopman & Meidlinger, 2000; Eisenberg, Baglia, & Pynes, 2006; Miller, Geist-Martin, & Beatty, 2005; Smith & Keyton, 2001). Stories travel through organizational grapevines and flavor everyday interactions just as they inform mission and vision statements, specification and user manuals, and newsletters (Boje, 2001, 2008). Stories connect people to one another in social groups, encouraging members to identify and divide, cooperate and compete. Indeed, Mumby (1987, 1993) argued that organizational life would be impossible if not for our capacity to order and embody lived experience in narrative form. By adopting narrative sensibilities, scholars and practitioners can reveal the processes through which the creation of a sense of the natural, necessary, and appropriate takes shape and gains traction.

Narrative represents a performative strategy with particular significance for advocacy organizations (Lindemann, 2007, 2011). Politically, storytelling can restructure institutional and communal life. Activists position narratives as central resources in their attempts to raise awareness about hardships and inequities (e.g., Bridgewater & Buzzanell, 2010; Buzzanell & Lucas, 2006; Clair, Chapman, & Kunkel, 1996; Harter, Scott, Novak, Leeman, & Morris, 2006; Mattson, Clair, Sanger, & Kunkel, 2000). "Stories are not only legitimating but evaluative," argued Poletta (2006), "they are lenses through which opportunities and obstacles, costs and benefits, and success and failure are assessed" (p. 48). Plots connect events and agents of causation in consequential ways, revealing and generating moral visions of how to live. In other words, stories have strings attached—they demonstrate what counts and the peril of missing it. Not surprisingly, advocacy-based organizations use "narrative forms for envisioning and articulating goals," stated Solinder, Fox, and Irani (2008), including but not limited to "revitalizing the environment, reclaiming history, encouraging civic engagement, and, most generally, for creating opportunities to build coalitions and take concerted action" (p. 3).

Importantly, health activists often draw from *biographical narratives* in articulating problems and prioritizing modes of action (Zoller, 2012). Biographical narratives reveal personal experiences and, when shared publicly and chained across time with others' stories, rhetorically function to render abstract hazards personal, concrete, and immediate. Consider Diane's motivations for founding S4M:

> *It is hard to imagine that if Colleen were here, she would be turning 13 today. It is also hard to believe that while incredible medical centers, our area hospitals still struggle to provide quality, emotional support to children with cancer and their families. As I reflect on 2011, I am grateful for the opportunity to have an impact on other families as they navigate the dreadful diagnosis of childhood cancer. Nationwide, a family learns that their child has cancer every 3 ½ minutes and more than 200 children are diagnosed with cancer each year at UNC and Duke alone. It eases the pain of losing Colleen to know that* **Striving for More** *is making a difference.*
> (Diane Moore, S4M Blog, December 14th, 2011, emphasis in original)

At the time of her diagnosis, Colleen was an 8-year-old girl with a seemingly healthy body and relatively uncomplicated future. Prior to her death, osteosarcoma had spread to her lungs, pelvic bone, spine, right shoulder and ribs, and every major growth plate in her body. The Moore family's story of navigating complex healthcare terrain with little socio-emotional support serves as what Hart (1992) and Jacobs (2002) termed a *mobilizing narrative* for S4M. Mobilizing narratives create collective identities for advocacy-based organizations and function as strategic resources for organizations that work toward social change (Miller et al., 2005). By politicizing personal experiences, members bring organizations into existence.

As an advocacy-based organization, S4M is imagined and known in stories people tell about it (see also Glover, 2004). In other words, its inception is grounded in storytelling. Diane relies on storytelling to reformulate thinking and reorder priorities in pediatric oncology.

Many parents of children who have not survived are not like me as they find it difficult to remain within a community of families still fighting the cancer battle.

The lack of psychological support for families is a huge problem that exists in the healthcare system. In fact, a couple of them [parents] joined our cyber community, one of them sent me a message telling me, "I can't do this, it is too difficult for me. I can't do it. I have been a basket case. I don't know how you do this every single day of your life. It is way too hard." So, I realize my story is a unique one. My ability to stay engaged is different. Dr. Wechsler told us over and over that people don't come back after their child dies, they just can't. So it seems like parents who have lost a child don't come back, they just go on with their life, and I get that. And the parents with surviving children move on to find funding for research and a cure. They are associating themselves with organizations that are trying to find a cure. Clearly I understand why, and I completely support that. They have children who are still fighting the battle and they are terrified every morning that they wake up that their child is going to relapse or that their child has another spot on their lung. So, frequently when I speak to people who have not been on this journey they are shocked that children are not getting the psychological and emotional care that is needed. Because that is just not what people are talking about—they are talking about a cure. (Diane Moore, Interview)

Diane's story—and its departure from contemporary childhood cancer activist stories—gave rise to S4M. "There is a need for more than a cure," stressed Diane, "and that is what we are about. We are striving for more than a cure." As S4M attempts to reimagine, reconfigure, and ultimately expand pediatric cancer care, it confronts not only the real material limits of care but also the established social order. For example, the popularity of "movements for a cure" makes it difficult to support efforts guided by different motives (see critiques by King, 2006, 2010; Pezulla, 2003). A social preoccupation with a "cure" inadvertently channels attention toward high stakes medical research to the virtual exclusion of other needs.

Taylor's (2007) concept of the *social imaginary* usefully illuminates the symbolic and material challenges faced by S4M and similarly situated advocacy organizations. Taylor maintains that we all operate within certain normative assumptions (largely unquestioned and invisible) that determine how we construct, know, and articulate our shared world. Borrowing from Benedict Anderson (1991), he refers to this understanding of our social world as our social imaginary. Taylor explains that the social imaginary encompasses the "ways people imagine their social existence, how they fit together with others, how things go on between them and their fellows, the expectations that are normally met, and the deeper normative notions and images that underlie these expectations" (p. 23). The efficacy of S4M's efforts is tied in large part to its rhetorical capacity to invent other spaces of discourse. "Rhetoric opens inventional spaces," argued Hauser (1999), "places where ideas, relationships, emotional bonds, and courses of action can be experienced in novel, and sometimes transformative ways" (p. 33).

Diane's motives, the problems S4M seeks to redress, and its endorsed corrective actions are reflected in its vision and mission statement.

The Problem: Although children are often surrounded by loved ones when they are ill, they frequently hide their feelings of fear and anxiety from those they love in an attempt to protect them. Qualified emotional support should be an integral part of treatment, ensuring that both child and family have the resources they need to get through this often terrifying journey.

Insurance companies do not easily reimburse this type of emotional support. Unless you live in a community with a large children's hospital where corporate benefactors or grants have been dedicated to fund emotional support, families are left to fend for themselves when it comes to the emotional well being of their children.

After personally experiencing the dramatic gaps that exist in services today, Diane Moore founded Striving for More to pursue dedicated funding for support resources - so that no family has to endure childhood cancer alone.

Our vision: At Striving for More, our vision is a community where all children with cancer and their families receive emotional and spiritual support:
- Beginning from the moment of diagnosis
- Regardless of where they receive treatment
- Regardless of their socioeconomic status or insurance coverage
- And with seamless continuity and high quality

Our mission: Striving for More is dedicated to ensuring that children with cancer and their families receive quality emotional and spiritual support.

To what extent can individuals and groups envision otherwise within a normalizing social imaginary of medicine that positions hope as a "cure"? Our ability to imagine is not, for the most part, a free exercise to call a different world into being but rather a movement that finds footing in prior practice, or is made to appear as such. The gaps and fissures of dominant narratives can be exploited by individuals who seek to unsettle exclusionary practices (see Harter, Japp, & Beck, 2005). In this respect, change is not so much a process of revolution but a gradation.

Diane and S4M is reconceptualizing healthcare and boldly challenging the social imaginary of the biomedical model. The meta-narrative of "technology as progress" is engrained in the biomedical model and guides healthcare initiatives—the typical end goal of which is N.E.D., no evidence of disease (see Chapters 1 and 2). Diagnostic techniques and clinical trials, pharmaceuticals and surgeries remain crucial tools of the trade. Biomedical discourse produces an identifiable subject—the cancer patient—around which a particular system of possibilities and power/knowledge relations materialize (Foucault, 1979). Typically, patients are dosed with chemotherapy, irradiated, and sometimes amputated. Public conversations about cancer typically rely heavily (and often uncritically) on the language of "scientific breakthroughs" and "technological progress." For example, races for a "cure" occupy a prominent place in public health efforts, with financial support reflecting an overwhelming preference for research on detection, treatment, and genetic-based research (see King, 2006, 2010). While still appreciating the life-altering possibilities enabled by searches for a cure, S4M tells a different story and supports initiatives that otherwise might get lost with the endgame of N.E.D. In doing so, it unsettles dominant notions of "care" that too often remain tethered to a "cure."

– ORGANIZATIONAL INITIATIVES –

The stories individuals encounter in organizational life include archetypal characters, plots, and settings that function as what Burke (1973) might term *equipment for living*, sense-making structures that size up situations and chart possible actions. We live in light of canonical scripts, drawing on socially sanctioned interpretations to guide our actions. Narratives articulate both possibilities and preferences that social actors invoke, reproducing and/or resisting them in daily routines and rituals (Mumby, 1987). When leaders seek to build trust or negotiate shared meaning, win support for an initiative or position, or act as change agents, they often turn to narrative reasoning and practice. Advocacy organizations arise to counter or provide alternatives to dominant, often taken-for-granted, ways of relating and organizing (Quinlan & Harter, 2010). Although Diane Moore supports efforts focused on a "cure" and the life-sustaining benefits that can ensue, S4M was conceived to support initiatives that too often get neglected or dismissed altogether when priorities and strategic choices are funded. S4M supports initiatives that do not rest comfortably under the "cure" umbrella of care.

Healthcare activists are narrators who focus attention on and interpret experience, creating a representation from raw experience. In so doing, they transport contemplators into another world, encouraging them to grasp another's experience. Consider the following story shared by Diane during an interview:

> The nurses come in to check on your child, doing vitals and other things every couple of hours or so and I was a light sleeper because I was pretty worried about Colleen—any light would disturb me. I realized very quickly that it is hard to get an uninterrupted night of sleep. I realized pretty quickly that surviving on this little amount of sleep was not good for me and I had the idea to bring in a sleeping mask. This worked like a charm and I actually still sleep with one today because I became so accustomed to sleeping with one during the 80+ nights we spent in that hospital room with Colleen.

With its concern for continuity and disruption, stories allow narrators to make sense of disconcerting episodes and co-orient tellers and listeners alike to action steps. In this case, Diane's story gave rise to one of S4M's initiatives—the creation of *care kits* for families with a member being treated for pediatric cancer. Among other things, the care kits include sleep masks to help parents try to get a better night's rest. "The ideas contained in this kit came from parents who have been where you are now. Some of the items you will need and some of the items you will want," stressed Diane, in a letter to families included in care kits. "We hope they provide you some small comforts during this difficult journey."

Photo credit: Lynn M. Harter

Care Kit

Many initiatives supported by S4M offer informational and material resources for families. For example, families can access PDF versions of "Feeling Faces Journals," and "Pain Journals" to encourage kids to express their feelings. During the period of Colleen's treatment when neither she nor her family were getting the emotional support they needed, a family friend who was a professional therapist suggested starting a "Feeling Faces Journal." Each day, Colleen chose a feeling face that matched her mood, and then wrote down three good things and three bad things that had happened that day. "The journal became a regular thing for Colleen," reflected Diane. "Although she occasionally refused to participate and still resisted talking much about her feelings, the journal became part of Colleen's nightly routine. At least once a day, it gave her the opportunity to reflect on her emotional ups and downs." Stories indicate what is thinkable, doable, and possible. A case in point: Inspired by Colleen's experiences, S4M works to ensure that other kids have access to resources like "Feeling Face Journals."

Photo credits: Robin Conway

Colleen and Diane

Colleen

Rhetorically, narratives can elevate people's consciousness, inviting them into the reality of the characters populating the setting (see Chapter 1). At S4M, Diane and other staff and board members move between biographical experiences (i.e., illness narratives) and organizational initiatives (i.e., Feeling Face Journals). In reflecting on her motives, Diane shared, "I hope the resources we provide will help families figure things out quicker than I did . . . Everything starts moving so fast. You are learning a whole new vocabulary. It took me a few months to figure out how to organize everything." As a result, the website of S4M functions as a clearinghouse of resources for families facing a similar journey, including helpful hints (e.g., make extra copies of forms with relevant information to streamline intake process), links to other helpful websites (e.g., summer camps for kids), PDFs of articles published in medical journals, and downloadable forms (e.g., calendars to record appointments, blood tests, and other relevant information).

In summary, the potency of storytelling is revealed in how it sets the terms for strategic action, rendering some courses of action reasonable and fitting while positioning others as ill-considered or impossible (Polletta, 2006). In observing how storytelling guides S4M initiatives, two points merit extended attention: *narrative scaffolding* and *narrative indeterminancy*.

NARRATIVE SCAFFOLDING

Narratives rarely have a solitary existence; instead, they function concurrently in relation to others' stories. Arthur Frank (2004) suggested, "Stories stand better together, each increasing the resonance of others like it" (p. 7). Resonance does not imply universal truth. Instead, stories gather strength in their ability to pose questions and offer examples that inform and enrich lives lived apart from any story's particular telling. In this way, retrospective accounts of experience function as *scaffolds* for future activities. "The examples that stories offer—their heroes—do not tell readers what to do," stressed Frank, "rather they are examples of struggling to figure out what has to be done and gather the resolve to go about doing it." We read, listen, and engage the accounts of storytellers from where we are, amidst our own bodies' vulnerabilities and uncertainties. Stories of others can help us envision what is possible.

Certainly, the Moore family's experiences continue to shape the efforts of S4M. Even so, Diane remains acutely aware of how people experience suffering in differing ways and with differing needs.

> *I am constantly trying to track down other families touched by childhood cancer in this area and figure out what they need based on what they are going through…I remember when Colleen was diagnosed, I felt so alone. I had a lot of people in my family with cancer, but never a child with cancer. And when I meet people, I always ask about their story, and I ask for their CaringBridge site, because people post their stories there. And I follow their stories. I connect with them. My goal is to connect with them, connect them with others and with resources and organizations that can help.*
>
> *I met a woman with a son who has a brain tumor. When we had dinner one night, I learned that I really could not represent all families with kids with cancer, because this child was not in pain. Children with brain tumors don't typically have pain. And Colleen was in an incredible amount of pain, so our experience was very different. So listening to her, I realized the importance of listening to other stories, because although there are similarities there are also differences.*

Diane witnesses and responds to the stories of others, accounts that are layered upon each other in what Jameson (2001) described as a *storybuilding process*, and creating a *scaffolding effect* for health advocates. As stories dovetail, the past and present are linked to imagined futures.

Diane turned to the Association of Cancer Online Resources (ACOR), a network of virtual support groups, in an effort to identify diverse needs of children and families living with cancer. Consider the following example:

> When I did research through the ACOR board, I surveyed patients and asked them in the emotional realm, where were your biggest gaps, and a resounding response came back. The biggest gap was in the area of emotional support programs for adolescent and young adults. The hospitals have a lot of art programs for young children but not for adolescents. But digital art is something that speaks to all ages, the little kids love it and the adolescents love it, too.

Participants' accounts led Diane and the board of S4M to help fund a digital art therapy program at UNC.

> That program actually began with a grant from a different organization... they had one iPad and then we helped them expand their program by giving them seven additional iPads and a printer. This allows the art therapist to leave the iPads with the kids so they could do art. The program is fantastic... I don't think they would have been able to help as many patients when they only had one iPad because they couldn't leave them with the kids. The patients hold onto the iPads for longer periods of time and they can also print their digital creations. Before the patient could only use it under the supervision of the art therapist and then she had to take it with her when she left the room.

Some of the initiatives sponsored by S4M arise from unexpected sources and in unpredictable ways. For example, S4M started a community-based support group for parents of kids with cancer.

> Over the last year, Striving for More has started the Triangle Childhood Cancer Support Group. There was never one before and I identified that when I was on Colleen's journey with her, that there was never really a support group for parents of children with cancer. The North Carolina Children's Hospital had a small group but Duke didn't have a support group at all, and there was never anything community-based. The need is especially as the move to treat more kids as outpatients is beginning. As treatment is starting to become more outpatient, the need to have a support group in the community is becoming greater. We are trying to fulfill this need and bridge the gap between the two local clinics with our community-based support group.

Interestingly, conversations that have unfolded during meetings have fueled other initiatives sponsored by S4M.

> Some of the ideas that have emerged from the support group are about items that should be included in the care kits, things I never would have imagined. The care kit has gotten bigger and bigger and bigger. There are now like 40 items in it. And the items going in the bag

are coming from the patients and families and staff at the hospital. I started the kits but then this group is coming up with ideas I never would have thought of, so the list has just grown. For example, some of the ideas, I went, "Huh, why would they need that?" Like for example, one suggestion was to include a lint roller. One of the nurses suggested an adhesive lint roller should go in the bag, and I just said, "Why would they need an adhesive lint roller?" And, she said, "It's because the children lose their hair so fast and we [nursing staff] can't keep up with changing the sheets, so the parents use that to remove the hair from the sheets, and to keep the children comfortable." And it is just a brilliant idea, and I just remember being brought to tears. What a comfort you could bring to a family.

Since its inception, Lynn has witnessed S4M emerge as a collective storytelling system in which the performance of stories—the telling and hearing and writing and reading of stories—is a key part of organizational sense-making. Individuals' retrospective accounts of the past and the here-and-now function as a *scaffold* for prospective activities. Of course, stories are differently intelligible, authoritative, or useful, and some generate a limited range of responses (Polletta, 2006). Meanwhile, stories do not stand still. Stories move and shift—and meaning-making remains indeterminate.

NARRATIVE INDETERMINANCY

Like most cancer patients, Colleen needed to undergo a surgical procedure to place a port-a-cath in her chest, allowing medicine (including chemotherapy) to be pumped through a vein that led directly to her heart. Needless to say, this was a terrifying prospect for Colleen and her parents.

Enter the sock monkey. A child life specialist gave it to Colleen and helped her "operate" on it to install the port-a-cath. Then she took Colleen on a field trip to the radiology department to x-ray the monkey. "While we're here," said the radiologist, "let's just get one of you, too." This cleverly eliminated the frightening buildup to the x-ray and helped make the whole port-a-cath procedure a little less scary.

Photo credit: Lynn M. Harter

The sock monkey became Colleen's favorite stuffed animal. Throughout her treatment, it was her "practice patient" for other procedures. Sadly, it also became a symbol of her emotional turmoil. Later in her treatment, she became depressed and noncommunicative. In a moment of particular frustration, she took a pair of scissors and dug into the monkey, cutting out the port-a-cath. (http://www.striving4more.org/section/colleens-story)

Individuals' storytelling is not static; rather, it shifts as they continuously refigure experience through reflection (Harter et al., 2005). Likewise, in advocacy organizations, meaning-making is subject to revision as individuals recast happenings through reflection and in light of contemporary knowledge and circumstances. People live stories, and in the living of stories, reaffirm them, modify them, or craft new stories altogether.

For example, Diane drew from her own experience with Colleen and the expertise of child life specialists in envisioning the "medical play doll" project as a viable alternative to sock monkeys and then shifting their support to "chemoducks."

We have changed our strategy recently. This is part of having a successful organization. You have to be flexible about what is the right thing to do for the patients. And what the capacity of the hospital and staff is. UNC had the sock monkeys. And they had volunteers who organized this. Duke never had anything. What we decided to do was have volunteers make medical play dolls, because the National Child Life Association guidelines recommend that medical play dolls are better to use because other dolls (like sock monkeys) look to much like other stuffed toys that kids have. The child life specialist on my board felt that sock monkeys were just too much of a pop culture icon. However, we recently came across a program called Chemoducks, and we've partnered with them and we are now funding Chemoducks at both UNC and Duke. They are targeted for younger populations. And we are doing this because both UNC and Duke like the Chemoduck program. The reason we like it is because the port-a-cath or hickman catheter is already embedded in the duck, and sometimes that is difficult to cut into the doll. At Duke, they have a shortage of child life specialists, since this program comes with great resources, their website is fantastic, and it was started by a parent of a child with cancer. The duck is delivered with a DVD and the parent can actually go to the website. There is also a parent-to-parent guide that we are putting in our care kits. We love it because the chemoduck doesn't need a child life specialist to navigate the child through its use. So a parent can help a child use it properly. It can be used in conjunction with the website. (Diane, interview)

New and different interpretations and initiatives emerge as standpoints and situations unfold and change. The evolving use of "medical play dolls" and "chemo-ducks" (see www.chemoduck.org) illustrates the tentative and revisable significance of past experiences based on the contingencies of present circumstances, the present from which we narrate (Ricoeur, 1984).

In summary, storytelling remains the coin and currency of advocacy organizations and helps health activists prioritize initiatives. Stories gain traction as they *stand together*, connecting past experiences to future actions. Yet, narrative accounts do not *stand still* in a way that allows for certainty. Shifting standpoints and stories may seem risky to practitioners and activists, yet we agree with Diane, "This is part of having a successful organization. You have to be flexible about what is the right thing to do for the patients."

— NARRATIVE CAPACITY —

The ultimate success of S4M rests in part with (1) its own narrative capacity, and (2) in developing the narrative capacity of its stakeholders. At an organizational level, narrative capacity refers to an advocacy group's efficiency at circulating narratives throughout its network (Atkinson, 2009, 2010; Atkinson & Cooley, 2010). Meanwhile, S4M also works to create space for patients and families to account for their own experiences. Although these storytelling efforts are interconnected, for analytic purposes we discuss each domain respectively.

ORGANIZATIONAL CAPACITY

Like other health advocacy organizations, S4M hosts a range of face-to-face fundraising and social support events (see http://www.striving4more.org/section/events1). Diane serves on the editorial board and as a freelance writer for *Touched by Cancer*, a free bimonthly publication circulated in central North Carolina. Jill Trotta Calloway (2010) chronicled the Moore family's journey as narrated through the eyes of her daughter, Katie. Calloway's book is accessible for children and adults alike and serves as a resource for parents, and teachers who are grappling with how to talk about why kids get cancer and involved treatments. Each of these moments and venues stretch the narrative capacity of S4M, inviting audience members to enter into and feel involved with the activities of the organization.

Meanwhile, S4M has developed a visible and robust online presence to enhance its narrative capacity. Americans increasingly seek and share health-related information via online channels (Sundar, Rice, Kim, & Sciamanna, 2011), a shift that architects of the first Health Information Trends Survey described as a "tectonic shift" (Hesse et al., 2005). The landscape of e-health is vast, and includes both clinical and nonclinical applications. Diane, with the help of a virtual assistant, has capitalized on the tectonic shift and relies heavily on blogs, Twitter, and Facebook to connect with constituents.

> *Diane: We need to be visible in cyberspace. So, I hired a virtual assistant and she is basically my voice into the world. She is very passionate about our mission and she knows exactly what we are trying to do. So she speaks as if she were me. She never does the commentary, it's always my words. So I will still write all my own blogs and all my own articles. But she helps get my story out there. And she helps post information I find that is relevant to what we do. I have Google Alerts set up, for example, for things related to our mission and she will post those. I will search quotes relevant to our organization and she will post those on Twitter. So, she has taught me a lot about social media and how to get people to follow us on Twitter. But it is a lot of work to keep up with that, so she helps out. And she keeps up with the content on the web, to make sure it's relevant and fresh and that our events are posted and things like that. I get the events moving and make the public appearances, do the speaking, write the articles and all that, and then she takes care of the administrative stuff on the back end, getting it out to a wide audience.*
>
> *Lynn: It seems like she enhances your narrative capacity in terms of disseminating your story?*

Diane: Yes, she does. That is a very good way of putting it. And she re-purposes things for me. So, I'm on the editorial board for a cancer magazine. They do a magazine every other month, so I do the column. And as soon as the magazine hits the delivery points that it is going to hit, the pharmacies and doctors offices, I get the publisher to send me and her the final version and then she blasts it out everywhere on the internet. So if you Google "childhood cancer," I now come up pretty high. She will put it in my blog, in e-zine a source on the web, like 10 different places. She also manages me. So she will find out when the next due date is and what the topic is and she will send me reminders about deadlines and stuff.

By disseminating information through a variety of media, S4M expands its opportunity to reach a network of individuals. One such opportunity is through search engine optimization (SEO). SEO is a strategy used widely in our networked world; the goal of SEO is to increase an organization's exposure to its target publics by triggering key aspects of a search algorithm. By repeating the phrase "childhood cancer" in the coding of a website, linking to other childhood cancer–related websites, and re-tweeting articles written about like subjects, web authors can push their site higher in the search results. Thus, rather than being the tenth site listed about childhood cancer, strategic SEO can push you closer to third or second.

This is an additional avenue for resistance, but not one without struggle. SEO is a moving target, as search engines such as Google attempt to make their results more "organic," or less susceptible to these strategies. By creating a ranking system, Google is placing narrative constraint on S4M. S4M resists this through a proactive, multichannel approach to messaging. The challenge presented by this back-and-forth is that it only further perpetuates the system. Furthermore, organizations with greater resources available who do not share S4M's mission or purpose could be more likely to push S4M down, thus limiting its narrative capacity.

Another opportunity for organizations like S4M to increase the effectiveness of their narrative capacity is through analytics. Analytics provide means for an individual or organization to identify demographic information such as age, gender, location, and search terms used. This information allows organizations to better target their messaging; if, for example, S4M discovers that a majority of its visitors are adults of children with cancer in the greater Charlotte area, they can create resources that more specifically tailor to the needs of people there as opposed to Winston-Salem.

Online modes of communication have several advantages for an organization like S4M: They expand the organization's reach by eliminating some geographic limitations inexpensively; foster a richer sense of interactivity and enmeshment in a narrative structure; and allow audiences to engage more richly with the organization and its members. A great example of this is Diane's Pinterest profile. Pinterest is a relatively new social network that emphasizes sharing; users "pin" photos to their virtual board. These pins are then pushed out to their connections. Diane's profile constructs a complex yet particular narrative told through what others have created. One of her "boards," or grouping of pins that are topically related, is called "Prayers Needed," and on this board Diane has pinned photos of children who are currently battling cancer. These photos do more than tell—they show.

CONSTITUENT CAPACITY

The mission of S4M is to provide socio-emotional and spiritual support for families facing pediatric cancer. Among other initiatives, it creates space for individuals to story their experiences. As indicated earlier, S4M sponsors a social support group. Group meetings provide opportunities for individuals to take stock of and handle life's adversities. Although supportive communication takes numerous forms (see Goldsmith & Albrecht, 2011, for an overview), for the purposes of this chapter we emphasize the therapeutic potential of storytelling.

Beyond face-to-face support groups, S4M connects constituents to social networking sites like CaringBridge. In one of her blogs, Diane emphasized how such sites can ease the emotional burden often accompanying the storytelling process:

> *You call your parents and your siblings and your best friend and you tell the story over and over. It is emotionally and physically exhausting. You figure out very quickly that although everyone wants to be kept in the loop, you will not be able to keep repeating yourself over and over.* (December 10, 2010)

Storytelling in social networks is clearly important when facing life-threatening and life-changing illnesses. Under the right conditions, it can improve family's coping skills, connect them to similarly situated individuals, create openings for individuals to enter each other's lives, and communicate health information.

Of course, individuals can narrate their experiences in multiple forms. Narrative scholarship emphasizes oral storytelling, often to the neglect of other aesthetic renderings of experience (see Chapter 3). Over the past year, working in partnership with Arts for Life, S4M has extended arts programming in both inpatient and outpatient settings.

> *The artist at Duke Colleen loved. But she had only been able to work with patients in the outpatient clinic and so we have given her a ton of resources. She said, I don't need crayons, and I don't need paper, and I don't need paint. Everybody wants to give me those things. I need equipment." So, we bought her a MacBook, a digital camera, an iPad, and a printer/scanner/copier. We are also sponsoring two interns and we are able to, and I think I got this term from you, increase her capacity and the capacity of that program so they can go into the inpatient clinic. During the growth of this organization, I have learned that we can give the hospital money but the hospital bureaucracy makes it difficult to get them to add needed resources. There are roadblocks everywhere. What I have learned is that it is better to establish relationships with likeminded non-profit organizations that have already successfully worked through the bureaucracy . This way, I can provide them funding to help them increase their capacity. Because it's not about giving me the glory, it's about helping the patients get the services that they need. So let's partner with the organizations that have successfully gotten into the hospitals and patients love them but let's help them do more than what they are currently capable of doing. Arts for Life is an excellent example of one of these partner organizations.. They have been there for years but they have been shackled for life in the outpatient clinic. And now, starting in 2012, they are going to be in the inpatient clinic, and we helped make that happen. Striving for More has increased their capacity to increase arts programming and their ability to reach more children.*

As indicated in Chapter 3, by fostering creative expression *among participants*, art-making allows individuals to *engage* with fellow sufferers, family, and friends. Artful encounters in clinical settings also can function palliatively by alleviating various types of suffering, making circumstances more bearable.

Over the past 2 years, S4M also has partnered with local hospitals to integrate the Beads of Courage program. Beads of Courage describes itself as a resilience-based intervention for children and families coping with serious illness.

> Through the program children tell their story using colorful beads as meaningful symbols of courage that commemorate milestones they have achieved along their unique treatment path. (http://www.beadsofcourage.org/pages/beadsofcourage.htm)

From Diane's perspective, the program "helps children gain ownership of their story along with various tools to retell it...[Beads of Courage] helps children express their feelings during a difficult time."

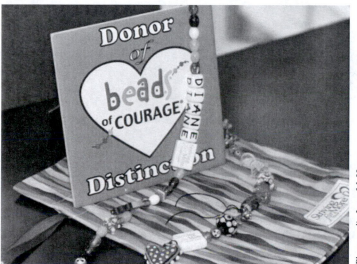

Photo credit: Lynn M. Harter

Finally, Diane helps constituents develop their narrative capacity by encouraging them to make sense of life by writing.

> I'm also on the advisory board by the Touched by Cancer magazine and I write some of the columns on childhood cancer. But I don't write all of them and it is because I don't want to be the sole voice on childhood cancer. This past month the article was on "surviving survivors' guilt," and I couldn't have written that article because I don't have survivors' guilt. My daughter didn't survive. But it is an important topic, so I needed someone else to write this. I met a mom through the Triangle Childhood Cancer Support Group who writes a wonderful blog so I invited her to write it. She lives this everyday and I knew she could speak to the topic beautifully.

Storytelling can be therapeutic for both writers and readers (see Keeley & Koenig Kellas, 2005), fostering sense-making about suffering and helping individuals navigate difficult terrain.

– CONCLUSION –

They gave me a tour. The nurse manager of pediatric chemo gave me a tour. She is managing the child life staff. When Colleen was there, they had two child life specialists across 12 units and now they have ten. And, she really spent a lot of time showing me different things. We delivered some beads of courage bags to patients. And she introduced me to a child life specialist and a nurse in charge of quality of life work there and the nurse said she had heard so much about me. And she said they now do weekly quality of life rounds. And I was fine until the quality of life nurse and the nurse manager said to me, "I want you to know how much this unit has changed since you and your daughter were here, and it is because of you. And it's not because of the money that Striving for More has necessarily given the hospital, but it is more what you have accomplished and the movement you started and what you have said, and the actions you took to increase awareness." And I became very emotional. I felt like a benefactor or celebrity or something. But I'm not that. I'm just a grieving mother. That's it. I'm just a grieving mother. I'm trying to take something senseless and turn it into something meaningful. (Diane, Interview)

The inception of S4M arose from Diane's recognition of a problem—a lack of socio-emotional and spiritual support amidst a rapidly growing and evolving repertoire of cancer therapies. When Colleen was diagnosed with osteosarcoma, Diane Moore had no templates, no trove of memories, to call on to navigate the "what ifs" and "what thens." The unvarnished truths of cancer make little sense amidst the inflammatory processes that foster its growth and the overwhelming severity of its treatment. Even so, the distance between senseless and meaningful can be a support group, a prayer chain, an art program, a website away.

S4M consists of collectively constructed and shared meanings, interpretations, and commitments. Like other advocacy organizations, it is imagined and realized through storytelling (see Glover, 2004). By transforming problems into stories, narration links the past to a possible future. The adventures of a story's characters, the settings in which action occurs, and the consequences of characters' behaviors co-orient tellers and listeners around family needs. As such, personal stories—including but not limited to the Moore family—direct the initiatives supported by S4M. Diane and S4M realize in practice what Fine (2002) theoretically argued, a social movement is "a bundle of narratives" (p. 229). Stories account for why and how the organization came to be and the programs it supports. Facebook, websites, blogs, Pinterest, Twitter, and search engines such as Google remain critical in enhancing the narrative capacity of S4M and that of its constituents. Even so, S4M will continue to evolve alongside shifts in social media, cancer therapies, and the self-identified needs of families.

We close by thanking Diane for allowing us to highlight the inception and development of Striving for More. Its communicative labor and initiatives are challenging, refining, and enlarging pediatric cancer care.

– REFERENCES –

American Cancer Society. (2012). What are the key statistics for childhood cancer? Retrieved from http://www.cancer.org/Cancer/CancerinChildren/Detailed

Anderson, B. (1991). *Imagined communities*. London: Verso.

Atkinson, J.D. (2009). Networked activism and the broken multiplex: Exploring fractures in the resistance performance paradigm. *Communication Studies, 60*, 49–65.

Atkinson, J.D. (2010). *Alternative media and the politics of resistance: A communication perspective*. New York: Peter Lang.

Atkinson, J.D., & Cooley, L. (2010). Narrative capacity, resistance performance, and the "shape" of new social movement networks. *Communication Studies, 61*, 321–338.

Boje, D.M. (1995). Stories of the storytelling organization: A postmodern analysis of Disney as 'Tamara-land.' *Academy of Management Journal, 38*, 997–1035.

Boje, D.M. (2001). *Narrative methods for organizational and communication research*. Thousand Oaks, CA: Sage.

Boje, D.M. (2008). *Storytelling organizations*. Thousand Oaks, CA: Sage.

Bridgewater, M.J., & Buzzanell, P.M. (2010). Caribbean immigrants' discourses: Cultural, moral, and personal stories about workplace communication in the United States. *Journal of Business Communication, 47*, 235–265.

Burke, K. (1973). *Philosophy of literary form* (3rd ed.). Berkeley: University of California Press

Buzzanell, P.M., & Lucas, K. (2006). Gendered stories of career: Unfolding discourses of time, space, and identity. In B.J. Dow & J.T. Wood (Eds.), *The Sage handbook on gender and communication* (pp. 161–178). Thousand Oaks, CA: Sage.

Calloway, J.T. (2010). *There's an elephant in my room: A child's unforgettable journey through cancer proved hope was stronger than fear*. Bloomington, IN: Author House.

Chemoducks. (2012). www.chemoduck.org.

Clair, R.P., Chapman, P.A., & Kunkel, A.W. (1996). Narrative approaches to raising consciousness about sexual harassment: From research to pedagogy and back again. *Journal of Applied Communication Research, 24*, 241–259.

Coopman, S.J., & Meidlinger, K.B. (2000). Power, hierarchy, and change: The stories of a Catholic parish staff. *Management Communication Quarterly, 13*, 567–625.

Dempsey, S.E. (2009). NGOs, communicative labor, and the work of grassroots representation. *Communication and Critical/Cultural Studies, 6*, 328–345.

Eisenberg, E.M., Baglia, J., & Pynes, J.E. (2006). Transforming emergency medicine through narrative: Qualitative action research at a community hospital. *Health Communication, 19*, 197–208.

Fine, G.A. (2002). The storied group: Social movements as "bundles of narratives." In J.E. Davis (Ed.), *Stories of change: Narrative and social movements* (pp. 229–246). Albany, NY: State University of New York Press.

Foucault, M. (1979). *Discipline and punish: The birth of the prison.* Translated by Alan Sheridan. London: Penguin Books.

Frank, A.W. (2004). *The renewal of generosity: Illness, medicine, and how to live.* Chicago: University of Chicago Press.

Glover, T.D. (2004). Narrative inquiry and the study of grassroots associations. *Voluntas: International Journal of Voluntary and Nonprofit Organizations, 15*, 47–69.

Goldsmith, D., & Albrecht, T.L. (2011). Social support, social networks, and health. In T. Thompson, R. Parrott, & J. Nussbaum (Eds.), *Handbook of health communication* (2nd ed., pp. 335–348). New York: Routledge.

Hart, J. (1992). Cracking the code: Narrative and political mobilization in the Greek resistance. *Social Science History, 16*, 631–668.

Harter, L.M., Japp, P.M., & Beck, C.S. (2005). Vital problematics of narrative theorizing about health and healing. In L.M. Harter, P.M. Japp, & C.S. Beck (Eds.), *Narratives, health, and healing: Communication theory, research, and practice* (pp. 7–30). Mahwah, NJ: Lawrence Erlbaum Associates.

Harter, L.M., Scott, J.S., Novak, D.K., Leeman, M.A., & Morris, J. (2006). Freedom through flight: Performing a counter-narrative of disability. *Journal of Applied Communication Research, 4*, 3–29.

Hauser, G.A. (1999). *Vernacular voices: The rhetoric of publics and public spheres.* Columbia: University of South Carolina Press.

Hesse, B.W., Nelson, D.E., Kreps, G.L. Croyle, R.T., Arora, N.K., Rimer, B.K., et al. (2005). Trust and sources of health information: The impact of the Internet and its implications for health care providers: Findings from the first Health National Trends Survey. *Archives of Internal Medicine, 165*, 2618–2684.

Jacobs, R.N. (2002). Narrative integration of personal and collective identity in social movements. In M.C. Green, J.S. Strange, & T.C. Brock (Eds.), *Narrative impact: Social and cognitive functions* (pp. 205–229). Mahwah, NJ: Lawrence Erlbaum Associates.

Jameson, D.A. (2001). Narrative discourse and management action. *Journal of Business Communication, 38*, 476–511.

Jemal, A., Siegel, R., Ward, E. Hao, Y., Xu, J., & Thun, M.J. (2009). Cancer statistics, 2009. *CA: A Cancer Journal for Clinicians, 59*, 225–249.

Kelley, M.P., & Koenig Kellas, J. (2005). Constructing life and death through final conversation narratives. In L.M. Harter, P. M. Japp, & C.S. Beck (Eds.), *Narratives, health, and healing: Communication theory, research and practice* (pp. 365–390). Mahwah, NJ: Erlbaum.

King, S. (2006). *Pink ribbon, Inc.: Breast cancer and the politics of philanthropy.* Minneapolis: University of Minnesota Press.

King, S. (2010). Pink diplomacy: On the uses and abuses of breast cancer. *Health Communication, 25*, 286–289.

Mattson, M., Clair, R.P., Chapman Sanger, P.S., & Kunkel, A.D. (2000). A feminist reframing of stress. In P.M. Buzzanell (Ed.), *Rethinking managerial and organizational communication from feminist perspectives* (pp. 157–174). Thousand Oaks, CA: Sage.

Miller, M.Z., Geist-Martin, P., & Beatty, K.C. (2005). Wholeness in a breaking world: Narratives as sustenance for peace. In L.M. Harter, P.M. Japp, & C.S. Beck (Eds.), *Narratives, health, and healing: Communication theory, research, and practice* (pp. 295–310). Mahwah, NJ: Lawrence Erlbaum Associates.

Mumby, D. (1993). *Narrative and social control*. Newbury Park, CA: Sage.

Mumby, D.K. (1987). The political function of narrative in organizations. *Communication Monographs, 54*, 113–127.

Pezulla, P. (2003). Resisting "National Breast Cancer Awareness Month": The rhetoric of counterpublics and their cultural performances. *Text and Performance Quarterly, 89*, 345–365.

Polletta, F. (2006). *It was like a fever: Storytelling in protest and politics*. Chicago: University of Chicago Press.

Quinlan, M.M. (2010). Fostering connections among diverse individuals through multi-sensorial storytelling. *Health Communication, 25*, 91–93.

Quinlan, M.M., & Harter, L.M. (2010). Meaning in motion: The embodied poetics and politics of Dancing Wheels. *Text & Performance Quarterly, 30*, 374–395.

Ricoeur, P. (1984). *Time and narrative*. Translated by K. McLaughlin & D. Pellauer. Chicago: University of Chicago Press.

Smith, F.L., & Keyton, J. (2001). Organizational storytelling: Metaphors for relational power and identity struggles. *Management Communication Quarterly, 15*, 149–182.

Solinder, R., Fox, M., & Irani, K. (Eds.). (2008). *Telling stories to change the world: Global voices on the power of narrative to build community and make social justice claims*. New York: Routledge

Sundar, S.S., Rice, R.E., Kim, H.S., & Sciamanna, C. (2011). Online health information: Conceptual challenges and theoretical opportunities. In T. Thompson, R. Parrott, & J. Nussbaum (Eds.), *Handbook of health communication* (2nd ed., pp. 181–202). New York: Routledge.

Taylor, C. (2007). *Modern social imaginaries*. Durham, NC: Duke University Press.

Zoller, H. (2005). Health activism: Communication theory and action for social change. *Communication Theory, 15*, 341–364.

Zoller, H. (2012). The narrative politics of health, risk, and illness in environmental health campaigns. *Journal of Applied Communication Research, 40*, 20–43.

PART 3

FUTURE DIRECTIONS

CHAPTER 9

SUBJUGATED STORIES OF PAIN AND ILLNESS

— MARK LEEMAN —

When I had my cancer, man, I was completely out of my mind. I was completely freaked out. They talkin' all these options, all these things that could happen, all these big words and [stuff], I didn't understand none of it. I lost it man. I was like, "Oh my God, I have no idea." I didn't know what to do. I could hardly even keep it together enough just to get to where I was supposed to be when I was supposed to be there. Finally one day I said to the surgeon, I can't remember his name, but he seemed like a

good guy, so I looked him in the eye and said to him "Doc, you gonna take care of me, right? You got this, right? I'll just trust you to take care of me." So I had the surgery.

That is how RJ unfolded the story of his prostate cancer treatment to me. As I have gotten to know RJ better I can imagine how "freaked out" he must have been. RJ can rarely keep track of what day of the week it is. He has a grade-school education, and administration of details is a constant struggle for him. However, in his contexts, and amidst his native interpretive community, RJ is an insightful, witty, and relationally intuitive man. He is one of my most valuable guides to understanding as I continue living in a neighborhood riddled by generational poverty. He is one of my instructors in my apprenticeship with the oppressed, through which I hope to better understand the discourses, meanings, and realities of people in poverty. But I would not want RJ making complex medical treatment decisions for me. As hinted at by the discourse above, RJ was overwhelmed and felt almost assaulted by all the information, situations, "experts," and monumental decisions he was being called to deal with at a time when he was especially "freaked out" due to his serious illness. As RJ has unfolded the larger story to me, it is clear that he felt unheard largely because the situation rendered him unable to speak. He knew that big issues with long-term consequences were on the table, but he was too scared and felt too ill-equipped to take his seat around that table to dialogue. So what did he do? Rather than roll within the epistemological parameters of the many health-care providers attempting to communicate with him (parameters like survival rates, treatment side-effects, research on quality of life, and life expectancy without treatment), he clung relationally to a doctor whom he perceived to be interpersonally a "good guy," and trusted that man with the decision. He felt a connection with that doctor, so he granted him autonomy over his health. He cried out to someone he discerned to be trustworthy. He cried out, "You gonna take care of me, right?" He trusted someone who looked him in the eye confirmingly and said, "I got this. I got you." He trusted someone who happened to be a surgeon, and so he got surgery instead of chemotherapy, or radiation, or both, or nothing at all (a choice currently gaining much support for prostate cancer).

RJ's choice may seem irrational to some, and I must admit that when I first heard the story it echoed in my experience as the narrative of someone from a marginalized population making a big decision based largely on the powerlessness of the subject positions he found himself occupying. Then I got sick myself, and my interpretation of RJ's story changed.

My reading of RJ's story changed because my experience of subjugation changed. From the Latin a plausible definition for the way I am using the word subjugation is "to make submissive." Illness has been described by Frank (1995, 2000) and others as a disruption of expectations. Because you are expecting, and hoping for, a different plot to play out, the disruption of pain and illness makes you submit to a new plot that is usually not of your choosing nor liking. You are made submissive to this new story. The disruption of expectations I went through thrust me into a position of subjugation. I went down hard and suddenly, and I could not get back up. I was literally on my knees in submission. In some ways I felt in submission to a new identity as I "lost it."

I, and my story, were subjugated in multiple ways. I was subjugated to my pain in ways I could never have imagined. It ruled me. The people around me who were both living and wanting for me the old "norm" subjugated me, in a sense, when I had lost my usual way of being. Out of love or out of professional concern they wanted something for me that was not happening, and it amplified my feelings of submission to the new norm that no one wanted. The powers of healthcare and insurance and money also subjugated me mightily. Then there was my sense of individuality, which subjugated me, and had to be subjugated, as I was forced to be reliant on others. At times I could not rise off of the floor, and that prostrate feeling of lowness was metaphorical of the helpless submission in which I suddenly found myself. I learned a lot about submission, and much of it turned me to uttering the same sentiment that my friend RJ had expressed to his surgeon. I found myself crying out to many people, "You gonna take care of me, right?" My helplessness in the face of the powers I've listed above, the systems, the cherished discourses, the physiological struggles, and different hopes and expectations, all worked to seem to steal my old voice. I couldn't tell a good story, or tell my story well, along any of those familiar plot lines. But just as RJ was rendered speechless in the midst of his illness, and so reached out relationally to his surgeon, I began to fight through my "loss of story" to forge some new ones, and to form new connections with people who could hear those new narratives.

By being forced, or subjugated, into positions where I cried out for care so often and to so many, I have begun to learn the beauty of some new normals. Just as Kathy Ferguson (1984) claimed that it takes perspectives born of subordination to "resist the official definition of reality" (p. x), and Paulo Freire (1970) argued that only the oppressed have the power to free themselves *and* their oppressors, so I have begun to learn from my recent submission to illness (as well as from the stories of subordinated folks) that new norms born out of subjugation can bring real freedom.

– JUST A LITTLE PAIN IN THE HIP –

I am an activist researcher who collects, studies, and learns from experiences and stories of people trying to communicate and cooperate across major areas of difference. I am particularly interested in meaning management across the divides of class, race, and gender. I believe we all have a lot to learn from others who are different from us. Therefore, as part of my academic and personal life I live and work in a neighborhood that is among our nation's poorest. There I cooperate with others to do what is sometimes called "community building." To "build" community can be a strain, and in doing rehabs of old buildings, neighborhood cleanups, and other activities I sometimes stress my body. I have had my share of aches, pains, and minor injuries, but nothing I really gave much thought to. So when it came time for me to fly across the country for a national communication conference, I was a bit sore, but felt fit for the journey. Little did I know what journey laid ahead for me.

It was a cool and pleasant evening in late autumn as I walked with my old friend and former office-mate from our PhD-school days. We strolled casually down the streets of New Orleans headed from a famous cafe toward our hotel, not far from Bourbon Street and all the tourist hot-spots associated with it. As we walked I began to feel a small, but sharp and deep, jab of pain in my left hip. Nothing debilitating, so we walked on. Upon arriving back at our room we relaxed and watched a little TV for an hour or so until we were to meet some friends for dinner. My hip hurt a bit, but not badly. When it came time to head out for dinner I got up and walked to the lobby, but my hip was too sore to go further. I wasn't that hungry anyway, and so I would just chill in the room and see my friend later. I returned to our room, laid down on the bed, and determined to just relax and let the nerve-like pain in my hip subside. As I look back on what transpired over the next 2 hours, it is like mentally watching a shadowy, dark, noir horror movie. As I lay on the hotel bed recycling redundant "headlines" from CNN, ESPN, and other cable stalwarts, instead of relaxing, all the muscles in my lower left side began to tighten, and tighten, and then tighten some more. You know how when you have a muscle cramp in your calf it is so convulsingly tight and painful that you can hardly stand the pain for the few seconds it takes to grab your toes and pull the cramp out? It was not long until my buttocks, thigh, calf, and part of my left foot were in such a cramp-up, and would not release. I would have been writhing wildly in pain, but for the other painful devilry simultaneously gripping me. For while my muscles were rocklike hard in tonic spasm, something deep in my thigh and leg also was tightening in such a way that my hip was contracted, forcing my knee up against my chest, and it was permanently held that way by a deep spasm of what felt like a steel cord (I learned later it was a nerve) in my leg being pulled as tight as a bowstring, and revolting violently with pain if it was moved.

I was stuck. Laying there hugging my left knee tight to my chest with both arms, but at the same time needing those arms to rub, grasp, squeeze, and do anything else that one instinctively does to groups of large muscles in overloaded spasm. Unable to move for the pain, unable to be still for the pain, I was trapped alone in a sterile hotel room 800 miles from my home. As I look back on it the feelings and thoughts I remember are summed up pretty well by RJ's sentiments when he learned he had cancer. "I was completely out of my mind. I lost it man. I was like, Oh my God, I have no idea. I didn't know what to do."

At this point in the story I must admit that a decent chunk of my day-to-day preferred identity could be summed up (although rather harshly) as "tough guy." I was raised in a high-crime steel town; I like cars, cigars, football, and construction. I even sport a "biker's" handlebar mustache (although I assure the reader its purpose is largely to blur and bring into question class distinctions marked by such symbolic artifacts). All that came into play as I laid in that hotel gritting my teeth and succumbing to fear over what was happening to me. I did not want to submit myself to medical caregivers—I have always struggled with mistrust of them and the system. I did not want to burden my old friend with whom I was sharing the room. But even more, I did not want to admit that I couldn't fight this off, that it wouldn't go away if I toughed it out, that I could avoid that hassle and embarrassment if I just stayed put, hid, and bore up harder. But as time went on and the pain intensified instead of diminishing, I can almost remember the exact moment that the non-tough-guy part of me took over. For another large part of who I am deeply believes in and values interdependency with others, community, and caregiving. That is the part of me that draws me to feminist scholarship and is spurred on by Patrice Buzzanell (1994) claiming that organized life can be about cooperation, relationships, and caregiving, by Stanley Deetz (1992) proclaiming, "We are morally obligated to try to create a discourse that invites participation" (p. 346), and by Mikhail Bakhtin's (1984) encouragement that good communication can prevent the "absolute death" brought on my being "unheard and unrecognized" (p. 287). Besides all that, I couldn't stand the pain anymore, I could see that I had to cry out to someone for help in my helplessness, "You gonna take care of me, right?"

So what did I do? I called my wife. She is the one person that I have learned not to be afraid to call out to, and to whom I can be vulnerable without having to fight to legitimize my story. We have learned to help each other, to depend on one another, and to bear one another's pain. So I struggled to reach the phone and explained the situation to my wife as best I could amidst my shortness of breath and agony. She, of course, replied, "CALL 911 THIS MINUTE!"

I resisted a bit, but soon called 911. As I did I felt the growing burden of trying to explain and justify what was going on, and that I had a legitimate need. My struggle was that I had no idea what was going on—"my hip has suddenly contracted and locked so tightly that my knee is in my chest and it hurts like hell" just seemed kind of far-fetched and lacking credibility—but I did my best. Then as I lay there in my tightly half-balled-up (my right leg was fine) state, convulsing the way people in agony do, the wait for the ambulance seemed to go on forever. I began to almost hallucinate about the paramedics entering, seeing the extreme pain I was in, springing in action and giving me some giant pill, or shot, or gas that would unlock my muscles and nerves, or just knock me out. Instead, the moment the paramedics entered the room and I made eye contact with them, I knew I was in trouble.

By this point, I had subjugated my tough-guy impulses and realized my need, and was reading and willing to embrace the value of caring connectedness with others. The paramedics didn't seem to have gone there. These were not heroic, intense, nor compassionate faces. The faces I saw looking down at me much more resembled the jaded, lifeless, bored, hassled, and suspicious faces of bureaucrats (I found out when it came time for paying the bills that they were employees of the city of New Orleans, and by the way, 8 months on, the ambulance charges are still in dispute between them and my insurance company). They looked at me like I was a pain in *their* butts! Ferguson (1984) argued that "bureaucracy separates people from one another" (p. 13), and that it prevents people from acknowledging one another as entire persons. One look in these faces and I felt separated, and like much less than a whole person. These paramedics surely cannot afford, emotionally, to enter into the pain of all of their clients, but I sorely could have used a bit of compassion, or even just professional curiosity and courtesy. Instead, I got what my roommate (he had returned from dinner) and I later could only make sense of by reckoning it to be suspicion that I was another Bourbon Street tourist who was a victim of his own abuse and stupid decisions. Whatever it was, I was in a very vulnerable position and I was getting strong negative vibes from the people who were about to exercise great power over me. It reminds of me of Arlie Hochschild's (2003) observation of "both the downward tendency of negative feelings and the upward tendency of positive ones" (p. 85). This idea, and my experience there in that New Orleans hotel, are summed up well by the old plumbers' adage "poop flows downhill" (n.p.). These paramedics (and more medical providers to come) had the "upward" power position and I was at the shortest of ends of the power stick. They were clearly expressing their distrust and distain "downwardly," while my roommate and I were working overtime to let them know that we were in the area for an academic conference, that we were PhDs of reputable character, that the pain was real, and so on. Even in my intense pain I discerned that I had to be very careful about crying out like RJ had ("You gonna take care of me, right?") to these folks. They were venting "downward negative feelings" and I was fighting for survival trying to justify myself, and my story, "upward." My story felt hyperintense to me, yet as expressed to them I was shocked by its lack of efficacy. Their faces and stories look bored and skeptical. Mine was, of course, subjugated to theirs.

The paramedics gathered all the most vital technical information (heart rate, blood pressure, insurance coverage numbers), but administered no care. They simply asked where we wanted to go. Where did we want to go? Just as we had no idea how to tell my story physiologically, nor in a way that would elicit compassion, we had no idea where in this unknown city such a story should take us, geographically. We knew nothing about medical care in New Orleans. So they muttered the name of some "infirmary" (that word scared me) and said they would take me there. Who was I to say differently?

You have to remember that while my left lower half was spasming and contracting strongly, my nerve there was enflamed and rifled pain through my body when moved in ways it did not like.

Such was my tenuous situation when it came to moving. A situation brought to a head when we encountered the small flight of about 10 steps that lay between our room and the hotel lobby and exit. At the top of those steps sat the ambulance stretcher. I was at the bottom. My roommate, a compassionate man from a large Polish family from Chicago who knows a good bit about caregiving, asked if there wasn't some way to get the stretcher down to us. The medics were in no mood for improvisation. I was caught—stuck in the nightmarish space between rock-hard waves of muscle spasms ever pulling against an overly taut and enflamed set of nerves, and now caught between the top of the steps where I needed to be and the rock-hard faces of two bureaucrat paramedics who chastisingly blurted at me, "You've got to get up there somehow!" As I looked up those stairs I was like a man without oxygen standing at the foot of Mount Everest. I hesitated in my despair, and that gave the medics their cue to grab me under the arms and attempt to lift me up the steps. That action pulled on my nerve and forced out of me a big scream. I immediately fell like a sack of potatoes on the floor in ever more agony. There I lay. In that pathetic situation—me basically flopping around on the floor—what could anyone have done with my story? My friend's face was in shock, the paramedics looked irritated (glancing at them I felt a strong sense that they had given up on me), and I felt alone and dazed. Nevertheless, I was forced to slowly and awkwardly crawl up the steps as they (and my horrified old friend) looked on. Just recalling how I had to strain and pause to gather myself at each step causes me much embarrassment and bewilderment. By the time I got to the top I was even more of a mess of pain, contraction, and convulsion.

By the time I was on the stretcher I was nearly unconscious from the pain, yet, I remember very distinctly the embarrassment of being wheeled through the hotel lobby as I squirmed, twisted, and clenched my teeth in my pain, much like I have seen Hollywood depict Civil War casualties when having their limbs amputated without anesthesia. I was embarrassed, the story of my preferred identities was warped, but I could do nothing about it. I got one thin sheet as shield and barrier between my vulnerability and onlookers' curiosity.

Of the ambulance ride I can only remember beseeching my attendant as to why it was taking so long. Upon arrival at the hospital I was attended to by nurses who put me in a curtained-off treatment room and administered a strong intravenous anesthetic. It had immediate effect and I was finally able to stop oscillating in pain and lay still, although with my hip still fully contracting my thigh to my chest. With the most intense part of my pain on hold, I was able to talk with my old friend. "What could possibly be going on with my body? Why was my hip locked? What the heck would cause all these intense muscle spasms?" and perhaps most frightening of all, "How am I going to get home when I am basically paralyzed into a ball?" We also processed the crawl up the steps and the paramedics. My old friend was obviously shaken and angry over their indifference and lack of help. But soon we would see a doctor and get some answers, so we thought.

Almost anyone in our medical system could feel that his or her story is subjugated just by the fact that no one seems capable of remembering it. The 911 operator, the ambulance people, and the emergency room staff all ask many of the same questions over and over; questions concerning my physical condition, and many questions concerning my financial and insurance situations. We experienced all that, but the bigger blow was when the doctor—the one you reason has real power to understand your story and help you—arrived. The doctor literally spent 5 minutes talking to us. She began with, "Hello, I am Doctor X. We are discharging you. We don't keep people with sciatica." My friend and I looked at each other in dismay and stammered trying to find words (keep in mind we are communication faculty) to prolong the "dialogue." I wish I had asked what sciatica is, but I couldn't think of it fast enough. My friend got out a question about what medical treatment would be needed next. Her reply was, "You need to get home and see your doctor." I thought I *was* seeing a doctor! And who is this person "*Your* Doctor," that I need to see? I then asked the question that was worrying me most: "How can I move or travel when I am locked in this very painful position?" Her reply was a question: "When are you scheduled to return home?" I told her my flight was in 2 days. She said back to me, "You may want to move that up and leave tomorrow." We got one more question in, inquiring whether the hospital could provide a wheelchair to aid toward getting me ambulatory. She replied, "We might have a list of places where you can rent a wheelchair." She then walked out. We were stunned and dismayed. Had these people not heard any of the plot that we unfolded to them? Were we being misunderstood, or not believed? Did no one understand or care that "we are discharging you" was a twist that caused more dilemmas than it solved? My insides boiled to near the point of panic.

At least our appearance at the hospital had accomplished one thing; it changed all the focus from getting medical attention, to getting me home (to seek medical attention). The emergency room staff called us a cab, furnished us with a prescription for pain pills, and a useless photocopied page listing medical rental businesses scattered throughout greater New Orleans. I felt unheard, unrecognized, and in my massive vulnerability, very much in submission.

When we got in the cab, however, we encountered the first person who truly listened to our illness narrative, and who processed and responded to it in a human way. Our story begged to be told, since I was riding in the back seat of the cab alone and crumpled up in a ball. The cabbie was an African American man around 40 years old. As he took us to a 24-hour pharmacy, waited for my friend to come out with my prescription, and then drove us back to the hotel, we told him all that had happened that night. His responses were extraordinary. He listened well, asked a few questions of clarification, and then gave us his reaction.

> *I'm really sorry for all the pain you been through, and I hope you get through it all right, but you know what? You got to be thankful for a friend like this. You got a friend that you know from work who is willing to go through all this with you? To take all this time in the middle of the night and watch out for you and take care of you like this and get your prescription and everything for you? Man, that is a huge gift. That is a blessing man. Real friends who help each other out like that are a huge blessing. You got to thank this dude man. You can be sick and all, but to have a real friend like that is a bigger and better thing man. That's beautiful.*

Wow. Even in my drugged up and pained state I was so warmed by that man's wisdom. Being sick and being well, caregiving and caretaking, life and death, it really is all a relational experience. A very personal and relational experience. I would not have traded my friend who was helping me, or my wife who had helped me (and I knew was waiting at home worrying), for anything in the world—not even a functioning left side without pain. Cab dude was right. What a blessing. As I told the story later I have been tempted to equate this cabbie with an angel sent to help me in a dark hour—reminding me how alone I was *not*, even if my medical story seemed to be an unheard mystery. My friend knew my story and ascribed to it, and to me, credibility. The cabbie did a bit of the same. He was like an angel for sure, he even suggested that I reward my good and faithful friend with a gift to let him know how much I appreciated it all. He said, "This is New Orleans, man, if I had a friend like that I would get him a whore, you need to buy your friend a woman for being so good to you man." My angel recommended I reward my caregiving friend with a prostitute. That probably made more sense than anything else that had happened that night.

The cab driver's call to heed my relational blessings multiplied as I was served well by my friend over the next 2 days as he was in constant contact with my wife. Then another dear friend helped me out of the hotel and all the way to the gate to board my flight. I remember little of the flight except clinging to my painful and fully buckled left leg as I stumbled down the empty isle (pre-boarding for "those needing special assistance"), leaning on and grasping the seat tops with my right arm. Once in my seat I was drugged up all the way to the city where my connecting flight was to be. Instead of taking that flight, yet another dear friend met me in the airport and drove me 4 1/2 hours to my home. I rode the entire way in the back seat on my hands and knees. In the days to follow, this would prove to be the only position that gave me any amount of relief from the searing pain. I was too torn up to tell my friend much of my story in the car, but seldom can I remember being so grateful for a friend doing a favor. I fear I could not have pulled off another flight. Perhaps I am indebted one more prostitute?

I was home at last. I had opioid painkillers and an order to see "my" doctor, but no real answers to what was going on or what might happen to me. Immediately, we were faced with some major obstacles to even the first step of getting my story heard. First problem, we had moved just months prior to this emergency and I had no established primary care physician. My wife enquired around, trying to find a hearing for my intense story of suffering, but it quickly became apparent that few primary care deliverers are willing to make space for a new patient in an acute state right before a holiday. It was just days prior to Thanksgiving. A bigger, happier, more restful story of American culture seemed to fully eclipse my story as we called for would-be appointments. Again my pain brought me outside of time and ordinary discourses. The holiday break I had been anticipating seemed now to be an inconsequential frivolity to me, yet it was powerful in blocking the new plot line I was living. My wife sold my story hard—and it was not hard for her to do as I was in constant pain, broken only by bouts of searing pain that would send me into Civil-War-amputee-without-anesthetics bouts from time to time. Two nights after I got home we again found ourselves in the emergency room, seeking relief from my screaming pain and answers to what was going on in my body to cause it. In the ER I again received intravenous anesthetic and an order to get to my doctor as soon as possible so he could send me to a spine specialist. Get to *my* doctor, and on Thanksgiving eve. Right. I was a relatively young man who had always been healthy. We had moved a lot, and I never saw the big need to establish a relationship with a primary care doctor. When I felt like I had strep throat or something, I went to a clinic or urgent care. Now I was going unseen and undiagnosed for lack of an ongoing relationship with a doctor who would be committed to see me despite acute symptoms and bad timing. Maybe my friend RJ had it right, it is making (eye) contact with a doctor and deciding if you can trust him to "take care of me" that really counts. Maybe the cabbie was right—it is all about people that know you and care about, and for, you.

My esteem has skyrocketed for the few highly trained and deeply indebted newly minted doctors who choose to serve as primary care physicians. I needed someone, besides my friends and family, to navigate and plug me into the system that could get at what was going on in my body. I needed someone inside that system who would both listen to my story and translate it to other medical professionals who would, in turn, listen to them as colleagues. We were finally able to use a connection with a medical student we knew to get us into a family practice doctor who was new to our city and therefore had appointment space. Another interpersonal connection served me. I am grateful that

I did not have to look a randomly chosen doctor in the eye, as my friend RJ had done, and decide whether he was "a good man" or not. I had a bit more to go on, because I had a lot of relational connections with people who had the power to argue my case, or drive to a distant airport to get me, or knew a doctor who knew a doctor. Folks with truly subjugated stories, like RJ and the folks in my neighborhood in poverty, seldom have those connections that help bring their stories to light.

At the time, however, I was not feeling well connected, listened to, nor cared for. It was much more like Bakhtin's absolute death—unheard and unrecognized—with a mysterious story of pain running through my head and body, a story that even I could hardly believe. I spent over 2 weeks in pulsating and paralyzing pain as I waited to see the primary care doctor, and then a neurosurgeon. Nearly half a month of stealing 15 minutes of sleep here and there, and that bit of sleep all on my hands and knees. My wrists became sore and fragile, and the skin on my knees raw, but those pains had to be given into as that position was the only one I could endure. I hardly knew when it was day or night, how much I had slept or eaten, or much else about what was going on around me. It was all pain, pain pills (which in retrospect I sorely underutilized out of my paranoia of becoming addicted as so many around me in our neighborhood had done), and waiting to get to tell my story to someone who might be able to successfully act on it.

It was during this dark period that I had the opportunity to experience a bit of life outside of time. There was no chronos, no hours or seconds, for me. I could do nothing, other than trying to keep my body as tame as possible. For much of it I was not even waiting to see a doctor or get treated—that story was on hold. It was just me and my still mysterious and powerful pain. My entire world had been shrunken down to those tiny boundaries. Time could not intervene into that dyad. I had once lived for nearly a decade in a polychronic culture, where my language teacher had refused to teach me to say "sorry I'm late" because it was a useless phrase I would never have need of. I have also spent much of my life living among people from generational poverty, and in those situations I have found that time has much less of a hold on lives than it seems to in my middle-class world. Yet my pain brought me a freedom from time that I could not have foreseen. An almost complete absence of the monochronic deity of my previous life experience. I can hardly describe it, but it was deeply profound and spiritual for me. The bondage of my pain brought me a glimpse of freedom from the yoke of an ever-ticking present melting into the unslowable past. I hope that experience forever impacts my post-pain story.

Finally, however, I did get to meet my new family doctor. Mine being a neurological problem precluded him from treating it, but he did offer up some plausible interpretations of the events of my story to that point, and some stronger painkillers to ease my suffering. Physiologically, something had probably broken loose in my back and was causing pressure on the nerves to my left side. That nerve pressure seemed much more severe than "usual," however, and this was a hint into interpreting the social plotlines of my narrative. The family practice doc conjectured that due to my unusually intense nerve and pain symptoms (read: *alleged* pain symptoms) the paramedics and ER doctors had probably been suspicious that I was "surfing for pain pills" and thus given me less than generous care. Sometimes a story can be *too* good. So "good" that it becomes hardly believable. This doctor confirmed that this was most likely what had happened to me. My story was so intense and my plot so "interesting" (and also mingled with the very different plots of countless pain pill addicts) that it had brushed up against fiction in the interpretation of my interlocutors. Sad, because to me it just hurt like hell.

For treatment, I needed to see a neurosurgeon as soon as possible.

After another good wait (specialists are even harder to get in to see than primary care providers) I was in the office of a neurosurgeon who was appalled that I had been left in such bad shape for so long. Appalled because he considered my 18 days of pain unnecessary (I wonder how he had spent his Thanksgiving?), but also because he feared permanent nerve damage from such an intense constriction of the nerve channel leaving my spine. To address both problems he would send me directly to a local hospital for an injection of steroid directly into the spinal column at the effected site. Three such epidural steroid injections given at 1- to 2-week intervals might release the pressure on the nerve enough to avoid surgical removal of the impediment.

FINALLY, someone seemed alarmed at my suffering! Finally someone heard my story and seemed to know what to do with it. Finally someone seemed to understand what was going on in my body and in my life due to this pain and fear. I nearly wept right there in the office. Just one quick call to clear my new (and "expertly" endorsed) story with the insurance company and we would be off to the hospital for treatment.

Wait, word comes from the neurosurgeon's office manager… "Treatment denied by insurance company, must wait a mandated three days from request date before spinal injections are cover-able." THREE DAYS more after all the waiting I had already endured! By the passing of that interval I could likely be both a cripple from the nerve damage and insane from the strain. I doubt I need to describe the incommensurability of my story (of human suffering), my doctor's story (of scientific diagnostics), and that of my insurance company (one of profits and the bureaucracy to assure them). A thinly trained call receiver at my insurance company had the power to rewrite all our plot lines in an instant. I sat in a chair in the doctor's office leaning forward on my crutches in an effort to find a less painful position, as I listened to the office manager plead my case. At least someone with credentials was now telling at least part of my story for me. Then something very moving happened. In desperation the office manager let my wife talk to the insurance worker and my wife moved the argument from science to human suffering and care. With a choked up voice she passionately unfolded my story like no one else could have, and pleadingly outlined what was on the line here for us. She turned the plot back to one akin to RJ's statement of interpersonal trust and pity: "You're going to take care of me, right?" In what still seems like a miracle to me, my wife's pleas did the trick and the woman on the other end of the phone bent some rules, called in some apparently seldom used power, and got my treatment OK'd.

I just had to pause my writing here in order to pull my emotions together just thinking about that moment. For at the same time my wife was talking on the phone with the insurance company a man limped over to me in the waiting room and said, "I can see you are in a lot of distress, so I just wanted to tell you that this doctor put me back together when my back was broken in eight places. Hang in there, he will fix you up. You will get through it." I was so numb I just replied, "thank you," but his words gave me strength, mostly because it was apparent that he could look at me and tell a good deal about my story, and that he knew firsthand how legitimate it was. Again, the human, relational side of the plot cannot be fully subjugated.

Two hours later I was having steroid, guided by a real-time video x-ray, injected into my spinal column. The steroid was administered at the point where a vertebral disk had burst, spewing the disk material in the dorsal (backward) direction, squeezing the nerves inside the vertebrae in an unusually stringent manner. The procedure cut my pain to about half of what it had been for the previous weeks. I went home and slept for 4 hours straight. Even I could keep track of it now.

Even though possible surgery and other unknowns still lay ahead, the "psychedelic" pain, the pain my wife equated to over 2 weeks in the contractions of childbirth, was substantially mitigated. The road from there was still rather long. Another spinal injection with very limited results, and then a third injection scheduled to either substantially reduce the nerve impingement or lead to doing that surgically.

This part of my story ended just 1 week before surgery on my back was scheduled to take place. I went to the hospital for the last epidural, which was my last nonsurgical chance to free my nerves before the damage to my lower left side would become permanent. The doctor was ready to proceed with the procedure when, again, my insurance company refused treatment. It seems that in their obfuscated mathematics a $1,000 spinal injection was not worth the risk of payment even to avoid a surgical procedure that would cost many times more. The anesthesiologist went into a tirade, bemoaning how much possibly avoidable pain and suffering I would have to endure, the "pathetic" state of medicine in the United States, and the politic state of our nation that seems to make changing any of that impossible. Finally the doctor, dressed in his surgical scrubs and gloves looked at me and the nurse present and said, "Alright, this never happened, no records, no bills, nothing. We will do it completely off the record and try to avoid that surgery." I couldn't believe it—a back alley, under-the-table, epidural steroid injection! Neither the doctor nor the hospital got paid (with money) for the procedure. It was done solely out of human kindness, and again human caring showed itself not to be completely dead. That doctor looked me in the eye in the face of a system that was subjugating his story of how he wanted to live and practice medicine, and he said to me, "I got you, I will take care of you." And he did "have my back" in the end, as that injection freed the vertebral canal over the next few days in a way that cancelled the surgery and soon had me walking with a cane.

Since then I have enjoyed a steady recovery, and one that keeps me thankful to walk to the bathroom every day I get out of bed. The intensity of the narrative is what marks it as so special in my experience. The intensity of the pain, and the intense feelings that my story was not being heard at a time I so needed to be listened to. I hope to learn and retain the lessons that this period of illness so ardently drove home to me.

– LESSONS LEARNED, AND LEARNING –

What were those lessons? First: *WHEN YOU ARE DOWN, IT FEELS LIKE NO ONE WANTS TO HEAR YOUR STORY.* It was because I was so far "down" that I needed so badly to be heard, and that I so badly needed some real generosity (see Frank, 2004). But that kind of intense need can also cause others—the would-be listeners—to recoil and buffer themselves from hearing and entering into the story. For to truly listen and hear an exceptional story may mean arousing in the listener feelings of responsibility, or guilt, or just more work they may have to do if they "go there." My story begged for others to go to places they would rather not visit. No one wants to look at that sort of pain, or think about how it feels or that it could happen to them or someone they love. I felt like no one heard me because my need was large, and my pain was exceptional. Yet I desperately needed to be heard *because* of the intensity of my pain and need. Real pain and suffering can cause that sort of a downward communication spiral. To let that sort of ironic spiral subjugate stories of human struggle is a shame, and a loss to all of us. My illness story picked up again 1 week after my last spinal injection. I developed blood clots due to the fact that my leg was locked stationary for so long. That 20 or so days of pain, when I felt my story went unheard, nearly killed me. They say my chances of death were about 30%. Looking back, I also felt about 30% listened to.

This experience of pain also beseeches me *TO NEVER UNDERESTIMATE THE POWER OF ANYONE'S PAIN*. Pain may be the loudest of all voices when it comes to the meaning-making discourses of our lives. Pain can be a trump card that supersedes rationalities, emotions, and other ways of being. I once heard a psychologist say that humans experience loss seven times more than we do gain. It seems a bit silly, or like a lot of hubris, to quantify it like that, but the sentiment rings true to my experience. Loss and pain seem to be magnified when it comes to the meaning worlds we are constantly building and rebuilding. Kenneth Burke (1954) wrote that "though the materials of experience are established, we are poetic in our rearrangement of them" (p. 218). I posit that pain may be a special, and even a "super" material of experience, one that carries extra "weight" and demands special "poetry" and handling to process, make sense of, and survive. Pain, or loss, or a big lack, can easily become the gorilla in the room of our sense-making. Just like pain dominated me when I was in unmitigated intense physical pain, so I want to remain aware that mental, social, emotional, physical, relational, and a whole list of other types of pain can often dominate and define people in ways, and to extents, I likely cannot imagine. This calls for support, for a rushing in to listen and to help translate, rather than silencing, shying away, brushing off, or denial. Isolation and silencing are the recipe for the powerful material of pain to morph into destruction.

Conversely, pain and illness given a hearing, shared, expressed, and processed, can be a powerful force toward making us more fully human. Arthur Frank (2004) argues that "we may need to be ill" (p. 9). Pain and illness may be parts of the human experience that we cannot do without. My pain experience has worked some powerfully good poetry in my life, and I would now like to make sure that I don't let the pain of those around me go wasted.

On a bit more of a personal note, it was driven home to me from this experience that *I CAN AND WILL BE BROKEN*. I will get old. I will get sick. I will die. This experience revealed to me a deep and meaningful layer of cherished discourse in me that was assuming that I could always count on digging myself out of trouble by working harder, by doubling down my efforts, and by "toughing it out." I have swallowed and embraced much more of the myth of American individualism than I was aware I had. I have often talked against that myth, but this experience has given me some new possibilities for different "poetic rearrangement" of it. I once had the opportunity to spend extended time with a group of folks with disabilities who often called folks like me "*temporarily* able-bodied." They understood what I could not. My newfound vulnerability has begun to open up for me new pathways to freedom that will allow me to live more in interdependence with others, in ways that allow me to embrace my weaknesses as I more fully appreciate the strengths and attributes that others bring to the table.

Finally, I will never again be disconnected from the system of primary care providers the way I was when this story began. That is the one place I found where the relational side of medicine is given a place within the larger discourses of science, profits, and efficiency. The system is flawed, for sure, but at least my family doctor has within his stated professional identity that he should *know* me in order to treat me and keep me healthy. I am now so plugged in with a practice of family doctors that I am part of their "quality assurance committee," helping to influence their office to be better listeners and consumers of, and responders to, the stories of their patients.

In retrospect, my illness was not a huge one, and it did not endure for long. But it has served as a strong reminder to me that pain is a special and very powerful thing. Further, I am compelled to remember that everyone on this planet is in pain, and that the pain they are in can easily work to subjugate their voices and their stories. Brunner (1990) and other narrative scholars have contended that to be human is to tell stories. Therefore, if we allow pain to sequester people's stories, we allow them to live as sub-human, to die really. Saul Alinsky (1971) wrote that the "denial of the opportunity for participation is the denial of human dignity" (p. 123). As scholars, teachers, doctors, friends, and colleagues, we can offer those who are suffering the opportunity to participate in the human life-activity of telling their stories and having them heard and recognized. That directly addresses the subjugating power of pain and can usher in human dignity. I hope my story of pain makes it less likely that I would allow those in distress around me to utter what RJ uttered: "I didn't understand none of it. I lost it man. I was like, Oh my God, I have no idea."

– REFERENCES –

Alinsky, S. (1970). *Rules for radicals: A pragmatic primer for realistic radicals.* New York: Vintage.

Bakhtin, M.M. (1984). *Problems of Dostoevsky's poetics.* Translated and edited by C. Emerson. Minneapolis: University of Minnesota Press.

Bruner, J. (1990). *Acts of meaning.* Cambridge, MA: Harvard University Press.

Burke, K. (1954). *Permanence and change: An autonomy of purpose* Indianapolis, IN: Bobbs-Merrill.

Buzzanell, P.M. (1994). Gaining a voice: Feminist organizational theorizing. *Management Communication Quarterly, 7,* 339–383.

Deetz, S. (1992). *Democracy in an age of corporate colonization.* Albany, NY: State University of New York Press.

Frank, A. (1995). *The wounded storyteller: Body, illness, and ethics.* Chicago: University of Chicago Press.

Frank, A. (2000). The standpoint of storyteller. *Qualitative Health Research, 10,* 354–365.

Frank, A. (2004). *The renewal of generosity: Illness, medicine, and how to live.* Chicago: University of Chicago Press.

Freire, P. (1970). *Pedagogy of the oppressed.* New York: Continuum.

Ferguson, K. (1984). *The feminist case against bureaucracy.* Philadelphia: Temple University Press.

Hochschild, A.R. (2003). *The commercialization of intimate life: Notes from home and work.* Berkeley: University of California Press.

CHAPTER 10

POETIC INTERPRETATIONS OF STORYTELLING

– LYNN M. HARTER, BRITTANY L. PETERSON, TIMOTHY MCKENNA, AND AMANDA TORRENS –

"When poems are well constructed we live them rather than read them"
(Faulkner, 2007, p. 226)

Humans make sense of experience through storytelling. Individuals act, account, and recount in response to others—imagined or present—and anticipate their responses, including subsequent retellings of their stories with variations. Ultimately, meaning is co-constructed in dialogue, whether in confirmation, revision, denial, or challenge of the original story. Across chapters of this book, authors witnessed the storytelling of others. They relied on diverse inquiry practices, listened and responded in different ways, and offered interpretations in an array of forms including ethnographic portraits, auto-ethnographic accounts, and composite/fictional narratives. Authors offered credible and compelling commentaries yet positioned their work as partial truths open to interpretation by readers. In this spirit, we reengage the stories presented in earlier chapters to illustrate how poetic traditions can inform narrative scholarship.

The authoring process is consequential for scholars, those they write about, and the publics they serve. Professors and students remain part of academic disciplines that privilege *prose* as the standard form of representing narrative discourse (see critiques by Ellingson, 2008, 2011). As word art, poetry represents a viable alternative and complement to conventional representations. Willis (2002) shared, "poetry is valued as good and useful when it opens up an insightful space that is shared between poet and reader," a space that may not be reached otherwise (p. 7). Poetry enhances the aesthetic qualities of language through creative placement of words on a page through line spacing, breaks, and stanzas (Richardson, 2002). And it opens up new doors for us to consider how poetry may inform our work and scholarship beyond traditional representations (e.g., Faulkner, 2007; Furman, 2006).

In interpretive research, knowledge claims rendered in poetic form have been referred to as *poetic reflections* (e.g., Willis, 2002), *ethnographic poetics* (e.g., Brady, 2004), *investigative poetry* (e.g., Hartnett, 2003), and *poetic transcription* (e.g., Carr, 2003; Glesne, 1997; Richardson, 2002). Common across each label and method is the creation of poems from research interviews, transcripts, field notes, documents, scholarly chapters, and articles. Some researchers create poems using participants' exact words in a condensed form (e.g., Ellingson, 2011) whereas others fuse together the researcher's generative responses with participants' expressions (e.g., Faulkner, 2007). In this chapter, we are not interested in adopting a singular term to reference the use of poetry in research representations, nor do we elevate one approach over others. Instead, we hope to demonstrate the potential of poetic interpretations as an alternative and complement to conventional scholarly forms.

Poetic interpretations rely on the selection and arrangement of artful phrases to convey meaning and emotion. Typically, scholars work with an entire story or distill the story into its most compelling parts (e.g., a bounded and chronologically ordered excerpt from an interview transcript) (Ellingson, 2011). Scholars then shape the story into a poem by identifying the most salient and powerful words from the prose, condensing long passages by removing excess discourse, and arranging the remaining words on the page (Ho, Bylund, Rosenblum, & Herwaldt, 2009).

How can poetic interpretation inform the work of narrative scholars, storytellers, and witnesses? As distilled representations of storytelling, poems teach us to reimagine something familiar in new ways (Faulkner, 2007). Poets reveal and emphasize epiphanies through sound and rhythm, punctuation and interesting diction. In this way, poetic interpretations can help narrative scholars create emotional connections between contemplators and those who narrate life-altering experiences. When done well, poetic interpretations magnify turning points in stories and invite readers to explore the relevancy of others' experiences in their own lives. Of course, poems created by narrative scholars are no less constructions than are excerpts of data interwoven into analytic explanations (Glesne, 1997). Any representation of storytelling—poetic or otherwise—ought to resist narrative closure and instead aim to increase space for different readings.

Each of us exercised our creativity by selecting, interpreting, and representing our understanding of a story in poetic form. The compressed nature of the task forced us to make decisions about what was most essential in the text. Meanwhile, we remained mindful of Faulkner's (2007) description of poems as "flexible enough to be written in pencil, acknowledging that our conceptions of good or effective poetry may alter through time, experience, and changing tastes" (p. 230). While representing the original discourse faithfully, we experimented with different forms and organizing patterns for aesthetic impact.

In the poems that follow, we refocus readers' attention on stories introduced in previous chapters. Each author provides a brief introduction to his or her composition and its inspiration.

– THE CANCER TRAIN –
BY BRITTANY L. PETERSON

Three poems, two narratives, one thread. Tim, Amanda, and I entered the stories of Rhonda and Abigail as originally shared in Chapter 1, and each of us reconstructed them from our unique standpoints. Even so, as you read my poem, and later Tim's and Amanda's, you will notice a similar storyline that runs through each representation. The poems interweave in ways that illustrate the mirrored renderings of experience yet depart through our individual poetic retelling and reframing of their stories.

My poetic transcription represents an interplay between two souls, a mother and her child, the former's words on the left and the latter's on the right.

I imagine these poems as being in conversation with one another. Read across the columns to best experience the journey from beginning to end.

It's cancer, 24/7	*Pain*
Living a new normal	*Biopsy*
I smell it	*Something just wasn't right*
It is the smell of fear, of loss of control	*Life was about to change*
	Journey started here
That smell makes me see	
I have to let her go and trust	*I had to fast all night*
Hand over my baby to them	*And my mom fasted*
I can't fix cancer, I can't fix it	*So we both fasted*
We were in the middle of the storm	*I wanted to be left alone*
Journaling about the experience	*I loved painting*
Became a therapeutic release	*It brought me out of myself*
	I just wanted to be free
Peace of having her at home	*In some ways it was all I could do*
Does come with anxiety	
But I loved it	*I had a 12-in metal rod in my leg and*
The anxiety is worth it	*I couldn't be physical or athletic*
I would still choose to do it	

Got off that cancer train
It dumped us off
We were still in fight mode

She is starting her new life
She doesn't have the stigma of cancer
Anymore

I was still stuck in the cancer
I have to forgive cancer
I had turned cancer into a person
Say that…acknowledge it…realize it…
Let it go

I was free… I was able to forgive it
The first time I shared my story
I was a wreck

It is a different story now when I tell it
The story has changed

I just wanted to be a kid.
I didn't want to be
The kid that had cancer

I was trying to get over and past it

A lot of people came up to me
I didn't know what to do
So, I was kind of mad…I was confused
After a while, I started to appreciate that
    I had cancer

I am glad that I went through
The journey of cancer
I got to advocate for myself

I kind of like being known as a survivor
It defines me in important ways

– FOREVER –
BY TIMOTHY MCKENNA

Like Brittany, I engaged Rhonda and Abigail's narratives as shared in Chapter 1. I synthesize and reorganize them to illustrate what I believe to be the most compelling storyline—how this family was forever changed. I drew from Rhonda's testimony to develop the first poem, while the second one emerged from Abigail's story of forever.

From Rhonda

It is not just your…
"Mommy, please don't leave us."
"And, how am I going to get…?"
Cancer is not the only thing happening.

It's the unknown.
I can't fix cancer
The hate in our heart,
the bricks on my shoulder,
the need to forgive cancer.

In the middle,
I needed to make sense of the storm.
We don't stop at 5,
as soon as those doors open,
I smell it.

To live in the pain.
To breath our own air,
not smell floor five,
a fire alarm,
would jolt me out of bed.
But I could cook,
clean.

It is a different now,
a day in my life.
I'm still passionate,
emotional,
but there is celebration.

As we finally got off
something as simple as coffee,
brought me to tears.
 "it's more than just coffee."

From Abigail

I looked at my mother,
her expression.
My life was about to change,
my journey started.

The only thing I heard,
"Abigail we are going to..."
They put me in a room
my pain disappeared.

Everything seemed perfect
until the doctor,
I didn't know what to do
besides accept,
they wasted no time.

Left alone,
the chance to paint.
It brought me out of myself,
it was all I could do.

I just wanted to be a kid.
Not the kid that had cancer.
After a while I started to appreciate,
 the journey.
It defines me.

— THE STORY CHANGED —
BY AMANDA TORRENS

My poem blended Rhonda and Abigail's stories together. I allowed their individual journeys to come through while moving back and forth across narratives, time, and settings. As argued in Chapter 1, our stories are never just our own. Particularly in times of acute vulnerability and scary change, the people who come alongside us share our story and become an indelible piece of fabric in the quilt of those times. In the midst of life's intensity, the punctuation of time and place can fade away leaving timeless phrases and unforgettable places in their wake. In this poem, I captured defining moments irrespective of when and where words were initially spoken. The beginning of a cancer story can sometimes feel like the end of everything else, but in Rhonda and Abigail's stories there was more living to do on the other side of their new normal.

Your child's life you are trying to save
Trying to save your marriage
Your mortgage
Doctors need to understand
Our lives changed forever
Diagnosis
A new normal
Other stuff, we drag it to our new normal
Cancer is not the only thing happening
Our world turned upside down
Flipped over
Deep fried

Moms having chest pains
They think they are having heart attacks
We have broken hearts
Hearts trying to mend
Broken hearts

We got off that cancer train and
We did not know
Where to go
Still in fight mode, what to do next?
Lost

Pray

The smell of fear
It is the smell of anesthesia
I have to let my baby go
Fear, vulnerability, loss of control
It's the unknown
I can't fix cancer
I can't fix it

Pain, chilling
Now waking up in a room of color
Smiling faces, my family
My pain disappeared until the doctor
Pulled me back to reality
Something wasn't right
Her expression…I was confused like
    never before
I accept the things thrown at me
Waste no time

Hate in our heart
"Who do you need to forgive?"
This ton of bricks on my shoulder
"Who do you need to forgive?"
I have to forgive cancer
Let it go
I was free, able to forgive it
Live in pain, function in pain
So much pain, but
I was able to live the pain better

Peace, having her at home
Breathe our own air
Get rest
But, anxiety…it comes with anxiety
Tired
But I loved it
The anxiety is worth it

I wanted to be left alone
But painting brought me out, I guess
I wanted to be free
So I drew the jumping fish
That fish was free and I loved it
I got closer to art, it was all I could do
But it was something

I just wanted to be a kid
I didn't want to be cancer
Get over and past it
I was mad a lot
Confused
But I appreciate
To this day I am glad
I like being a survivor, it defines me

She doesn't have cancer anymore
I was still there, stuck in cancer
You deserve handicapped parking
So I parked there
You can look, just don't say anything
"Ma'am, I need to see the driver's license for
    this handicapped placard"
Offended
Appalled
 "You know what mom,
I don't want cancer to be the only thing that
    defines me"
She taught me something
She is amazing

It's about giving back
Make it better
Something simple
Something so small
That is why I am here
Cancer gave me my story

The first time I shared my story, I was a wreck
I've spoken, and it is a different story now
Life now is different
I'm different
I'm passionate, I'm emotional
But celebration is different
It is different today
The story changed

— HOPE —
BY TIMOTHY MCKENNA

In this poem, I explored Chapter 3 and synthesized the text to illustrate humanizing medicine. I integrated both scholarly text from the chapter (plain text) and the narratives presented therein (italicized text). I sought to illustrate how readers can poetically distill and interpret knowledge claims presented in scholarly articles and chapters.

"Would you like to listen to the dictation process?
It's your choice,"
a vortex of emotions and "what ifs?"
Nod in unison.

You shouldn't be afraid…
As they enter the story
As they ask questions,
they engage and edit to make sense.

Address their concerns about next steps
pause
clarify treatment protocols,
ensure everyone is on the same page.

To set a story in motion
one must remap social existence,
grasp and honor meanings,
be moved to act on the patient's behalf.

But too often
patients' perspectives are minimized
to scientific and instrumental logics
entrenched in institutionalized scripts
and "good patients" voices go mute.

You're intimidated.
If I don't get those questions out,
If there's anything new,
you don't get smart talking to yourself.

Just one-page summaries
and shared calendars
that situate illness
in hopes to humanize medicine
to put yourself in their shoes.

— THROUGH THE CRACKS —
BY AMANDA TORRENS

In this poetic rendering, I blended the voices of participants with the scholarly voices presented in Chapter 5. I only distinguished between the two sets of voices when there are direct quotations participants shared about their healthcare experiences. For these women, the Community Health Program (CHP) is now part of their story and I wanted to reflect that in the poem.

Living in poverty, material scarcity, inhospitable environments
Unmet needs
Faces of the working poor
Many lack medical treatment
The shame and stigma prevents
Women from seeking healthcare

Community Health Program
Disrupts social and material barriers
Fully includes patients' voices
Reimagines healthcare
Shifting scenes
Healing relationships

Between stories by participants,
The agonizing choices women often face

Assembly line medicine
Falling through the cracks
Bleak terrain
Just trying to survive
"I had never seen it face to face
I was really angry about it"
Invisible to mainstream society
An already shaky foundation
The poverty closet

Compelling stories of falling through the cracks

Holly lost her job and her husband became ill
Katherine has no insurance since her husband died
Ignore the symptoms and the pain
The problem will disappear
A hopeless feeling
"I can't afford it; I can't afford it"

Peggy suffered a heart attack
"I can't afford to pay for my heart"

Scared and desperate
Patients are at the mercy of others
Fear prevents care
Stigma and pride
Judy did not choose life circumstances
Spoiled or tainted identities, difficult to repair
People have pride in taking care of themselves
And their own

Physicians make competing demands
Treat patients as people
Cost-effective and efficient medicine
"Doctors never have time; they don't listen
Doctors want money"
Treat and street
Assembly line medicine
Sub-par care

Community Health Program
Disrupts assembly line medicine
Reorganize space
Foster community
Invite storytelling
For some, this is the only chance they get
To tell their story
To have someone really listen
Denice, scared, embarrassed and uncertain
Felt she was "treated with dignity"
Patients and staff not separated

People are important enough to make an effort
To bring care to their doorstep
Join medicine with the spirit of community

— STRIVING FOR MORE —
BY LYNN M. HARTER

In Chapter 9, I invited readers into the world of Striving for More, a health advocacy organization founded by Diane Moore. Originally, I moved between Diane's stories and scholarly literature to illustrate the role of storytelling in health activism. Here, I focus on her words and represent them in distilled form to invite readers to learn more, be more, and strive for more.

Sit-com life.
Two daughters.
Two dogs.
Two-car garage.
Lives irreversibly changed.

I am. We are.

Harrowing 8-month journey.
Inconsistent and inadequate
emotional and spiritual support.
Haunts me.
Called to respond.

I am. We are.
Striving for more…

Fund research.
Find a cure.
I get it.
But I want more.
I am outraged.

I am. We are.
Striving for more…
than a cure.

Track families.
Invite stories.
Tell stories.
Similar yet different.
Identify needs.

Striving for more...

Bring comfort to families.
Flashlights.
Lint rollers.
Starbucks.
Chemoducks.

I am. We are.

Gain ownership of story.
Need tools to retell it.
CaringBridge.
Beads of Courage.
Art for life.

Striving for more...
than a cure.

I'm grieving.
Just a grieving mother.
Trying to take senseless.
Turn it.
Make it meaningful.

– REFERENCES –

Brady, I. (2004). In defense of the sensual: Meaning construction in ethnography and poetics. *Qualitative Inquiry, 10*, 622–644.

Carr, J.M. (2003). Poetic expressions of vigilance. *Qualitative Health Research, 13*, 1324–1331.

Ellingson, L. (2008). *Engaging crystallization in qualitative research: An introduction.* Thousand Oaks, CA: Sage.

Ellingson, L. (2011). The poetics of professionalism among dialysis technicians. *Health Communication, 26*, 1–12.

Faulkner, S.L. (2007). Concern with craft. Using *ars poetica* as criteria for reading research poetry. *Qualitative Inquiry, 13*, 218–234.

Furman, R. (2006). Poetic forms and structures in qualitative health research. *Qualitative Health Research, 16*, 560–566.

Glesne, C. (1997). That rare feeling: Re-presenting research through poetic transcription. *Qualitative Inquiry, 3*, 202–221.

Hartnett, S.J. (2003). *Incarceration nation: Investigative prison poems of hope and terror.* Walnut Creek, CA: Alta Mira Press.

Herwaldt, L. (2008). *Patient listening: A doctor's guide.* Iowa City: University of Iowa Press.

Ho, E.Y., Bylund, C.L., Rosenblum, M.E., & Herwaldt, L.A. (2009). Teaching health communication through found poems created from patients' stories. *Communication Teacher, 23*, 93–98.

Richardson, L. (2002). Poetic representation of interviews. In J.F. Gubrium & J.A. Holstein (Eds.), *Handbook of interview research* (pp. 877–892). Thousand Oaks, CA: Sage.

Willis, P. (2002). Don't call it poetry. *Indo-Pacific Journal of Phenomenology, 2*, 1–14.

INDEX

F

Faulkner, S. L., 189
"Feeling Faces Journals" (S4M), 157
Ferguson, K., 177
Fine, G. A., 152
Fiske, J., 71
"Forever" (McKenna), 190–192
form, as relational, 12–13
Frank, Arthur, 17, 59, 158, 174, 184
Frey, L. R., 49

G

Gergen, Kenneth, 35
Giddens, A., 56
Gilbert, Natalie, 36
Goffman, E., 55
Graff, Dawn McDaniel, 36
Gray, Janette, 131–137

H

"Hairy Situation, A" (Jack G.), *116–117*
Handbook of Health Communication, The (Sharf, Vanderford), 12
Harter, L.
    The Art of the Possible, 6, 54, 60, 61, 63–64
    Community Health Program (CHP) and, 87 (*see also* mobile clinics)
    "Striving for More," 198–199
    on "worlding," 16
Hauerwas, S., 9
Hauser, G. A., 154
Hayward, C., 6, 54, 60, 61, 63–64
healing, fitness and, 140
Health Information Trends Survey, 162
Healthy People 2010, 102
Hepworth, M., 112
Hochschild, Arlie, 177
"Hope" (McKenna), 195
Horrigan, B., 127
humanizing, of medicine, 53–68

"Hope" (McKenna), 195
narratives and social order, 54–56
perspective of, 56–57
shared calendar concept, 61, *62*
social constructionism, 56–57
Humiston, John, 134
Hyde, M. J., 99

I

identity, integrative medicine and, 140–141
"illness script," 58
"individual being," 35
Institute of Medicine (IOM), 100
integrative medicine (IM), 125–147
    Brazos Healing Center (BHC) case study, 137–144
    case study approach to, 131
    The Center for Health and Wellbeing (CHWB) case study, 131–137
    complementary/integrative medicine (CIM) *vs.* complementary and alternative medicine (CAM), 126–130
    defined, 127
    generally, 125–126
Integrator—Integrative Medicine and Complementary and Alternative Medicine News, The (Weeks), 132

J

Javits, Joy, 31, 32, 45, 46
"joining," 31

K

Kaplan, Sherrie, 63
Kenyon, G., 33, 109
Kirksville College of Osteopathic Medicine (KCOM), 70
"knowledge-making," 151

P

pain
    "Pain Journals" (S4M), 157
    subjugation and, 173–185
Patterson, Spencer, 70
Pechura, C., 127
pediatric care. *see* Striving for More (S4M)
Permanence and Change (Burke), 19
Peterson, Brittany L., 189–190
Pink, Daniel, 59
Pinterest, 163
"planned patienthood," 63
poetic interpretation
    Burke on, 12
    "poetic rearrangement," 184
    of storytelling, 188–200
Polletta, F., 153
poverty, mobile health clinics and. *see* mobile
    clinics
Prairie Meadows Senior Living (Kasson,
    Minnesota), 120–122
provider-patient interviews, 6
public health activism, 149–169
    generally, 149–152
    narrative capacity and, 162–165
    "Striving for More" (Harter), 198–199
    Striving for More (S4M) inception,
        152–156
    Striving for More (S4M) initiatives,
        156–161
Putnam, R. D., 39

Q

quantum energy, 142–143
Quinlan, Maggie, 45–46

R

Randall, W. L., 33, 109
rapport-talk, report-talk *vs.,* 100
Rawlins, W. K., 16
reiki, 142–143

"relational being," 35
role play, 69–83
    example, 75–78
    preparation for, 79–80
    standardized patient (SP) labs, or localized
        performances, 71–75
    standardized patient (SP) labs as pedagogy,
        70–75

S

scaffolding effect, 159–160
self
    arts programming for expression of self and
        engagement with others, 32–40
    self-expression by elderly, 117–119
    transforming, 16–19
sense making, 58
Sharf, Barbara, 12, 61, 88
social change, mobilizing narratives and, 153.
        see also public health activism
social constructionism, 56–57
"social imaginary," 154
social media, 162–166
society, transforming, 19–21
Society for Arts in Healthcare, 31
Soja, Edward, 129
standardized patient (SP) labs
    as pedagogy, 70–75
    preparation for, 79–80
    role play example, 75–78
State of the Field Report (Society for Arts in
    Healthcare), 31
stigmatization, 92
storybuilding process, 159
"Story Changed, The" (Torrens), 192–194
storytelling in health contexts, 3–27, 187–200.
        see also arts programming; role play
    "A Hairy Situation" (Jack G.), *116–117*
    "Forever" (McKenna), 190–192
    generally, 3–6
    "Hope" (McKenna), 195
    imagining new normals, explained, 5,
        14–21, *15–16*